Sign Language and The Deaf Community

Essays in Honor of William C. Stokoe

Edited by

Charlotte Baker
Robbin Battison

SIGN LANGUAGE AND THE DEAF COMMUNITY:
Essays in Honor of William C. Stokoe

CHARLOTTE BAKER
ROBBIN BATTISON

Copyright 1980 by National Association of the Deaf

Library of Congress Catalogue Number 80-82286

ISBN: 0-913072-36-2   paperbound
ISBN: 0-913072-37-0   hardbound

Printed in the United States

Contents

Foreword

Back in 1960 I was out West in the cattle and wheat country as a teacher and principal of the Montana School for the Deaf. Although we were somewhat isolated from the mainstream of happenings in deafness, we did get word that a gentleman by the name of William Stokoe had just published a "book on signs" called *Sign Language Structure: An Outline of the Visual Communication Systems of the American Deaf.*

As a profoundly deaf individual who had received all of his education in a residential school, I was keenly aware of the importance of signs in our daily communication activities. Because of this, I had long been concerned about prevailing attitudes toward Sign Language. Through my college days, this concern grew into a deep resentment toward those educators who perceived Sign Language as "back-alley" talk, fit "only for bathrooms" and other private places, away from the scrutiny of the public eye. These attitudes were passed on to parents of young deaf children and to the media in various subtle and not-so-subtle ways.

So when I learned about the work of Bill Stokoe, I felt an inner excitement. I ordered his book immediately. Somehow I had a feeling this man was going to light a fuse, bring to Sign Language a needed measure of recognition and dignity, and cause considerable controversy, although I did not then dream of the extent.

Here was someone, I dared to hope, who might blast open the pretense and ignorance of how deaf people communicate with each other; someone who would rock the boat and create waves in the field of deafness and in the Deaf community all over the world. I saw in Bill a potential ally for all deaf persons who felt that signs were a necessary part of their lives, and who objected to other people's oppressive insensitivity to this fact.

Since then, and all through these awakening years, I have felt that the field of deafness and even the Deaf community itself have not yet recognized the full extent and magnitude of Bill Stokoe's contribution to the quality of our lives, to the growing openness and recognition of our communication needs, and to the status of our incomparable American Sign Language. To know, once and for all, that our "primitive" and "ideographic gestures" are really a formal language on a par with all other languages of the world is a step towards pride and liberation.

This book is only one attempt to fully recognize a pioneer and a giant; one who established Sign Language as a linguistic and cultural phenomenon of the American and the world Deaf community. The work of Bill Stokoe has permeated all corners of the linguistic world. But more than that, it has created a renaissance among deaf persons everywhere. It has caused a rebirth of hope, pride, and confidence in ourselves as we take a more active role in the modern world. With every passing year, we will understand and appreciate even more the many contributions of William C. Stokoe, Jr.

Mervin D. Garretson
Special Assistant to the President,
Gallaudet College
Past President, National
Association of the Deaf

Introduction

In July of 1979, we sent out a letter to 15 individuals, asking them to contribute to a Festschrift (the German word for a "celebration writing") in honor of William C. Stokoe. Each of these individuals had worked with Dr. Stokoe or had been influenced by his work, and all were actively involved as professionals in research, teaching, or other uses of Sign Language. We told them that we wanted to describe the impact of Sign Language research on the Deaf Community, and we asked each of them to write a paper that would trace the historical development of their professional fields as well as to describe their own involvement in those fields and their personal and professional interactions with Dr. Stokoe. Their responses were enthusiastic.

This volume is, collectively, a "labor of love"—a tribute to a man who stubbornly continued his pioneering work on American Sign Language despite considerable political obstacles, public scorn, and little support from his colleagues. Now all of us are reaping the benefits of his determination and perseverance, and the world itself has begun to recognize the truth of his "shocking" claim that American Sign Language is a language worthy of full recognition, study, and use—on a par with all other languages of the world.

During the past ten years, this recognition of American Sign Language has had an increasing impact on the traditionally negative attitudes of professionals who interact with Deaf people—educators, teachers, interpreters, audiologists, therapists, and others. No longer are these professionals able to view Deaf people as "defective hearing people." With the recognition that Deaf people use a highly complex language that is elegantly structured to fit the capabilities of the signer's eyes and body comes the recognition that having a hearing loss means interacting in a *different* way, but by no means an inferior way. This new understanding of American Sign Language enables us to see that Deaf people have their own culture and values that are expressed in this language—and that this culture, its values and its language, deserve the respect of all individuals who interact professionally and personally with Deaf people.

This book talks about what has happened to people and to professions as a direct result of this new information and new attitudes about American Sign Language. It also talks about how much more must happen before Deaf people and their language receive the full respect that is rightfully theirs. We have worked very hard to make the information in this volume understandable to those who are not professionally involved in our fields of study. We want all people to have access to this information and to be able to share it with other people.

A few of the more visible events of this history are shown in the chronology that follows this Introduction. But what the chronology gives us is just like the cities marked on a roadmap: just as roads connect cities, there are personal histories that connect main events and make them possible. We begin this volume with a very short piece by Ruth Stokoe on her husband's life—before he became involved with Sign Language and Deaf people. Ruth shows us that Bill Stokoe is a man of many talents and many accomplishments, and we can begin to understand where his energy comes from. Next we launch Bill's career at Gallaudet College with an historical account by Gilbert Eastman. In the process of describing his own transition from student to faculty member at Gallaudet College, Gil colorfully portrays what happened during those early days, what the thoughts and feelings of the Deaf community were about Sign Language and Bill's work, and how Gil's own thoughts and feelings about Sign Language led to innovations in the field of drama.

We then enter the scientific realm and begin to describe some of the linguistic research on American Sign Language. Robbin Battison talks about some of Bill's early work on Sign Language structure and draws out some of the social implications of one of his greatest contributions: the idea that signs are not simple pictures drawn with the hands; they can be analyzed into parts, and act very much like the words of spoken language when you examine them. Ursula Bellugi then describes how signs express complex meanings—far more complex than anyone originally believed—and she outlines a plan for a future dictionary of American Sign Language that would reflect what we have learned since the publication of the *Dictionary of American Sign Language* by Stokoe, Casterline, and Croneberg in 1965, more than fifteen years ago. Charlotte Baker takes us one level further and explains why it is important to look at other parts of the body besides the hands: facial expressions, head and eye movements, and body postures all contribute information about the grammar and the structure of sentences in American Sign Language.

In the section titled "The Deaf Community," we shift gears from looking at language to looking at people and how they use language. Carol Padden, a Deaf linguist, discusses how Deaf people live, how they interact with other Deaf and hearing people, and what they value; she clarifies the central role of American Sign Language in the culture and community of Deaf people. Barbara Kannapell provides an intriguing story of her own personal awareness about language, and how this has shaped her social life as a Deaf person and her professional life as an advocate, researcher, and teacher. James "Woody" Woodward, a sociolinguist, reviews the history of sociolinguistic research on ASL, and discusses why people have different ways of signing and how Deaf and hearing signers often interact with each other.

The next section describes some exciting changes in the use of Sign Language in society, changes that reflect what we have learned in the last twenty-five years about the language and culture of Deaf people. Dennis Cokely outlines some of the issues that face three types of professionals: Sign Language teachers, Sign Language interpreters, and educators in schools for Deaf children. He describes the influence of Sign Language research on each of these fields, tracing their historical development and future directions. Carol Erting reviews some of the research on how Deaf children learn to communicate from adults and other children, how communication is influenced by the environment in schools, and what the role of "native signers" is in a language-learning situation. Raymond Stevens, the principal of a school for Deaf children, discusses some of the forces that shape the Deaf child's experience in school and some of the changes that need to take place in schools in order to truly educate Deaf children. Louie Fant, a skilled actor, author, and Sign Language teacher, describes his professional and personal awareness of Sign Language and how his awareness developed and changed over the years. He provides several examples of artistic interpreting in American Sign Language, and what must go through the mind of the performing artist. The contribution by Raymond Trybus, a psychologist and educational researcher, clarifies an area that has received little attention up till now: the relationship of cultural and linguistic aspects of Deaf people's lives to their mental health. He describes what mental health workers should know about Deaf people, their language and their culture, and discusses the professional role of Deaf people in the field of mental health.

In the final section, we remind the reader that the issues we have raised go beyond the American Deaf people and their American Sign Language; Deaf people in other countries are undergoing changes in their schools and communities that parallel many of the events in the United States. Schools for Deaf children in other countries are re-examining their attitudes and policies toward Sign Language. Researchers in other countries are aware of the pressing social need to answer many questions about Deaf people and their language. The idea that a new perspective is needed toward Deaf people and Sign Language is one that is catching hold in dozens of countries: teachers have put together a Sign Language dictionary in Australia; parents have fought to include signs in classrooms in New Zealand; researchers and Deaf teachers in Sweden have been successfully teaching Swedish Sign Language (and not just "Signed Swedish") to hearing parents of Deaf children; researchers in Taiwan, Japan, Portugal, and Italy have been attempting to describe the signed languages used in their regions, and to make that information available for professionals who work with Deaf children and Deaf adults. We wish that we could include a report of all our colleagues in every country, but that would be a separate book in itself. What we do have are excellent contributions from social and linguistic researchers in three countries: Bernard Mottez and Harry Markowicz chronicle the amazing growth of the movement behind French Sign Language; Mary Brennan and Allan B. Hayhurst describe how several different research groups in Great Britain have teamed up with Deaf associations and schools for Deaf children to produce changes; and Britta Hansen relates how Deaf people in Denmark have influenced, and have been influenced by, research on Danish Sign Language. Each of these national stories is fascinating in its own right. But each one also enables us in the United States to see parallel developments with our country as well as differences that we can learn from. And with each story, we learn once again that many of the initiatives and much of the momentum for the activities in other countries can be traced to Bill Stokoe and his ideas.

We end the book with an unusual move. Since we have been interested all along in how ideas about the language and culture of Deaf people have been transformed into social action, we do need to consider some of Bill Stokoe's own thoughts about his work. In the section called "Afterwords," we have pulled together a few paragraphs from a short article that Bill himself wrote about his early experiences with Sign Language. We have borrowed these paragraphs without informing Bill because we kept this entire book a secret from him until after it was published.

Finally, we would like to add one more tribute to a man whose ideas have been inspirational and whose actions have supported so many of us. The authors and editors have agreed that all of the proceeds from this book will go to a special fund to continue the work that Bill started almost 25 years ago: The William C. Stokoe Scholarship fund will support students who have a major interest in research on Sign Language. That's just our way of saying, "Thanks, Bill."

April 30, 1980   Robbin Battison
Washington, D.C.   Charlotte Baker

Editors' Note

Some of the authors in this volume have used the word *deaf* to describe people with a hearing loss and have used the capitalized *Deaf* to describe people who form a society or culture. In some cases, the words are highlighted to allow the reader to focus on this distinction.

Throughout the text, the names of signs are always written in capital letters, for example, LEAVE. Other conventions for writing signs are explained in each chapter.

Throughout the text, *signed language* refers to a type of language that uses signs, just as we use the words *spoken language* to refer to a type of language that uses words. On the other hand, we use the capitalized words *Sign Language* to refer to a particular language, for example, *Danish Sign Language.*

Acknowledgements

We are grateful for the generous efforts of the many individuals who volunteered their time to help prepare this volume: to Kathy Burton, Jingle, Linda Kohler, Barbara LeMaster, and Deborah Vitale for their assistance in typing—and especially to Beverly Klayman who worked long and late hours typing, proofing, xeroxing, and comforting; to Corrine Hilton of the Gallaudet College library and Ruth Stokoe who pulled together the photographs of Bill Stokoe; to Charlie Shoup who developed the copies of those photographs; to Melvin Carter and the National Association of the Deaf who enthusiastically sponsored this "secret project" and made the arrangements for presenting the volume to Bill; and finally to all of the authors who worked so hard writing, revising, and re-revising their papers to make this volume a useful and understandable "state of the art" description of Sign Language and the Deaf community.

Photos of William Stokoe courtesy of Film Media, Gallaudet College, and Charlie Shoup.

Illustrations on pp. 43-44 by Elizabeth Baird.

Illustrations on pp. 60-73 by Frank A. Paul.

Photos on pp. 77-78 by Tom Klagholz.

Photos and illustrations on pp. 251-261 courtesy of the Center for Total Communication, Copenhagen.

Sign Language in the 20th Century:
A Chronology

prepared by Dennis Cokely & Charlotte Baker

1913–1920 National Association of the Deaf (NAD) initiates a film project for the preservation of Sign Language—includes films of George Veditz, John B. Hotchkiss, Robert MacGregor, and Edward Miner Gallaudet

1957 American Council of Learned Societies awards research grant to William C. Stokoe for beginning analysis of American Sign Language (ASL)

1959 National Science Foundation begins funding Stokoe's linguistic research on ASL

1960 Publication of the first linguistic study of ASL—*Sign Language Structure: An Outline of the Visual Communication Systems of the American Deaf* by Stokoe

1964 Registry of Interpreters for the Deaf (RID) is established, with Kenneth Huff as its first president

1965 Publication of *A Dictionary of American Sign Language* by William Stokoe, Dorothy Casterline, and Carl Croneberg

1967 Communicative Skills Program (CSP) is established at the NAD with a grant from the Vocational Rehabilitation Administration. Terrence O'Rourke is first director of the CSP

1970   National Theater of the Deaf (NTD) is established with funding from the Department of Health, Education and Welfare (HEW)

Laboratory for Language and Cognitive Studies is established at the Salk Institute for Biological Studies in San Diego with a grant from the National Institutes of Health (NIH). Ursula Bellugi is director of the lab and begins research on ASL

Stokoe offers first graduate course on the structure of ASL at Gallaudet College

1970's   "Total Communication" begins to be accepted by educators in programs and schools for deaf children

1971   Linguistics Research Lab (LRL) is established as an autonomous unit at Gallaudet College. William Stokoe is director of LRL

Stokoe begins publishing a newsletter on topics relating to Sign Language, called "Signs for Our Times"

First presentation of information on ASL at a Linguistic Society of America conference, by James Woodward

Special Study Institute on "Psycholinguistics and Total Communication" is held at Western Maryland College, sponsored by the CSP with a grant from the Bureau of Education of the Handicapped (BEH)

1972   Special Study Institute on "Psycholinguistics and Total Communication" is held at Lewis and Clark College in Oregon, sponsored by the CSP with a grant from BEH

Stokoe begins publication of the journal *Sign Language Studies*

First text on teaching ASL is published by Louie Fant (*Ameslan*)

American colleges and universities begin to accept ASL as a language that can be used to satisfy language requirements for Ph.D. programs. Some of the first to accept ASL are American University, New York University, and the University of Minnesota

RID begins national certification of interpreters

Gallaudet College begins testing the signing skills of its teachers

1973   Congress passes the Rehabilitation Act of 1973 in which Section 504 mandates the provision of interpreters for deaf people in educational and occupational situations

First Linguistics Ph.D. dissertation on ASL is written by Woodward (Georgetown University)

A section on Sign Language is established at the annual conference of the Linguistics Society of America

First play which focuses on attitudes toward ASL ("Sign Me Alice") is written and produced by Gilbert Eastman at Gallaudet College and published the following year

1974   A symposium on Sign Language takes place at the American Anthropological Society annual conference in Mexico City

A conference on Sign Language is held at Gallaudet College, co-sponsored by the Linguistics Research Lab and Sign Language Programs

Language Perception Laboratory is established at Northeastern University by Harlan Lane and begins research on ASL

1975   Congress passes the Education for all Handicapped Children Act (Public Law 94–142) which asserts the child's right to an instructional program agreed upon by the school and parents, and requires that assessment of the child be in his or her own native language or most comfortable means of communication

World Federation of the Deaf (WFD) meets in Washington, D.C. and includes papers on attitudes toward Sign Language and cultural conflicts in the Deaf community

First International Symposium on Sign Language interpreting meets in Washington, D.C., following the WFD meeting

National Interpreter Training Consortium (NITC) is established by a grant from the Vocational Rehabilitation Administration

First organization of Sign Language teachers—Sign Instructors Guidance Network (SIGN)—is established through the Communicative Skills Program at the NAD

1976   National Center for Law and the Deaf (NCLD) begins petitioning HEW for acceptance of ASL under the Bilingual Education Act

SIGN begins certifying Sign Language teachers at the NAD convention in Houston

National Science Foundation awards a grant to the University of Rochester to host a Conference on Sign Language and Neurolinguistics

1977   First National Symposium on Sign Language Research and Teaching is held in Chicago, organized by the Communicative Skills Program at the NAD

Ohlone College in California sponsors a two-week intensive course for Sign Language teachers on the linguistics of ASL

Second International Symposium on Sign Language Interpreting is held in Copenhagen, Denmark

National Technical Institute for the Deaf and Gallaudet College host a conference in Kansas City on how to implement "Manual/Simultaneous Communication Instructional Programs in the Educational Setting"

Pre-College Programs at Gallaudet adopts a policy that includes a description of ASL and states that teachers' ASL skills will be evaluated

1978   Pre-College Programs at Gallaudet begins evaluating the ASL skills of its teachers

First credit course for Gallaudet undergraduates on the Structure of ASL is offered

Gallaudet's summer Sign Language program begins offering a course on the Structure of ASL

First conference on ASL poetry is held at the University of Indiana in South Bend

Second National Symposium on Sign Language Research and Teaching is held in San Diego, with the theme "Bilingual and Bicultural Education"

1979   Rehabilitation Services Administration (RSA) awards a grant to the CSP to establish a National Consortium of Programs for the Training of Sign Language Instructors (NCPTSLI)

Gallaudet's undergraduate faculty officially recognizes ASL as a viable means of communication which may be used in classes

First course for Gallaudet faculty and staff on the Structure of ASL is offered for graduate credit

"Rainbow's End," a series of instructional programs for deaf children with a cast of deaf actors using ASL, is televised nationally

At the RID board meeting, terminology is clarified so that "interpreting" becomes defined as taking information from one language and transmitting it in another separate language (as opposed to "transliterating")

First International Symposium on Sign Language Research is held in Stockholm, Sweden

A NATO Advanced Study Institute on "Sign Language and Cognition" is held in Copenhagen, Denmark

A Linguistics Department is established at Gallaudet College

1980 William C. Stokoe is honored at the centennial convention of the National Association of the Deaf and presented with the volume *Sign Language and the Deaf Community: Essays in Honor of William C. Stokoe*

I
PERSONAL HISTORY

William Clarence Stokoe, Jr.:
The Person behind the Story

by Ruth Stokoe

Bill Stokoe was born on July 21, 1919, in the little town of Lancaster, New Hampshire. He is very proud of his birthplace even though his family left New England for West Virginia less than a year later. This began a series of moves which led them at last to a white farmhouse in Livingston County in western New York. Bill's father had given up his career as a county agricultural agent for full-time farming, so Bill and his younger brother Jim attended school, joined the 4H Club, raised calves for exhibition at the county fairs, and raced around the country lanes on Bill's old Harley Davidson motor bike.

In 1937, with the aid of a New York state scholarship, Bill entered the College of Arts and Sciences at Cornell University. He planned to major in English and to support himself with part-time jobs. These varied from 'hired hand' for an Ithaca couple, to kitchen helper in a fraternity house where he learned to cook from a fiery little chef named Rosie, to maintenance man for an engineering lab.

These were the years of Hitler's buildup in Germany and Bill joined the ROTC. In the summer between his junior and senior years he became seriously ill while at ROTC camp—so ill that he returned home, unable to go back to Cornell that September. He remained out of school for a year to recover his health.

In the fall of 1941 he returned to Cornell and felt well enough to resume his intercollegiate fencing, which earned him his Cornell "C." He was co-captain of the fencing team and was elected to Phi Beta Kappa and Phi Kappa Phi.

In the spring of 1942, Bill and I were introduced. We became engaged in the beautiful setting of an Ithaca springtime and graduated together from the College of Arts and Sciences that June. After graduation, Bill worked for a time in a factory in Rochester, New York, not far from his home. We were married in Sage Chapel on the Cornell campus in November of that same year. The following September found us back in Ithaca where Bill was a graduate assistant and later an instructor in English while working for his Ph.D. His field of study was Old and Middle English and his dissertation dealt with three medieval romances: *Sir Launfal, Sir Degaré*, and *Richard Coeur de Lion*.

After earning his doctorate, Bill accepted an offer of an assistant professorship at Wells College, and in 1946, the family moved a few miles north along Cayuga Lake to the little lakeside village of Aurora. Bill later became chairman of the Department of English and remained there until 1955. Our children, Helen and Jim, were born in these pleasant surroundings.

In 1953, Bill was granted a full-year sabbatical leave from Wells and this took the whole family to Britain. He had intended to spend the time preparing a new edition of the Scottish bishop Gavin Douglas' translation of the *Aeneid* into Middle Scots. But while working in the library of the University of Edinburgh, he became interested in linguistics, thus preparing the way for his future life's work. He also took advantage of the time and the place to learn to play the great highland bagpipe and bought himself a kilt.

Back at Wells College in 1954, he received an offer from an old friend—George Detmold, then Dean of Gallaudet College—to come to Washington, D.C. as professor of English and chairman of the English department at Gallaudet. In the summer of 1955, the Stokoes and their old "woodie" Ford station wagon, piled high with children and possessions, arrived in the capital area.

The new job at Gallaudet turned out to be one more adventurous path for Bill Stokoe, as other essays in this volume will describe. But Bill has never shied away from either adventure or new challenges and his private life offers many examples of his unusual energy, his talents, and his many diverse interests. He has traveled widely, and at different periods in his life he has been an accomplished swordsman, hunter, aircraft pilot, and licensed ham radio operator. For a long time, he was also a proud member and Pipe Major of the bagpipe band of the St. Andrews Society of Washington, D.C.

Needless to say, life with Bill has meant something new every day, and it's been fun.

As a young faculty member at Gallaudet College, 1956

As a professor at Gallaudet College, 1965

As Piper at the Conference of Executives of American Schools for the Deaf, Spring 1968

As Marshall of the Gallaudet College Commencement, May 1977

As Director of the Linguistics Research Lab, January 1980

From Student to Professional: A Personal Chronicle of Sign Language

by Gilbert Eastman

Introduction

Years ago the professionals in deafness gave their full attention to the *disabilities* of deaf people. Then came Dr. William Stokoe, a linguist who studied Sign Language; he gave his full attention to the *abilities* of deaf people.

In this paper I would like to talk about Dr. Stokoe as a college professor (even though he never taught me), as a colleague in the English Department (even though our offices were in separate buildings), and as an advisor on Sign Language. Also, a bit about myself as a college student, Sign Language instructor, stage actor, director, playwright, and professor of the Drama Department at Gallaudet College in Washington, D.C.

Gilbert Eastman is presently chairman of the Theatre Arts Department at Gallaudet College. He has a B.A. in art from Gallaudet (1957) and a M.F.A. in drama from Catholic University (1963). He was a founding member of the National Theater of the Deaf and has taught courses for NTD's summer program. Gil has been an actor, stage manager, translator, or director for more than 40 plays and wrote the plays "Laurent Clerc: A Profile," "Hands," and "Sign Me Alice" (published in 1974). He teaches courses on Visual-Gestural communication as a Sign Language base and has given talks and workshops on these courses in Sweden, France and Canada as well as across the United States.

This paper will describe actual events at Gallaudet College. While I have relied on my memory for events of the last 25 years, throughout this history I quote from articles from the "Buff and Blue," the Gallaudet student newspaper.

Remembering . . .

One September day in 1952 I rode on a train to Washington, D.C. from a little town in Connecticut called Cromwell. I was on my way to a new world . . . away from my home, my family and my friends. I arrived at Union Station. On a paper pad I wrote with a pencil, "Gallaudet College" and I handed it to a cabdriver. He took me to the college without looking at a map. I got out of the cab and looked at the famous buildings . . . Chapel Hall . . . College Hall . . . Fowler Hall. The campus was beautiful and quiet. There was a farm behind the great buildings.

Some time later, an issue of the Buff and Blue (our student newspaper) announced . . .

> This year Gallaudet is given the privilege to boast of its recordbreaking total of eighty-five new enrollees which includes forty-three men and forty-two women.

I was one of the members of the Preparatory Class . . . I was fascinated by the upperclass students' signing—there were flying hands everywhere. And I, too, had the opportunity to acquire "refined" Sign Language from college professors, especially Elizabeth Benson. Everything was so different from the American School for the Deaf that I had attended. Leonard Elstad was our college president then.

In the same Buff and Blue (B & B) issue another article stated:

FOUR NEW MEMBERS ADDED TO FACULTY

The Buff and Blue Staff is very happy to introduce all of you to our four new faculty members.

Dr. George E. Detmold, our new Dean of Instruction received his B. A. in 1938, his M. A. in 1940 and his Ph.D. in 1943 from Cornell University. He was an English Instructor at the Cornell University from 1939–1942. In 1941 he was called to active duty in the United States Army, where he served chiefly in China, Indian, and Burma until 1946. Upon completion of his Army career, he returned to Cornell, where he was once again an Instructor of English. In 1947, Dr. Detmold went to Wells College as an Assistant Professor of English. Then, in 1952, he went to Teacher's College, Columbia University as Assistant on Admissions and studied for a professional diploma in the administration of higher education.

I was told that Dr. Detmold was different; I did not understand what they meant. Maybe he was different from other Gallaudet professors. I decided not to bother with him and avoided meeting him. I went on with all of the traditional activities. The following month (November) there was a stirring talk.

STUDENT ONE:	Have you read the Buff and Blue?
STUDENT TWO:	What will become of Gallaudet College?
STUDENT THREE:	I totally disagreed with him.
ME:	Him . . . who?
STUDENT THREE:	Detmold. D-e-t-m-o-l-d.

The announcement in the B & B was:

DR. DETMOLD GIVES OUTLINE FOR NEW CURRICULUM PLAN

Gallaudet College should have a new curriculum by September, 1953, according to Dr. George Detmold, Dean of Instruction. Plans now under discussion with the faculty, provide for a two-year program leading to the degrees of Associate of Arts and Associate in Applied Science, as well as a four year program leading to the Bachelor of Arts and Bachelor of Science degrees. There will also be a graduate program leading to the Master's degree in Education.

Dr. Detmold stressed that present plans are only tentative and are subject to modifications as the faculty work out details. Guiding principles in the construction of a new curriculum have been offered by two recent surveys of the College's offerings: the report of the Federal Security Agency in 1950 and the evaluation report made in 1952 by the Middle States Association of Colleges and Secondary Schools.

The fundamental purpose of a new curriculum, according to the Curricular Prospectus, now under discussion, is that it "should provide all our students with a basic training in the liberal arts, preparing them to assume intelligently, their roles as men and women in modern society and that (as far as our resources permit) it should prepare each of them for the profession or vocation which he is best fitted to follow."

The students' argument about the new curriculum lasted through the rest of the academic year. In the fall of 1953, the Gallaudet Freshmen invaded Dr. Detmold's office to protest his drastic changes in curriculum . . . We were lost in chaos . . . we had to take brand-new courses that had never been offered before . . . we said that it was not fair to the past students. It was a tough program. We often planned a boycott which never happened . . . Several months later we became used to the changes but we still did not like Detmold's transformation. Another protest arose when there was another announcement.

FUSFELD, DETMOLD GET TOP RANK PROMOTIONS

Dr. Detmold, Dean of Instruction since 1952, has been named to succeed Dr. Fusfeld as Dean of the College. He will have supervision over all instructional activities.

I went through the Sophomore year with Detmold's modern curriculum. We complained constantly. We often threatened to leave the college . . . I decided not to come back next year . . . But I returned anyway. I declared art as a major in my Junior year. I began to like the college and became involved in several extracurricular activities. My favorite was the Dramatics Club and I was selected as the President.

The Buff and Blue of October 1955 announced:

GALLAUDET FACULTY BOOSTED TO SEVENTY

Gallaudet College, the world's only college for the deaf, has added twenty-four new staff members, including three replacements, for its ninety-second academic year, it was announced by Dr. Leonard M. Elstad, President.

The faculty now numbers seventy. There are eleven graduate, and 301 undergraduate and special students—the largest enrollment in the history of the Federally sponsored institution. The new staff positions are provided for in the expansion program recently authorized by the Eighty-first Congress.

Among the newcomers was someone named Stokoe:

William C. Stokoe, Jr. becomes Professor and Chairman of the Department of English. Formerly Chairman of the Wells College English Department, Professor Stokoe has a Ph.D. from Cornell.

STUDENT
ONE: Wells College? I have heard of the name. Cornell, too.

STUDENT TWO:	Detmold's friend!
STUDENT THREE:	Not fair! Why did he hire his own friend?
STUDENT ONE:	Oh, I see. Stokoe is Detmold's friend.
STUDENT TWO:	I don't understand Detmold. He also hired several deaf professors.
STUDENT THREE:	Maybe Detmold recognizes the skills of deaf professors but why did he hire Sto------e?
STUDENT TWO:	I am not going to take a course under him.
STUDENT THREE:	I heard he is a tough teacher.
STUDENT TWO:	I prefer deaf professors in the English Department.
STUDENT ONE:	Stokoe just learned Sign Language. Why should I waste my time watching him sign slowly and stiffly?

In 1956, the January issue of the B & B reported:

During the vacation Dr. Stokoe attended the annual convention of the Modern Language Association in Chicago. Dr. Stokoe has been appointed contributing editor of the forthcoming revised edition of John E. Wells' *A Manual of Writings in Middle English*.

STUDENT ONE:	Why should he go to the convention? He wasted his time. He should have studied Sign Language during his Christmas vacation.
STUDENT TWO:	I don't think he will stay here. Gallaudet students are too much for him.
STUDENT ONE:	Hey! You know Detmold's new curriculum. Well, have you heard about the new plan for our campus? Elstad and Detmold's plan? (Shows him a ground plan)
STUDENT TWO:	Wow! You can't call this Greater Gallaudet.
STUDENT ONE:	I don't think E.M. Gallaudet would like it.

STUDENT TWO:	I won't be surprised if Stokoe agreed with the Elstad-Detmold Plan.
STUDENT ONE:	Let's look at the plan. Look! New classroom and lab building . . . P.E. building . . . Cafeteria . . . women's dorm . . . men's dorm . . . Oh, no, speech and hearing center . . . even an auditorium.
STUDENT TWO:	I can't believe it. Only 300 students here. Why do we need those buildings?

In the fall of 1956 I shouted: "Now I am a Senior! My last year at Gallaudet!" The new library was being constructed—a very modern building as opposed to the Victorian Gothic buildings. I was still in dramatic activities . . . Several students still criticized their professors.

STUDENT ONE:	Do you know why Stokoe has difficulty learning Sign Language?
ME:	No.
STUDENT ONE:	I don't believe he actually studied Sign Language.
ME:	I have seen him practicing signing in his office in the basement of Kendall School. He tries hard to put signs in grammatical order.
STUDENT ONE:	Maybe he knows signs but not the Sign Language.
ME:	Give him time.
STUDENT ONE:	Why doesn't he join us in the Reading Room every night? It is the best place to learn Sign Language. We often stay there all night and we sign and sign and sign about everything . . . international news . . . national . . . and of course, campus news. We often have good bull sessions, too. I think it is a good idea to have electricity turned off at 11 p.m. so we will move from our rooms to the Reading Room to talk.
ME:	What does that have to do with Stokeo.
STUDENT TWO:	(Corrects him) S-t-o-k-o-e.
ME:	Stokoe.
STUDENT ONE:	I came across an article in the B & B about him.

STUDENT	
TWO:	Yes, I've read it.
STUDENT	
ONE:	He joined the Washington Scottish Band.
ME:	Scottish?
STUDENT	
ONE:	Yes, and he wrote about Scotland. Read it.

Dr. Stokoe was a member of a pipe band during the summer, the Clan MacNaughton, in Rochester, New York, and piped during his spare time. He is now piping for the Washington Scottish Band.

He is also writing a bibliography of medieval Scottish literature for the Modern Language Association. He says that playing the pipes is a good change from studying Scottish Literature of 600 years ago and a good way of "blowing off steam." "What I like about playing bagpipes," he adds, "is that I have to do so many things at the same time that it keeps me in condition for teaching."

ME:	Very interesting . . .
STUDENT	
ONE:	No, he's not interested in us. He prefers to learn pip-ing than signing! No wonder he's a lousy signer.

One day in December 1956, I went to one of the art classes. The instructor came up to me and told me that Dr. Detmold wished to see me. I thought, "What have I done?" I was scared to go to the administration office . . . maybe, bad news from home . . . maybe, my courses . . . no, not my courses . . . why did he want to talk to me? . . . So I went to Dr. Detmold's office and he welcomed me, leading me to a chair. I sat down, shaking all over.

DR.	
DETMOLD:	I remember you when you were in "Macbeth" two years ago.
ME:	Yes.
DR.	
DETMOLD:	I really enjoyed helping the cast and coaching those two players in fencing. Remember? I saw you per-form a small part . . . Seyton. I was pleased with your performance.
ME:	Thank you.
DR.	
DETMOLD:	You have always worked in student productions and you were president of the Drama Club. Right?
ME:	Yes.

DR. DETMOLD:	(Pauses) Well, I have been thinking . . hmmm . . . for a long time . . . of a person . . . a deaf person, I mean . . . who might be interested in teaching drama at Gallaudet.
ME:	Oh?
DR. DETMOLD:	Are *you* interested in teaching drama here?
ME:	Me???
DR. DETMOLD:	Yes.
ME:	But . . . but I'm majoring in art.
DR. DETMOLD:	Great. You can major in drama at Catholic University.
ME:	Me? At a hearing college? Impossible! No. No. I can't.
DR. DETMOLD:	Sure you can.
ME:	But . . . I already have a job ready for me in Hartford . . . as a commercial artist at the Travelers Insurance Company.
DR. DETMOLD:	I see . . . Well, it's up to you.
ME:	It's hard to make a decision.
DR. DETMOLD:	You don't have to make it now. Come back next month and let me know your answer.
ME:	May I ask you a question?
DR. DETMOLD:	Sure.
ME:	If I stay here, where will I teach? And for which department?
DR. DETMOLD:	The English Department. Dr. Stokoe will arrange everything for you.
ME:	Oh, I see . . . thank you. I'll be back in January. I'll talk it over with my family.

I went out of his office, thinking, "Stokoe, no, no, no, Stokoe, no, no, no. Should I accept Detmold's offer? . . . or go back to Connecticut? I don't know . . ."

Gallaudet College was finally accredited in May 1957, and we, members of the Class of 1957, had the honor of being the first to receive our diploma from the "new Gallaudet." I accepted the teaching position the following fall and I took part-time graduate work at Catholic University.

One day in the spring of 1958, several professors were discussing some incredible research.

PROFESSOR: Do you know that Dr. Stokoe is going to study Sign Language?
ME: Yes, he had better.
PROFESSOR: I do not mean that he is learning Sign Language. He actually *studies* Sign Language.
ME: So?
PROFESSOR: He is doing a linguistic research.
ME: Linguistic?
PROFESSOR: Study of language . . . science of language . . . He will analyze our Sign Language!

DR. STOKOE UNDERTAKING A LINGUISTIC RESEARCH

At the moment, Gallaudet College has three research projects underway; one of them being a linguistic research headed by Dr. William C. Stokoe, Jr. who began it with six weeks at the University of Buffalo last July and August. Its purpose is to make a scientific analysis and description of the structure of the sign language.

In preparation for the research program, Dr. Stokoe attended a workshop on the structural analysis of English at the University of Buffalo. The information derived from the workshop could be applied in studying any language, but Dr. Stokoe was especially interested in applying it to the language of signs.

In his research program, he is applying the principles of scientific language analysis to the study of sign language. This study is being made on the basis that all languages have a systematic structure which can be discovered and described. For example: A professor of English at Oxford and Mexican laborer in the Southwest United States speak the language very differently but both their dialects can be explained in terms of the structure of the English language. Perhaps too, the signing of a Gallaudet graduate and of a deaf person without much schooling, will be seen to be explainable as variations of a central pattern.

One of the aims of the research is to find the relationships between sign language and other languages an individual knows. It asks and tries to answer such questions as: (a) Does using good English damage one's signing and (b) Does using good sign language affect one's spoken or written English in any way?

My colleagues and I laughed at Dr. Stokoe and his crazy project. It was impossible to analyze our Sign Language. One professor reminded me that people used to laugh at Thomas Edison.

Some of us were concerned about the hearing professors' skills in Sign Language. In the same March 1958 issue in which the article on Stokoe's research appeared; another article was published—this one written by a very concerned student, Bert Shaposka.

IS GALLAUDET LOSING ITS POWER OF THE SIGN LANGUAGE?

Gallaudet is supposed to be the center of the language of signs. As deaf students, we are presumably the cream of the crop. We are supposedly capable of assuming many responsibilities and one is certainly the evaluation of our original language of signs.

Unless remedial measures are taken soon, this essential element in the culture of the deaf, the sign language, may become warped. We are the deaf leaders of tomorrow. Who else but us can keep our unique method of communication alive and functioning as an effective medium?

In recent years, the Gallaudet College faculty has undergone numerous changes. There were formerly quite a number of deaf instructors on the staff who knew the sign language by heart. Although a few of them are still around today, many have been replaced by hearing newcomers.

The faculty is no longer the guiding force it used to be in respect to the sign language. Today they are more dependent on the students to confirm its correct use. Formerly the instructors were looked upon as the authorities in the language of signs and they insisted upon correct signs. One of the courses which had an important role in stressing the correct application of the sign language was public speaking. It is no longer given.

A possible answer to this problem is an organization to preserve the language of signs. Membership could include both students and faculty members. Although a large number of students skilled in the language would be most welcome, we would settle for a handful of interested people.

I began to wonder what the language of signs was. What was Sign Language? The teachers at the American School for the Deaf kept telling me to use Sign Language. Now the older professors warned me to preserve the beauty of the language of signs. I remember when I was introduced to Dr. Elizabeth Peet, an authority on Sign Language. I stared at her signing gracefully about the play she recently saw. She advised me to sign properly and clearly. "Always select right signs," reminded the matron. "Each sign has its meaning. When you fingerspell, do it moderately and clearly." I wished I could sign as well as she did.

Whenever I saw a new professor on the campus, he usually signed awkwardly. I always thought it was easy for everyone to learn Sign Language. I didn't understand why they couldn't sign well. Dr. Stokoe was still a "no-good signer," yet he was analyzing our language of signs.

A Buff and Blue report about Dr. Stokoe's project in October 1959:

> Dr. William C. Stokoe, Jr., head of the Department of English, has penetrated further in his linguistic research on the language of signs, it was learned recently.
>
> The purpose of this research is to use the methods of the modern science of structural linguistics to analyze all that can be discovered about the sign language.
>
> The results obtained so far in this research project are a fairly complete description of the basic symbols of the system called the "sign language" and the principles of their combination into signs. A system of written symbols for their basic visual symbols so that the sign language can be written down for records and for further study is vital.
>
> Research on the language of signs began in 1957 with a grant from the college budget along with another grant from the American Council of Learned Societies to Dr. Stokoe, George L. Trager and Henry L. Smith of Buffalo, New York.
>
> Dr. Stokoe, with the help of his assistants, Mr. Carl Croneberg and Miss Dorothy Sueoka, plans a study of the grammatical and syntactic principles—how sentences in the language are established and so forth. This study should then prove of value in teaching English to the deaf.
>
> This research will continue as long as any other branch of anthropological sciences continues.

I did not believe Dr. Stokoe would succeed in his project and I thought these two deaf assistants were wasting their time signing before the camera. I had seen one book published in 1918 by Rev. J. Schuyler Long that had many pictures of Long showing signs. That was sufficient. The subject of linguistic research was continuously discussed among the students and professors. In January 1960, Dr. Stokoe was out of town—this time to Los Angeles to attend a four-day meeting on "Machine Translation" at the University of California. I wondered what he was trying to do with our Sign Language. Later, we were surprised to learn of his progress.

LINGUISTIC RESEARCH GETS $22,000 NSF
GRANT FOR PROJECT

Gallaudet College has been awarded a grant of $22,000 by the National Science Foundation for the support of basic research entitled "Linguistic Structure of Sign Language".

The grant will enable a research team headed by Professor William C. Stokoe, Jr., to continue its analysis of the sign language of the deaf in the United States. Professor Stokoe, Mr. Carl Croneberg, and Miss Dorothy Sueoka of the college will investigate the sentence patterns and the dialect difference of the language during the two-year period of the grant . . .

More progress: Dr. Stokoe prepared and wrote a new textbook on English composition for Freshman students. It was called *The Calculus of Structure*. This book used symbols to clarify problems of grammar and syntax for those students whose hearing loss prevented them from a natural acquisition of language. The students protested about the strange book. Some of the students refused to take this special English course instructed by Dr. Stokoe. Those who took it had shown me their assignments. They were alien to me and I thought Dr. Stokoe was eccentric.

In the Buff & Blue issue of November 1960, it was stated:

"WRITTEN" SIGN LANGUAGE MADE POSSIBLE BY RESEARCH

In a new book by Professor William C. Stokoe, Jr. chairman of the Department of English, the language of signs acquires linguistic status. This book, *Sign Language Structure,* marks the first stage of the continuing research program in linguistics of which Dr. Stokoe is director.

Coming hard on the heels of the publication of an English textbook *The Calculus of Structure,* the new book deals with the basic elements of the sign language used by thousands of deaf people in the United States and Canada. Dr. Stokoe isolates these elements and gives symbols for them, so that for the first time what is "said" in this language can be written down.

A table of these symbols is included in the book. A new font, designed by Dr. Stokoe and made by the Vari-Typer Corporation, will make possible the preparation and publication of clear and convenient dictionaries, grammars, and textbooks of the language of signs.

Further research in linguistics is being supported by a National Science Foundation grant, and will examine the grammar and syntax of the sign language.

Sign Language Structure was originally published in a special issue of "Studies in Linguistics" at the University of Buffalo.

I became close friends with Dr. Detmold because of our work in theatrical productions. Between classes and rehearsals I went to Catholic University. Once I had to write a term paper for one of the drama courses and I went to see Dr. Detmold for advice. He suggested that I see Dr. Stokoe, which I did. After reading my term paper, he got excited and suggested that I do a little more research on the history of the theatre. I followed his advice, did more research on my paper, then handed it in. I got a good grade on my paper! After several meetings with Dr. Stokoe, I began to admire him for the advice he gave me. I respected him for treating me as a human being—not as a deaf person. Sometimes he would stop me and asked me for a specific sign and I signed it to him. He did not discuss his linguistic research. He occasionally went out of town for meetings, giving speeches or doing research. In the spring of 1961, he was out of the country.

DR. STOKOE EXTENDS RESEARCH ON SIGNS TO BRITISH ISLES

To investigate visual communication among adult British deaf persons, Dr. William C. Stokoe, professor of English at Gallaudet College, left the United States on March 21 for a five-month stay in the British Isles.

The particular interest of this study is the British sign language as it differs from and is similar to American sign language and the relationship of visual language structure to the national and regional dialects.

Dr. Stokoe's main centers of work will be with the welfare centers, clubs, and missions for the deaf in London and Birmingham, England; in Belfast and Dublin, Ireland; and in Edinburgh and Glasgow, Scotland.

His research trip is being sponsored by the American Council of Learned Societies and is part of the long-term program of structural analysis of sign language under Dr. Stokoe's direction.

American Sign Language? That was the first name I ever heard for our own language of signs. I was afraid that the new term might be misunderstood for the Sign Language used by the American Indians.

The next year Dr. Stokoe received another grant for his study of Sign Language.

$23,200 GRANT FOR LINGUISTIC RESEARCH

A grant of $23,200 to prepare a dictionary of the American Sign Language used by deaf persons has been granted to Gallaudet College by the National Science Foundation.

The dictionary will be the first attempt to record signs systematically and to describe the grammatical features of the language.

Under the terms of the grant, the dictionary will be published as a report on a five-year program of linguistic research, and will be edited by a research team of Gallaudet faculty members, including the following: Dr. William C. Stokoe, Jr., director of the research program, as editor; Dr. Leonard Siger, as Associate Editor; Assistant Professor Carl C. Croneberg and Mrs. Dorothy Sueoka Casterline, as Assistant Editors.

The signs listed in the dictionary will have a strange look, for this language has never before been written. But the symbols used to write it follow the structure of the language so closely that many Gallaudet students and other interested visitors to the Gallaudet Linguistic Research Laboratory have learned to read and write the signs in half an hour or less.

The text will be set on a varityper, using for the signs, a font of type developed especially for writing American Sign Language.

But in the meantime, there were other developments on campus. The Drama Department was established in September 1963.

GALLAUDET DRAMA DEPARTMENT FOUNDED

A Drama Department was established last summer with Instructor Gilbert Eastman as its chairman. Its purpose is to install in the students an intellectual grasp of the art of the drama, with emphasis on the public presentation of the play . . .

Under the Drama Department, the student will work in the classroom, the laboratory theatre and the Gallaudet College Theatre. He will study play production, the history of the theatre, world drama, and a project in the field of special interest.

Finally, a new dictionary of signs was published and distributed . . .

DICTIONARY OF SIGNS HAS 2000 ENTRIES

Dr. William C. Stokoe, Mrs. Dorothy Casterline and Professor Carl C. Croneberg have been working for the past seven years on a new book on the sign language, which is to be distributed in 1965.

A *Dictionary of American Sign Language on Linguistic Principles* will describe and photographically illustrate the elements of the language of signs and analyze their combination into signs. Some two thousand entries in the dictionary will list the signs in symbolic notation and give information on their etymology, regional distribution and usage.

Dr. Stokoe states that this dictionary will be a source of scientific information about the language of signs and is not meant to compete with the many manuals and phrase books intended for everyday use. The language described in the dictionary is that used by Gallaudet students, many of who cooperated as informants, and to some extent that encountered in field studies.

And in the same issue that announced the new dictionary . . .

RESEARCH STUDY REPORTS SIGN LANGUAGE HELPS DEAF

Teaching a deaf child the language of signs will help him learn English later, reports a research team at the University of Pittsburgh.

This, they said, refutes the argument that early use of the language of signs inhibits a deaf child from learning to talk, write and lipread . . .

Among their findings:

1. Deaf children taught the language of signs from infancy tend to read, write and lipread better than other deaf children.

2. The very young deaf child needs a method of communication and can learn signs much faster than speech.

3. Parents may communicate via the language of signs with preschool deaf children without fear they are jeopardizing the later learning of English . . .

Dr. Birch and Dr. Stuckless found the early use of the language of signs teaches a child the value of communication and gives him an advantage over a child with no means of expressing himself.

The year 1967 saw a new chapter of sensational happenings. First, Dr. Herbert R. Kohl came to Gallaudet College to give a speech about methods of education for deaf people in the United States.

The main point of Kohl's thesis is that none of the methods of educating the deaf in the United States today has been of very great success. He argues that the sign language appears to be a "natural language" to deaf children, and that the deaf child should be permitted to use this natural mode of communication from the very beginning of his schooling. He emphasizes the need for further study along these lines, and subsequent refinement and improvement of the sign language.

Kohl further states that this suppression of the sign language by schools for the deaf has blocked the emotional development of the deaf child, and contributed to his present lag of four to seven years and that the social, emotional, linguistic, conceptual and intellectual problems of the deaf are inextricably bound together.

Second, a new kind of communication called Cued Speech, was introduced at Gallaudet College by Dr. R. Orin Cornett.

This communication, called Cued Speech, involves signs close to the mouth that show only what is missing or cannot be easily distinguished on the lips. The signs mean nothing in themselves.

The method employs twelve manual "cues" which do not show individual "phoneme" but give, instead, enough information in each to lead to correct identification of the phoneme from which is visible on the lips.

The central purpose is to aid the deaf person in lipreading and also the learning and mastering of the spoken language.

It was an artificial communication and it was absolutely not a language. It was like Morse Code. It caused much controversy. Deaf people, for the most part, did not support this new means of communication.

Third, the National Theatre of the Deaf was born with eight members including myself, my wife June, Bernard Bragg, and Lou Fant. Many people across the United States were exposed to Sign Language. Sign translating as an art was introduced.

Fourth, a unique course, "Sign Language Translation for the Theatre" was offered in the Drama Department at Gallaudet. There was no other course like it in the world.

Fifth, a National Program in Sign Language was established by a grant awarded to the National Association of the Deaf for the purpose of developing guidelines for teaching, testing, and evaluating Sign Language.

Finally, more of Dr. Stokoe's work was announced in the November issue of the Buff and Blue.

Dr. William Stokoe, Chairman of the English Department, has expressed hopes of beginning a study of the sign language sentence structure of the deaf. He is interested in the construction, the parts, the holding factor of the sentences and what the different arrangements of the same parts of a sentence have to do with the signaling of different meanings.

There is a new device that will be used to study filmed conversations in sign language. This method will allow short stretches of conversation to be repeated as often as desired in order to study the structural aspects of the sign language.

The description of language is divided between two rivals, one is the structural method used in "Sign Language Structure" (S.L. op: 8, 1961). The other is transformational grammar. Dr. Stokoe has not yet had the chance to try transformational grammar to see if it can be of any contribution to our knowledge of language although he is interested.

The present series of materials for the teaching of English to the deaf will be completed in a matter of months. Dr. Stokoe states that this series will probably be used for high school students. Dr. Stokoe has a contract with a publisher on a freshman English book that has to be revised.

We began to discuss some of these issues among ourselves. Here is a typical conversation I had with one of my colleages:

FRIEND: Listen to me carefully. I'll explain to you the difference between the Sign Language we are using and the Sign Language others are using.

ME: I know Sign Language.

FRIEND: You don't understand this.

ME: Neither do you.

FRIEND: Wait a minute. Let me show you. What we use is like this "Hey, Gil . . . I would like to take you out for a drink . . . How about it?" See, I use a sign for each word. That is one sign language. Or better to say, that is English.

ME: Yeah, I know that.

FRIEND: Another Sign Language . . . I don't like to use . . . is like this. "Me think car red expensive." That is not English.

ME: But it's Sign Language . . . ASL.

FRIEND: No, no, it's not. It is a low language.

ME: It is not a low language.

FRIEND: Damn! You not understand. Stubborn always you.

ME: See! You're using ASL.

FRIEND: I never use ASL.

ME: Good grief!

It was not the first time I had encountered this kind of conversation. Some people, including deaf people, were deaf to our true Sign Language . . . American Sign Language.

In the fall of 1969, Dr. Edward C. Merrill, Jr. was installed as the fourth president of Gallaudet College. In 1970 Elizabeth Benson retired. George Detmold resigned from the office of College Dean and became a faculty member of the Drama Department.

The name of Washoe, the chimpanzee, was frequently finger-spelled on the campus and the question of teaching a chimpanzee Sign Language was argued among the students and professors. Some of them angrily reacted to the experiment with Washoe and they feared that hearing people would think about deaf people as apes!

Dr. Stokoe left the English Department to take a new position in the newly-established Linguistics Research Laboratory.

Dr. William C. Stokoe, Jr. who has served as chairman of the Department of English since 1957, has been named as full-time Director of the Linguistic Research Laboratory. He will assume his new duties in July.

Dr. Stokoe will head a broad program of research, but the central concerns of the Laboratory will be American Sign Language and English. These two languages have prime importance for students and teachers at Gallaudet.

The author of several books on sign language and English language learning, as well as numerous articles and papers, Dr. Stokoe had carried on linguistic research at the College during his tenure in the English Department. With support from the American Council of Learned Societies, the National Science Foundation, the Office of Education, and the Center for Applied Linguistics, his research has gained for American Sign Language recognition as one of the languages of the world. It has also provided the basis for such innovative work as the Gardner's teaching of Washoe, a chimp, a large vocabulary of signs and Ursula Bellugi-Klima's longitudinal study of language acquisition by a deaf child. Now with a full-time director, the research planned and in progress is expected to enhance the prestige of sign language and add information to a special area of the language sciences.

The new appointment will also increase cooperation with Ph.D programs in special education, speech, psycholinguistics, and sociolinguistics. Dr. Stokoe has been a contributor to several university programs in Washington and New York City. Now on a full-time schedule, the Laboratory will be able to receive students and researchers for brief visits or for a period of study.

In 1971, a Sign Language Program was created under the direction of Willard Madsen. Sign Language courses including American Sign Language were offered. Common statements I heard about the ASL course were: "How can you teach ASL?", "It is impossible to learn ASL in a class," or "ASL is a language in its own right?! Prove it!"

During the same year, I joined the National Theatre of the Deaf Summer Program and was asked to teach a course called "Nonverbal Communication" to hearing students who knew little or nothing about signing. I had to develop an outline and material for students in gestures the way I would with foreigners. By the end of summer school, I began to realize how essential nonverbal communication is in our deaf society. I continued to develop the course, "Nonverbal Communication as a Sign Language Base," for the Sign Language Program at Gallaudet. Dr. Stokoe gave me full support in teaching this course and continued to encourage me. This led me to design this course for those who are not familiar with American Sign Language as well as for those who need to improve their signing skills.

In the fall of 1971, I took the title role in that season's play, *Cyrano de Bergerac,* and we had the difficult task of translating poetic dialogues. An aspiring reader, Dennis Cokely, read for the vocal character of Cyrano. He came to rehearsals as many times as he could to study Sign Language. We became close friends and co-actors. There were several fascinating tasks; one of those involved translating a "sword speech" into ASL (based on several English translations of the French play) and then having Dennis re-translate my ASL translation into English.

Also in 1971, Dr. Stokoe introduced a new monthly newsletter, *Signs for Our Times,* which published information on Sign Language and linguistics:

> *Signs For Our Times* is an experiment in communication to be continued if response warrants . . .

In 1972, Dr. Stokoe began to publish a quarterly journal, *Sign Language Studies,* which printed "research reports, articles, reviews, and brief notes of study in several fields. Anthropology, ethnography, psycholinguistics, psychology, semiotics, and sociolinguistics are some of the disciplines in which the use of motor signs and their organizing infrastructures have importance."

In 1972, Lou Fant—a former professor at Gallaudet College, a former actor in the National Theatre of the Deaf, and the author of *Say It With Hands*—came to visit Gallaudet and gave a talk on Ameslan (an acronym for American Sign Language). He said that "Ameslan is not a new sign language. It is nothing more than an accurate name for American Sign." A common question resulted: What is the difference between American Sign Language and Ameslan?

> After Mr. Fant's lecture on Ameslan language, there was a question and answer period. He was asked what his next book will be, and he replied it will be called *Ameslan,* published by NAD. It will be used to teach Ameslan and is arranged in conversational order. He believes in teaching signs first, and fingerspelling last. He felt they (students) must think from the picture or idea. This book will be used this fall in teaching Ameslan at SFVSC [San Fernando Valley State College, now California State University at Northridge], which will be an accredited course.

The result of Lou's new introduction to Ameslan led to recognition from some of the Gallaudet students. They formed the Ameslan Fan

Club in the Buff and Blue and some of them began trying to write in Ameslan. One of the letters to the editor said:

> Me like your article in B & B about your writing on Ameslan some weeks ago. You talk and write smooth. How do you do it?
>
> Please keep up to write our language in B & B so that we deafies enjoy, read, talk, and maybe write.

A tragic event struck when the first deaf research associate in the Linguistics Research Laboratory, Judy Williams, was killed in an automobile accident while traveling to her husband's parents' home in North Carolina. She had worked with Bill Stokoe in the Linguistics Research Lab, and she had already begun research on her deaf child's acquisition of Sign Language in their home; her work began to demonstrate that a deaf child could master more than one kind of language. Bill was shocked and grieved by her untimely death.

During the summer of 1972, I decided to translate a play in ASL by *writing on paper*. I converted six English translations of Sophocles' Greek tragedy *Antigone* into one comprehensive Sign Language translation. The readers were instructed to vocalize the signs, which followed the grammatical structure of American Sign Language. The characters used archaic ASL signs, and there were no initialized signs. After the production, some of my colleagues, including Dr. Stokoe, encouraged me to do more productions with that kind of translation, but others criticized the readers' presentation. However, the production was judged as one of the nation's ten best college and university theatre productions and was selected to be performed at the John F. Kennedy Center for the Performing Arts in Washington, D.C. This honor recognized both the beauty and the uniqueness of American Sign Language.

One day in the spring of 1973, Dr. Stokoe came to my office and introduced me to his friend, Dr. Ursula Bellugi. I had heard so much about her and her linguistic research on Sign Language at the Salk Institute, and she had written me several letters and even sent me several papers on ASL for me to read. I was honored to meet her and we had a wonderful conversation together. I realized that it was not only Gallaudet College that had linguists, but there were apparently Sign Language linguists from coast to coast.

At that time, I decided to write a play myself . . . something about deafness. It was called *Sign Me Alice*, based on George Bernard Shaw's *Pymalion* and Lerner and Lowe's *My Fair Lady*. It was about the life of the deaf mingling in the life of the hearing. The deaf characters did not ask for pity but for the right to a choice: to use the Sign Language that they preferred, rather than having new signs forced on them. Private jokes, playing with signs, and newly invented signs were included in the play.

After the performance Dr. Stokoe came and offered me his hand to shake. Another encouragement. People wrote to me and asked for my script of *Sign Me Alice*. I did not have a proper script then, and the original script was filled with notes, scribblings, changes and eliminations. But during the following summer I worked at the Linguistics Research Laboratory and helped Dr. Stokoe transcribe films made in 1913 of signing by deaf people. It was a fantastic experience for me, and later I asked Bill for technical advice regarding the development of word codes for publishing signs. *Sign Me Alice* was published a year later and Bill wrote a foreword for the play.

The new development of word codes for signs helped my work in the field of drama, especially for a course I taught, "Sign Language Translation for the Theatre." With patience and effort, my students were able to write down what they signed in ASL, and eventually, they were able to translate poems and plays into ASL using the word-codes.

The following year, 1974, the Buff and Blue stated:

> The Sign Language Programs Office and the Linguistic Research Laboratory at Gallaudet College held their first annual sign language conference in Hall Memorial Building No. 213 at Gallaudet College last Saturday, April 27th from 9 a.m. to 6 p.m. The theme of the conference was "What Lies Between the American Sign Language and Sign English?" The American Sign Language is the casual and informal sign language used by deaf people whereas the Sign English Language is the more formal sign language usually used by the hearing students and friends, teachers of the deaf, interpreters in educational or formal settings, and proponents of total communication.

The lecture by William Stokoe at that conference was also mentioned in the B & B.

> "The Ins and Outs of In and Out" by Dr. William Stokoe, Jr. He stated that the recognition of Sign as a language has been long and slow in coming, primarily due to the sociology of language and that the solid knowledge of language structure comes from groups that know and use a common language in their interaction. Through careful questioning, linguists discover which signs and which sentence structures are in a particular language (are acceptable). He stated that many signers accept almost any attempt at signing because of deference to hearing people

who speak the English language, and this double standard hampers the study of Sign as a language in its own right. Dr. Stokoe exhorted persons with a good Sign background to "take a harder line" with new signers to alleviate this difficulty.

The B & B of September 26, 1974 headlined:

DEAF RUSSIAN ACTOR SCORES BIG HIT

Gallaudet College Auditorium was the scene of one of the most re-markable cultural events in recent years when Michael Sliptchenko gave a lecture-demonstration on Tuesday, September 17.

Mr. Sliptchenko, a deaf Russian actor from the Moscow Theatre of Mimicry and Gesture, is in this country for one month. He was intro-duced to the audience by Gilbert Eastman and then proceeded to show slides of the Moscow Theatre of Mimicry and Gesture and to answer many questions from the audience. Mr. Sliptchenko gave his lecture using International gestures, with Jane Wilk serving as his interpreter. Miss Wilk was aided in interpreting by Yerker Andersson and Simon Carmel.

Michael was my house guest and he shared his home experiences with my family. We used an interesting way to communicate, using gestures only. He chose several places he wished to visit and he had to use many gestures to indicate each place. One of the interviews I arranged was at the Linguistics Research Laboratory with Dr. Stokoe and·Robbin Battison. We discussed the difference between Russian Sign Language and Sign Russian, similar to our languages, ASL and Sign English.

In the fall of 1975, I developed another play, *Hands*, which was an original piece created in collaboration with Gallaudet drama stu-dents. The play grew out of the life experiences, observations, and fantasies of the actors. There were incidents relating to family affairs, hearing-oriented events, communication problems, and school memories. These compositions were refined for the stage, using the actors' creativity and signing talent.

This "art form" signing has been acted out mischievously in school dormitories, heartily shared among deaf families, used as entertain-ment at deaf parties, and secretly used among ourselves. It has long been supressed and unrecognized by the general public and educa-tors of deaf students. This art form, a definite part of our deaf culture, has passed from hand to hand, generation to generation, through storytelling. It is the traditional deaf folk sign and is still popular in deaf society. It will never die because it is our own way.

In 1976, during my sabbatical leave, I wrote a historical play about Laurent Clerc, the Frenchman who became America's first deaf educator. I did extensive research in Washington, D.C. and in Hartford, Connecticut to gather information on Clerc. I examined not only his life, but also the Sign Language that Clerc brought to America from France. I contacted several people for more information on Clerc and several times I came to see Dr. Stokoe for advice and suggestions. We stayed in his office for hours talking about Laurent Clerc and French Sign Language.

In the spring of 1977, the National Symposium on Sign Language Research and Teaching was held in Chicago; the entire program was sponsored and arranged by the Communicative Skills Program of the National Association of the Deaf. Linguists, teachers, administrators and other interested people from all over the country attended lectures in the morning, workshops in the afternoon, and entertainment in the evening. The majority of participants recognized American Sign Language as a true, respected language used by deaf citizens of the United States.

The following year a group of French people (linguists, psychologists, Sign Language teachers, school teachers) came to Gallaudet College for five weeks to learn about the education of American deaf people. Preparations were made by Harry Markowicz, a former researcher at the Linguistics Research Laboratory and now a linguistic consultant in Paris. The French participants attended many programs, including a class in Nonverbal Communication which I taught.

In the same year a new course, "Structure of American Sign Language," designed by Carol Padden and Charlotte Baker, was finally offered for undergraduates at Gallaudet. And in 1978, due to popular demand, the course also began to be offered at the graduate level for Gallaudet faculty and staff.

Courses with the title "Nonverbal Communication" were offered at universities and colleges in the United States but the subject matter in these courses was entirely different from my developed course because they emphasized body language, behavior, personalities, clothing, etc. So I changed the title of course, "Nonverbal Communication as a Sign Language Base," to "Visual-Gestural Communication as a Sign Language Base." In that way it more accurately reflected the course content.

The Second National Symposium on Sign Language Research and Teaching took place in October 1978 in San Diego. Many of the same participants were there, and many new people came for the first time. At the closing of the symposium I had one of the greatest, richest, experiences I ever had when I interpreted for Harlan Lane, who gave his talk on Laurent Clerc.

In 1979 at Gallaudet, the Linguistics Research laboratory began to organize informal brown-bag lunches for people who were professionally interested in Sign Language. During those lunches, we shared our Sign-related experiences and discussed problems, attitudes, questions, developments, and results of our experiences.

In the summer of 1979, my wife June and I had the opportunity to attend the first International Symposium on Sign Language in Stockholm for a week, and I gave a speech about nonverbal communication as a Sign Language base and how to translate into Sign Language for the theater to sixty participants from other countries. Three other delegates from Gallaudet College also gave talks on the terms "verbal" and "nonverbal" (Charlotte Baker), on bilingual materials for teaching English (Barbara Kannapell), and on Sign translation (Eric Malzkuhn). After the convention, June and I toured Europe and I conducted a workshop in Paris.

I would like to close this informal history by saying that Dr. Stokoe taught me to be aware of Sign Language and to appreciate its beauty. I developed basic Sign Language courses, wrote plays, and went all over the country to conduct workshops on Visual-Gestural Communication and to give speeches about my work. But it was Bill Stokoe who helped me to develop pride in my language and my activities, and it was he who encouraged me to tell the truth.

Dr. Stokoe is not a fluent signer, yet he has never stopped learning our Sign Language. He has never stopped teaching us what he has observed about our language. Dr. Stokoe was the first linguistic researcher in ASL, and he became an internationally known advocate of deaf people and Sign Language. We should all honor him as the Father of Sign Language linguistics.

II
THE
STRUCTURE
OF SIGN
LANGUAGE

Signs Have Parts: A Simple Idea

by Robbin Battison

It was December of 1971 and I was flying from San Diego to Europe to attend some meetings and see some friends. I had been working with American Sign Language for about a year, and one of the books that I kept going through again and again was the Dictionary of American Sign Language. *I decided to meet the principal author of that book as long as I was stopping in at Washington, D.C. Who knew when I would have a chance like that again? I called up Bill Stokoe and he invited me to lunch. At lunch, we chatted; he was friendly and full of ideas and wanted to know about mine.*

He later surprised me when he wrote to offer me a job that summer (the Watergate summer of 1972) in the Linguistics Research Lab. Of course I accepted; the salary he offered was twice what I would have asked for. I made several false starts that first summer and actually wrote up very little of my research or my ideas; but the following year Bill asked me to come out again. After the second

---

Robbin Battison first became interested in Sign Language in 1970, while studying linguistics at the University of California, San Diego, and working in Ursula Bellugi's laboratory at the neighboring Salk Institute for Biological Studies. He spent the years 1973–1976 at the Linguistics Research Lab, Gallaudet College, and received his Ph.D. in Linguistics from UCSD in 1977. His dissertation, Lexical Borrowing in American Sign Language, *was published in 1978. From 1976 to 1979, Robbin conducted research and taught American Sign Language in the Psychology Department of Northeastern University in Boston. Since 1979, he has pursued his interest in bureaucratic language and language comprehension as Manager of the Document Design Center at the American Institutes for Research in Washington, D.C. He edits a newsletter,* *Fine Print, *and other publications which discuss the language and design of public documents.*

summer in the Lab, I did not return to graduate school in San Diego.
After all, I had finished my course work, and at Gallaudet College I
could write my dissertation while surrounded by hundreds of
skilled signers, the people who could help me discover new things
about this very peculiar language that I had chosen to study. I had
some ideas but very little direction at this point. Bill gave me the
support I needed to develop my ideas and to shape my work into
something coherent. It took years . . .

Introduction

The thing that interested me most about Bill Stokoe was that he
had hold of an exciting idea, one that clearly was going to lead
somewhere. He said that Sign Language was a language like any
other language and that it could be analyzed as a language. This
simple idea contradicted many popular beliefs: for who could see
similarities between the movements of hands and body and the au-
dible sounds produced by speaking? What possible basis of comparison was there? And, as the argument went, even if they did have
some casual similarity, we would still know that signed languages
were fundamentally different from spoken languages: after all, signs
are like pictures drawn in the air with hands, aren't they, while
words are quite abstract?

This is actually the crucial part of the argument, and the basic idea
that Bill developed. Bill believed that the basic way to think of a sign
was *not* as a picture, but as a complex and abstract symbol that could
be analyzed into parts. This heretical idea contradicted what most
experts had always said about signed languages, but eventually it
took hold, because it opened new doors of understanding. Analyzing
signs into parts allowed us to develop new theories about how
signed languages work, where they came from, where they are going,
what is the best way to teach them. This simple idea also later influenced the way in which Sign Language is used in classrooms, and
how it is used by interpreters. In this chapter I would like to give a
short history of how this simple idea developed, the scientific in-
quiries that it inspired, and the social action and professional
policies that derive from it. The story is not yet at an end.

Signs as Pictures

There are perhaps several reasons for the tradition of thinking of
signs as pictures: they are visual; they involve space and size and

shape; and they sometimes seem to represent things wholly and directly, just like a picture or a drawing. I would not argue against any of those very common observations. Signs are like pictures in many ways. But to stop there is to miss an important point. Saying that signs are like pictures is like saying that speech is like music. Spoken languages certainly have their musical aspects, but there are so many things about words and connected speech that are not like music—especially how they transmit meanings. There is more to signs than meets the eye; even if a sign does seem like a picture, that may not be the most important aspect of a sign to investigate.

There are several kinds of evidence which demonstrate that the pictorial or graphic nature of signs is not the most important aspect of Sign Language. First, several different kinds of experiments show that people who don't know Sign Language have a hard time guessing what very common signs mean, even in a multiple-choice test. Second, if we compare signs from different countries, we find that not everyone uses the same kind of gesture to represent the same meaning; in other words, different signed languages may represent the same thing with different kinds of gestures. Third, if we look very carefully at written and filmed records of older signs, we find that very often these signs have changed to become *less* graphic or picture-like, and have become more like a standardized gesture that must be pronounced in a particular way to be "just right." For example, the sign STUDENT (based on the sign LEARN) originally was made so that it seemed to create the image of taking something from a book and absorbing it into the mind; however, the modern sign looks very much like taking something and tossing it away! Fourth, sometimes even if you know what a sign means, you may find it hard or impossible to decide just exactly what pictorial image connects the meaning with the gesture. Some signs are just less pictorial than others.

For all these reasons and others (which are reviewed more carefully by Klima and Bellugi in their 1979 book) it is evident that we cannot learn very much or explain very much about Sign Language by depending on the weak idea that they are graphic pictures written in the air with the hands. There has to be something more.

Writing about Signs

Bill Stokoe had a lot of faith in his ideas; that is, he always was a stubborn man, unwilling to change his opinions just because very few people agreed with him. Faith and stubbornness are sometimes just two ways of looking at the same thing.

At first his ideas didn't make sense to anyone. Many respected experts (including some of the authors in this volume) dismissed his ideas as worthless; he was wasting his time. But knowledge comes step by step, and Bill Stokoe had a plan for studying Sign Language. First, he would need to describe the language in an elemental sense: he must write a dictionary. But before he could do that, he would need to write signs down on paper, in order to "capture" them accurately and describe how they are made. So first he would have to invent an adequate writing system—and that's where the idea began to take real shape.

In order to develop a transcription (writing) system for signs, Bill was forced to take a good hard look at how signs are made: what parts of the body move or don't move, how the fingers bend or extend, how the hands contact the body, where they touch, the speed and repetition of movements, and so on. If he could just think of a written symbol for each of the *important* elements in making signs, then he could write them down, collect signs, and begin even further analyses that could provide important information about these very strange communication systems.

Very early on, he proposed that every sign had at least three independent parts:

location — where on the body or in space is the sign being made? On the cheek, the chest, in front of the body, etc.?

handshape — how are the fingers extended and bent in this particular sign? Is the hand a fist, or does it have some fingers extended, etc.?

movement — how does the hand (or hands) move? In a circle, up-and-down, forward, etc.?

From his experience and training with other languages, Stokoe then made an assumption that turned out to be true. He assumed that within each of these three categories, there were probably a limited number of different ways of making these sign parts. For example, there might be ten different handshapes, or there might be one hundred; the important thing was that he could probably develop a list of all the possibilities, and then develop symbols for each one of them—the list was not going to be infinitely long. The same would be true of different locations and movements. The possibilities were not endless. There was probably a system to it, waiting to be discovered.

In the end, he came up with a system that worked: he had 19 different basic symbols for handshapes, 12 different basic symbols for locations, and 24 different basic symbols for types of movements. In much the same way that the symbols 0123456789 allow us to express any number, Stokoe now had a system that would allow him to express any sign on paper. He published a list of symbols and some of his early thoughts about how to use them in a thin volume in 1960 called *Sign Language Structure.* Table 1 shows the chart he published.

Regardless of how well this system captured the important parts of signs, it was an advance for the time, and it gave us some new tools to work with in probing Sign Language further. There were also practical applications. Using a transcription system, for example, a dramatist could use the transcription system to record exactly the signs needed for a play, a poem, or some other dramatic presentation; a Sign Language teacher could begin to organize lesson material according to which signs are similar, or which signs are different. The most important thing that Stokoe went on to create, however, was the first true dictionary of Sign Language. With Carl Croneberg and Dorothy Casterline, he collected, organized, and described more than 2000 different signs from the language he had begun to call American Sign Language. The dictionary was published in 1965.

We must remember the social and intellectual climate of fifteen years ago: many people were still denying that there was such a thing as a signed *language.* Certainly there was nothing that deserved the elegant title of American Sign Language (displayed in capital letters like that). And whatever kind of language it was, it was certainly nothing like the very large, complicated, and elegant spoken languages that were known in the world. As a matter of fact, some people belittled the language by referring to the dictionary and saying, "Only 2000 signs? This clearly indicates the impoverished, simple nature of Sign Language." What these people forgot is that our scientific knowledge of spoken languages has been developed and refined over several thousand years. By contrast, the scientific study of signed languages has only been progressing for twenty years, if we date it from Stokoe's first publication in 1960. We were only scratching the surface, so far.

Why was the dictionary so important? Surely there were other books that listed signs that deaf people use? But none were like this.

KEY

Tab = location
Dez = handshape
Sig = movement

Tab symbols

1.	Ø	zero, the neutral place where the hands move, in contrast with all places below
2.	∩	face or whole head
3.	∩	forehead or brow, upper face
4.	⊃⊂	mid-face, the eye and nose region
5.	⊔	chin, lower face
6.	3	cheek, temple, ear, side-face
7.	Π	neck
8.	□	trunk, body from shoulders to hips
9.	⅃	upper arm
10.	∠	elbow, forearm
11.	ɑ	wrist, arm in supinated position (on its back)
12.	D	wrist, arm in pronated position (face down)

Dez symbols, some also used as tab

#	Symbol	Description
13.	A	compact hand, fist; maybe like 'a', 's', or 't' of manual alphabet
14.	B	flat hand
15.	5	spread hand; fingers and thumb spread like '5' of manual numeration
16.	C	curved hand; may be like 'c' or more open
17.	E	contracted hand; like 'e' or more clawlike
18.	F	"three-ring" hand; from spread hand, thumb and index finger touch or cross
19.	G	index hand; like 'g' or sometimes like 'd'; index finger points from fist
20.	H	index and second finger, side by side, extended
21.	I	"pinkie" hand; little finger extended from compact hand
22.	K	like G except that thumb touches middle phalanx of second finger; like 'k' and 'p' of manual alphabet
23.	L	angle hand; thumb, index finger in right angle, other fingers usually bent into palm
24.	3	"cock" hand; thumb and first two fingers spread, like "3" of manual numeration
25.	O	tapered hand; fingers curved and squeezed together over thumb; may be like 'o' of manual alphabet
26.	R	"warding off" hand; second finger crossed over index finger, like 'r' of manual alphabet
27.	V	"victory" hand; index and second fingers extended and spread apart
28.	W	three-finger hand; thumb and little finger touch, others extended spread
29.	X	hook hand; index finger bent in hook from fist, thumb tip may touch fingertip
30.	Y	"horns" hand; thumb and little finger spread out extended from fist; or index finger and little finger extended, parallel
31.	8	(allocheric variant of Y); second finger bent in from spread hand, thumb may touch fingertip

Sig symbols

#	Symbol	Description	Action group
32.	˄	upward movement	vertical action
33.	˅	downward movement	vertical action
34.	N	up-and-down movement	
35.	>	rightward movement	sideways action
36.	<	leftward movement	sideways action
37.	z	side to side movement	
38.	⊤	movement toward signer	horizontal action
39.	⊥	movement away from signer	horizontal action
40.	H	to-and-fro movement	
41.	ɑ	supinating rotation (palm up)	rotary action
42.	p	pronating rotation (palm down)	rotary action
43.	ꝫ	twisting movement	
44.	□	nodding or bending action	
45.	◦	opening action (final dez configuration shown in brackets)	
46.	#	closing action (final dez configuration shown in brackets)	
47.	ᴀ	wiggling action of fingers	
48.	◦	circular action	
49.	⤬	convergent action, approach	
50.	×	contactual action, touch	
51.	⊠	linking action, grasp	
52.	↑	entering action	
53.	◦	crossing action	
54.	÷	divergent action, separate	
55.	ᴄ	interchanging action	interaction

Table 1. Stokoe's Transcription Symbols

A dictionary gives several different kinds of information about the words (or signs) of a language. For each *lexical entry* (separate word or sign), it gives: a coded physical description, telling us how to physically reproduce (pronounce) the word or sign; the meaning of that word or sign, including special nuances; the grammatical functions and properties of that word or sign, telling us how we might use it in a sentence and what variations we might expect depending upon its grammatical form; something of the history of that word or sign, especially a history that relates to other words or items in the language. The *Dictionary of American Sign Language* gave us all that. Previous books had given us only scattered and incomplete (and sometimes misleading) information about signs and Sign Language. Without a writing or transcription system, signs cannot be faithfully reproduced, unless especially clever photos or illustrations are used (and they usually were not).

The *Dictionary of American Sign Language* was remarkable for another reason: the signs were arranged according to a principle of the language. Just as spoken language dictionaries arrange their words alphabetically (according to the order of the first letter, then the second letter of the word, and so on), Stokoe arranged his sign dictionary according to the parts of the signs that he used for transcription. Thus, this idea that signs are complex objects with parts not only led to a writing system, but also led to a principle of *organizing* all the signs that could be related to each other, depending upon which parts they shared. This is like the way we think of different words as being related if they share the same sounds, particularly at the beginnings of words. This arrangement also shows a lot of *respect* for the language.

Considering the obvious usefulness of Bill's analysis, the reader might expect that he received a lot of support for his work from members of the Deaf community and from professionals in the field of deafness. But this was certainly not the case. Why didn't his ideas catch on more rapidly? Why was there such resistance and even hostility to his ideas about analyzing, transcribing, and describing signs?

There are two interesting reasons for this lack of support that are not usually considered. The first reason concerns the prevailing attitudes among educators of deaf people and deaf people themselves. At that time, you must remember, Sign Language was only accepted if it could be justified as a contribution to the educational system. Any new idea about Sign Language was discussed as a tool for classroom use. As several stories have it, students and faculty at Gallaudet and at some residential schools mistakenly assumed that they were going to be forced to learn this new transcription system for signs, and that all their books would be written in these complex symbols. Of course, nothing was further from the truth: the transcription system was intended as a scientific tool. But there were enough rumors and feelings going around to prevent anyone from really seeing the transcription system as Bill had intended it.

The second reason was a strategic error on Bill's part. Bill gave new technical names to the things he was describing. Perhaps he didn't realize that he was creating resistance to learning when he gave complex names to simple and familiar things. He referred to *dez, tab,* and *sig* when he could have simply said *handshape, location,* and *movement.* Some people were probably put off by these strange words and had some difficulty learning what they meant and keeping them separate; I certainly did, and I worked hard at it.

Parts of Signs

Comparing, grouping, and classifying signs according to what parts they have in common and what parts they don't is not simply a convenience for organizing dictionaries. Like words, signs must be broken up into parts in order to perceive what they mean. This is especially true of the kinds of complex signs that Ursula Bellugi describes in the next chapter, but it is also true of very simple signs.

Just as we know that the two English words 'skim' and 'skin' are different words with different meanings, we know that they are *minimally different.* That is, the only difference between these two words is the final sound unit: 'm' or 'n'. Of course we can find thousands of these *minimal pairs* (pairs of words that differ in only one *minimal* way). From them we can determine what types of sound units play an important role in distinguishing meanings in a spoken language. We can do the same with a signed language.

We can find minimal pairs of signs that differ in only one aspect of their production. For the aspect of handshape, there are pairs of signs that are identical except for their handshape. An example is the pair of signs CAR and WHICH (Figure 1). The only difference between them is that CAR has a fist with the thumb closed against the knuckles, while WHICH has a fist with the thumb extended. In the case of location, a minimal pair of CHINESE and SOUR (Figure 2). The two signs are identical except that CHINESE is made on the temple or high on the cheek and SOUR is made near the mouth.

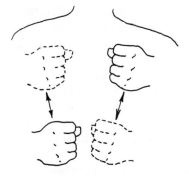
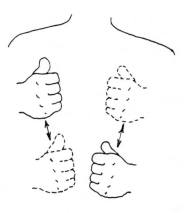

CAR/DRIVE   WHICH

Figure 1

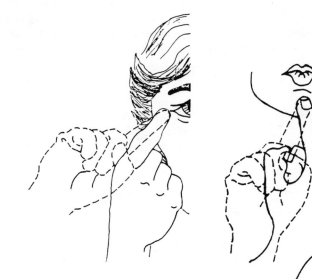

CHINESE   SOUR

Figure 2

A minimal pair for movement is found in NAME and SHORT (Figure 3). NAME is made with simple contact (sometimes repeated), while SHORT is made identically except for its brushing motion of the upper hand. Figure 3 also shows that the *orientation* of the hands might also be a distinctive aspect of signs. The pair of signs NAME and CHAIR differ only by their orientation: in NAME, both palm surfaces point towards the body, but in CHAIR the palm surfaces point downward. These and many other examples of minimal pairs show that there are critical parts of a sign that allow us to distinguish it from other signs.

There is also reason to think that this is not just a convenient way to speculate about words and signs. This kind of division into parts seems to reflect the way deaf native signers think in signs. Several memory experiments with both spoken and signed languages have shown that the errors people make when trying to recall lists of vocabulary items are frequently related to the other member of a minimal pair. In a spoken experiment, for example, someone who heard 'vote' might later recall it as 'note'; in a signed experiment, someone might see the sign TREE (with the hand completely open and fingers extended and spread, the entire upright forearm shakes on its axis) but later recall it as the sign NOON (same gesture, with-

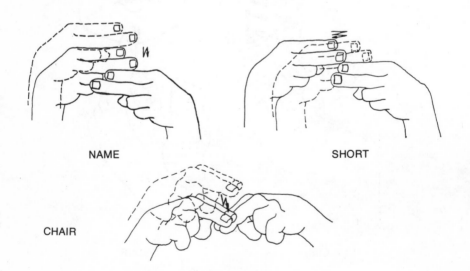

NAME   SHORT

CHAIR

Figure 3

out the shaking). The same principles of analysis into parts seem to guide the structure and use of signed languages and spoken languages.

There are several other different types of constructive arguments that are based on an analysis of signs into component parts like the one that Stokoe proposed. If we are trying to argue that signs are not simply random gestures that our bodies just happen to be able to perform, and if we also want to argue that a sign does not have to be a "picture" and does not have to "graphically" represent an idea or an object, then we might look for some other factors or forces that determine how signers use their hands and their bodies to make signs.

From work with spoken languages, it is well known that the individual sounds in a language and the way those sounds can come together to make words in a language are always only a small portion of what humans are able to articulate. Not every possible vocal sound is used in a spoken language. Of the sound units that a language uses, not every possible combination of these units is used to form syllables or words—many are unlikely or impossible combinations, such as 'frtps'. This is because sounds and their combinations are governed and limited by psychological and physiological laws relating to the speech organs, and by the way that the ear takes in and processes information.

It is easy to show that the same kinds of principles determine how the different elements of signs—handshapes, locations, and movements—can come together (or *co-occur*) to form complete signs. Of course, some things are quite impossible to do with the hands because of physical limitations. But what about things that are *possible,* but *too complex and unnatural* for the kind of rapid signing that is common in conversation? Are there such things? Linguistic research has shown that there are.

The example I will offer here is from some work I did while studying how signs limit the ways that different parts can occur together. (At that time, I was looking for something parallel to what we call *morpheme structure constraints* in spoken languages.) In ASL, as in all signed languages that we know about, many signs are made with both hands. Logically then, the handshapes could either be the same (for example, two fists), or they could be different (for example, a fist on the left hand and a "V" shape on the right hand). As it turns out for the signs that I studied, there are a number of rules and predictions that you can make on the basis of the handshapes used in signs made with both hands. For example, if the two handshapes are different:

- only one hand will move during the sign—usually the "dominant" hand.
- the hand that does not move will not be just any one of dozens of handshapes—it will be one of the simplest, or most natural, handshapes (the closed fist, the open palm, the open hand with fingers spread, the fist with index finger extended, the "O" hand, or the "C" hand).

This kind of limitation, which is observed in other signed languages as well as in ASL, leads to several further observations. First, the limitation is systematic and excludes large numbers of possible hand arrangements; there are only a very few existing signs which break the two "rules" above. Second, there seems to be a physiological reason for the way these "rules" operate: complex and moving things are most often on the dominant hand; simple and static things will most often be on the non-dominant hand (the one that is usually not as skilled in doing things). Other reasons may include perceptual factors, such as how many different things the eye and the brain can take in and keep track of when a person watches signs. There is quite a bit of evidence that perceptual limitations play a role in "shaping" possible signs.

There is no need here to continue listing and describing the many different kinds of constraints that people have hypothesized for the structure of signed languages. For the purposes of this paper, the important theoretical point is that these constraints are like those that explain how spoken languages operate: the forms of a language are constrained by physiological and perceptual factors on the production and perception of spoken words and gestural signs.

There are practical observations that are linked to this small set of rules. Consider the problem that faces many professionals who work with signs, especially teachers of young deaf children. Very often teachers will want a sign for a particular word or a concept, but they don't know what that sign is, or even know if it exists. Occasionally, they will appropriately ask several skilled signers to determine what they should sign. Much more often, they will either fingerspell the word or invent their own sign.

Now, what about all these signs that get invented? Many schools have continuing discussions in committees whose main purpose seems to be to invent signs. But are these invented signs appropriate? Do they fit the natural rules of how signs can be constructed out of parts? The answer is that many of the invented signs, particularly the signs that have been invented to transliterate English words, are unnaturally complex. Many of the signs that have been invented for children, including the names of animals and toys, violate some of the rules that natural signs obey. The results of this situation have been observed by many people in many different places: both children and adults have difficulty learning how to make the signs; both children and adults tend to change the signs, to pronounce them in a little more natural way; and experienced signers often view some of these signs as being unnatural ("they don't fit in"), and in some cases peculiar, silly, or even crude. The lesson is quite clear: we should study how deaf people use signs in a conversational context, and we should pay attention to the detail of how the signs are made. Only then, and only cautiously, should anyone attempt to invent a sign on their own — and only as a last resort.

Extending the Idea that Signs Have Parts

The first summer working in the Linguistics Research Lab was one of exploration and discovery for me. Contrary to what I expected, Bill did not order me to carry out a specific research plan; he didn't order me to transcribe videotapes, and he didn't have me compiling information from dusty books on a hot summer day. He allowed me to think about what I wanted to do, and to take it from there. I kept thinking about breaking signs down into parts and comparing them; I knew that this would be the way to discover all sorts of things about signing, and that this would provide a basis for comparing signs with words. That summer, Lynn Friedman (another summer research assistant) and I began to talk about another level of structure. We knew that it was interesting and useful to think of signs broken down into handshapes, locations, and movements . . . but what was beyond that? What was a handshape? What was a movement, really? These things could also be analyzed into finer parts, and perhaps that division would be useful too. We felt that if we could isolate the different levels of structure of a sign, we might compare them to the different levels of structure of a word. We felt that a word corresponded to a sign pretty well, and the three aspects that Stokoe had discovered might correspond roughly to individual sounds in a spoken word. But we also knew that even individual sounds were composed of finer parts called *distinctive features*, and perhaps we would also find a corresponding level of structure in signs.

Distinctive features in spoken language can refer to many things, but for our purposes here I might say that they refer to different *acts* that the vocal organs (mouth, lips, tongue, etc.) perform in order to make the sounds of language. For example, the feature of *lip rounding* is a distinctive feature of many sounds in many languages. We felt that we might discover a similarity, so we began by breaking down handshapes into features that we called *bent* (if the fingers were bent), *crossed* (if some of the fingers crossed each other), *spread* (if the fingers were not touching each other), etc. We eventually came up with a preliminary analysis of features for handshapes, locations, and movements, and we later pursued this track of investigation more thoroughly in our ways.

By now you may be asking yourself, "Why bother breaking down signs into finer and finer details?" The answer is that we were creating a tool for understanding how Sign Language works. Since all of us were continually trying to think of new ways to get valid and meaningful information about signs, it made sense to at least experiment with the very lowest, very finest level of description: how different parts of the body had to arrange themselves and move in order to compose a sign. It was also good practice for learning how to describe signs adequately, and eventually might help us sort out what were the important, as opposed to the unimportant, parts of signs.

The second set of reasons had to do with the general strategy among sign researchers at the time. We were always looking for familiar things that would help alert us to how signs really worked. Since spoken languages had been studied for many centuries, there was a set of traditions (sometimes misleading) and set of theories (sometimes conflicting) about how human beings managed to move their mouths and tongues and make sounds, and how they could listen to those sounds and somehow form the impression that the other person had given them information. There is something magical about it, after all. But for spoken languages, we had at least made a dent in the problem. There are large dictionaries of spoken languages and many scholars who study those languages. Even elementary school children learn something about grammar and composition in their classrooms. More importantly, there is a vocabulary of technical terms for discussing spoken languages. The natural thing to do, although cautiously, was to try to find things in signed languages that looked like, or seemed to act like, familiar things in spoken languages. In this way, we were trying to answer the question: "In what ways are signed languages like spoken languages?" If we kept finding similarities despite their different production mechanisms (the hands and body versus the voice) and despite their different perceptual mechanisms (the eyes versus the ears), then we would feel sure that we were somehow getting closer to discovering ways for producing and perceiving language that all humans share, regardless of whether a given human can hear or not.

Any time that a researcher did find a similarity, it might lead that researcher onto a very productive path. This was true of the distinctive feature analysis. As it turns out, allowing us to think about distinctive features of signs allowed us to make a connection to three different kinds of psychological studies that had been done with spoken languages. These offered researchers three new bases for comparing signs and words as people actually used them.

The first kind of study concerned psychological processes like perception and memory. Experiments had showed that the "inner language" of the mind may operate in terms of something like distinctive features. This led to a whole series of investigations by various researchers on the memory and perception of signs.

The second type of study concerned the effects of brain damage on language production and perception. Some of the descriptive work on hearing people who have suffered brain damage used an analysis of distinctive features; this work could now be extended to studies of deaf people (usually elderly) with brain damage.

A third type of study was even more exciting than the other two. People who study "slips of the tongue" (everyday speech errors) have found that these errors help us understand how the brain controls the parts of the body that express speech and language. One of the only ways to describe some of the errors is in terms of distinctive features. This suggested a new avenue of investigation for sign researchers, who then began to study "slips of the hand," or sign errors.

The point of these little anecdotes is not to inform you about distinctive features. The point is to show the logical progression of ideas leading to further ideas and action.

I think it is very easy to show, for example, that the original idea that signs have parts influences the ways in which we think about the grammar of a signed language. Just to take one point, many writers have said (even into the 1970's) that a signed language has no distinction between nouns, verbs, and adjectives, as spoken languages do. The truth is quite the opposite, as Ursula Bellugi explains in the following chapter; we just weren't paying attention to the right parts of the sign. Normally, a spoken language will add some additional sounds to a word (a suffix or prefix) to indicate whether it functions as a noun or a verb in the sentence. For example, 'claw' can be either a noun or a verb, but 'claw<u>ed</u>', 'claw<u>ing</u>', and '<u>de</u>-claw' can only be verbs. Anyone who looked for signs that "added on" bits of signs in this way was disappointed, because there weren't any. But as Ted Supalla later noticed, there are systematic differences between nouns and verbs in American Sign Language: they are expressed as different types of movement. Bellugi describes this in greater detail in her chapter. I only raise the point now to show how one observation can build on, and make use of, another. Once movements had been separated (in a sense) from other parts of signs, it became easier to notice different roles that individual movements might play.

Another way that we can use the information about the structure of individual signs is when we try to decide if two different "pronunciations" of a sign make two different signs, or if they are just alternate pronunciations of the same sign. This becomes an issue when we consider what an "idiom" is in American Sign Language. Without discussing it in any great detail, we can show that things that are often called sign "idioms" are often just ordinary signs that are difficult to translate into English (see similar comments in Hansen's paper on Danish Sign Language), or are signs that are confused with other signs. For example, some people claim that the sign SUCCEED has an idiomatic or special meaning, "finally" or "at last." But these two signs are made differently: SUCCEED has two distinctive movements, while the sign that I call AT-LAST has only one sharp movement. If two signs are made differently, and have different meanings, this is good evidence that they are separate signs. So AT-LAST is not an idiom, even though it might historically derive from the sign we call SUCCEED. One of the ways ASL expands its vocabulary is through such changes in movement. Again, we see one more reason for paying attention to the fine details of how signs are formed.

This is just one example of how the term "idiom" has been often misused when it is applied to Sign Language; the effect is often to obscure how the language really works, and to make it seem as if the language is unstructured and simple. Of course, nothing could be further from the truth.

Conclusion

In this essay I have described some of the research findings that have come out of the last twenty years of thinking about the structure of signed languages. This description has pointed out a few general principles and a few practical results that have sprung from a very simple idea: signs have parts. The discussion has also shown that when we investigate signed languages, we find many parallels to the structure of spoken languages. I think that this will become a very significant factor in how we hearing people think about deaf people, and in how deaf people think about themselves. It is becoming harder and harder these days to maintain that Sign Languages are very "simple" and "primitive." On the contrary, they are very rich and complex systems. Future investigations in which signing and speaking are compared will tell us more about the wonderful capacity the mind has to deal in abstract symbols.

In closing, let me say that simple ideas are usually the most valuable ones. The work that Bill Stokoe began more than twenty years ago, and which he continues today, has produced ideas that have generated interest among scholars everywhere. They have led to a re-examination of policies and attitudes towards deaf people; they have contributed to the emergence of deaf people as a cultural group; and they have let all of us, deaf and hearing, come a little bit closer to each other.

References and Selected Bibliography

Battison, R., *Lexical Borrowing in American Sign Language.* Silver Spring, MD: Linstok Press, 1978

Battison, R. & Cogen, C., The Implications of Teaching American Sign Language as a Second Language. Paper presented at the 2nd Annual National Symposium on Sign Language Research and Teaching. Coronado, CA, October, 1978

Klima, E. & Bellugi, U., *The Signs of Language.* Cambridge, MA: Harvard Press, 1979

Stokoe, W., Sign Language Structure: An Outline of the Visual Communication Systems of the American Deaf. *Studies in Linguistics: Occasional Papers 8,* 1960. Revised 1978, Silver Spring, MD: Linstok Press.

Stokoe, W., Casterline, D., & Croneberg, C., *A Dictionary of American Sign Language on Linguistic Principles.* Washington, DC: Gallaudet College Press, 1965. 2nd Edition, Silver Spring, MD: Linstok Press, 1976

How Signs Express
Complex Meanings

by Ursula Bellugi

Introduction

In 1965, William Stokoe and his colleagues published *A Dictionary of American Sign Language on Linguistic Principles* (DASL). This book represents a landmark in the analysis of the special linguistic properties of signed languages that has not been superceded or surpassed in the fifteen years since its publication. Although the field of Sign Language research has blossomed since that time, the publication stands as the single outstanding contribution to the understanding of the structure of the signs of American Sign Language

Ursula Bellugi is Director of the Laboratory for Language Studies at the Salk Institute for Biological Studies and is an Adjunct Professor of Psychology at the University of California at San Diego. Dr. Bellugi received her doctoral degree in Education in 1967 from Harvard University, where she investigated the native acquisition of English by hearing children. She is currently researching the grammatical structure of American Sign Language and its acquisition as a first language. She recently collaborated with Edward Klima and others on a book entitled The Signs of Language, *which surveys much of the recent work in American Sign Language.*

This work was supported in part by National Institutes of Health Grant #NS15175 and HD13239 and National Science Foundation Grant #BNS79–16423 to The Salk Institute for Biological Studies. All drawings were made by Frank A. Paul, copyright Ursula Bellugi, 1979.

(ASL). The DASL was significant in two ways: (1) it is the first extensive listing of signs of ASL with explanations of their meanings and usage, and (2) it is the first and most complete linguistic analysis of the sign into its component parts.

The DASL is not organized alphabetically, as are all dictionaries of spoken languages, but according to the elements of signs that Stokoe first identified and described. Today, fifteen years after the publication of the DASL, the field of Sign Language research is in an exciting and agitated stage; there are new hypotheses about the structural properties of signs cropping up with impressive regularity; all are suggested hypotheses, partial analyses. Up to now, however, none has yet been worked out with the precision of this original work.

In his introduction, Stokoe spells out briefly the principles underlying the construction of the DASL. These principles were first described by Stokoe in 1960. As he points out, American Sign Language had never before been written. It could be written in the DASL for the first time, because of Stokoe's analysis of the structural components of signs. As the preceding chapter of this volume shows, Stokoe specified three aspects of each sign that distinguish it from all other signs in the language: the place where it is made (location); the distinctive configuration of the hands in making it (handshape); and the action of the hands (movement). Entries in the DASL give several different types of information: the components of each sign; possible variations; the nature of the sign (e.g., pantomimic, imitative, metonymic, indicative, name sign, initialized sign); notes on how the sign is made; syntactic value; meaning; notes on usage and examples; and cross references.

It is important to remember that the DASL is a pioneering work, the work of one small lone group of investigators working over a period of a few years to collect the materials for a dictionary, for a language which had never before been written. These investigators were laying out the basic groundwork for a linguistic analysis at the same time as they were presenting the first detailed listing of the basic lexicon of a visual-gestural language. It is remarkable how well that work holds up and how solidly it stands even now, when there are many investigators all over the United States and in Europe studying the structure of ASL and other signed languages. Other dictionaries of foreign signed languages have been developed, built on the same principles Stokoe elucidated for ASL. In our research at the Salk Institute, we have consistently found that the seeds of all of our major findings are contained in 'hints' in its pages.

Comparing Dictionaries

Let us consider first, how the DASL compares with other dictionaries of spoken languages, and second, some of the ways in which we would now revise it if we had an army of scholars over a long period of time, comparable to those which have produced the major dictionaries of spoken languages like English. Of course, the most appropriate comparison would be with dictionaries of languages which have no commonly used written form. However, since I do not have information on these, I will contrast DASL with some general-purpose dictionaries of English.

A dictionary is a book that contains a selected list of words in a language. These words are arranged in alphabetical order, followed by an explanation of their meanings and other types of information. No dictionary records all the words of written language, and the number of entries of a dictionary depends on its purpose, the number of people and hours available to compile it, and the sources available. The earliest dictionaries were made by the ancient Greeks and Romans, but most were lists of rare and difficult words or specialized lists of words. More recently there have been general-purpose dictionaries which describe ordinary words, literary words used in formal writing, technical words, words that have dropped out of the language, words or phrases borrowed from other languages, idioms, abbreviations, and important place names. The words described in a dictionary are usually taken from written documents. The great dictionaries of English, such as the *Oxford English Dictionary*, have taken generations of scholars combining vast amounts of written documents to compile the list of words and the desired information about them. And they contain hundreds of thousands of items that are not part of current vocabulary, not part of speaking vocabulary, and not part of common knowledge.

Let us for a moment consider what items are given separate listings and how lexical items are listed in a general-purpose dictionary. *Webster's Third International Dictionary,* for example, lists nouns and verbs separately, even when they have the same form. Thus, 'act' (the noun) and 'act' (the verb) have separate entries. However, there are no separate listings for the inflectional forms of that noun and verb. For example, there is no separate listing for the plural of the noun 'acts', for the possessive of the noun 'act's', or for the third person singular present indicative of the verb, as in 'he acts'. These are presumably known by speakers of the language as regular inflectional forms which are predictable in meaning.

On the other hand, there are separate listings for a variety of *derived* forms of the item 'act': for example, 'acting' (the noun), 'action', 'active', 'actively', 'activist', 'activity', 'actor', and 'actress'. Furthermore, there is an entry for 'blue', but also entries for 'bluebell', 'blueberry', 'bluebird', 'bluebonnet', 'bluefish', 'blueprint', and more. These are all compound nouns formed from the word 'blue' in conjunction with other words of the language. Thus, there are separate entries for *derived* forms of a word in a general-purpose English dictionary. These forms illustrate ways in which the vocabulary of a language is enriched or expanded.

Most of the listings in the DASL are single lexical items of the language, although a small number of compounds are listed. Thus one might conclude, from counting the separate listings in DASL, that the vocabulary of ASL (and perhaps of other signed languages) is extremely limited, when compared with vocabularies of spoken languages. A dictionary of Israeli Sign Language by Cohen, Namir, and Schlesinger (1977) makes this point explicitly: "The vocabulary size of different sign languages has been variously estimated at anywhere between 1000 and 4000 signs—*far less than in spoken languages*" (emphasis added, p. 33).

From ten years of research in ASL, it is my experience that this view is far from accurate. American Sign Language has a vast vocabulary and is a fully expressive language. There are numerous grammatical devices—a rich variety of inflectional processes and a large number of derivational processes—all of which show that the vocabulary is far richer than many people have thought. There are mechanisms within the language which are used daily in conversation to expand the lexicon to encompass new concepts and ideas. For example, we have been studying the ways in which new concepts (such as 'microwave oven', 'laser beam', 'lunar module', 'satellite', 'genetic engineering', 'hang glider', 'Moped', and 'transsexual') are expressed linguistically in ASL. We have found a variety of grammatical devices in ASL which are used for this kind of lexical expansion.

But perhaps just as important, ASL researchers have only begun to describe the vast lexicon which deaf people regularly use. Consequently, many signs that should correctly be listed as separate lexical entries in dictionaries have been combined into single entries in the DASL, and many meaning distinctions which are regularly made by deaf signers are not listed.

For example, the single sign glossed as LOOK can be varied in specific ways to mean "reminisce," "sight-seeing," "watch," "look forward to," "prophesy," "look around aimlessly," "stare," "gaze at," and so forth. Many of these could be given separate listings in the dictionary that show that they are all *derived* from the basic root sign that means "look at."

Similarly, the sign glossed as WRONG can be varied by specific changes in movement to mean "error prone," "make many mistakes," "unexpectedly," "and then," "making mistakes all the time," and many more. The single sign CHURCH can be varied to mean "pious," "go to church regularly," "a row of churches," "narrow-minded," and many more, again by specific changes in movement. Furthermore there are a large number of compounds, such as TALK NAME meaning "mention," NAME SHINY meaning "fame," LOOK STRONG meaning "resemble," MONEY BEHIND meaning "money kept in reserve," THINK TOUCH meaning "keep thinking about," TIME SAME meaning "simultaneous," EAT NOON meaning "lunch," RED RECTANGULAR meaning "brick," and thousands more, all of which are candidates for separate dictionary entries.

The DASL does have a section on SEE and LOOK which lists some of the many related forms of that pair of verbs. For most other signs, however, as in all sign dictionaries and handbooks up to the present, the different forms of a root sign are under a single listing. We suspect that, in many cases, the derivational distinctions may have been overlooked.

Thus, it is clear that the vocabulary of ASL is far larger and more differentiated than had been thought; that there is no inherent limit on the vocabulary; and that there are a great variety of morphological processes within the language which are not derived from any spoken language. In fact, it is now apparent that ASL—like Navajo, Greek, and Russian, but unlike English and Chinese—is one of the "inflective" languages of the world.

Just as the primary pioneering contribution of Stokoe was to provide the first linguistic analysis of signs into their component elements, the major focus of the research of the Laboratory for Language and Cognitive Studies at the Salk Institute in the last several years has been on the morphological processes of ASL. That is, we have been studying how the form of a sign is changed to express different meanings. We have discovered that these changes (modulations) represent a rich system of morphological processes in ASL that use space in a structured way and that compress a great deal of information into a single sign unit.

In the rest of this paper, we will discuss the lexicon (vocabulary) of ASL in greater detail: how individual root signs can systematically become parts of larger, more complex signs; how the lexicon can be expanded by systematic morphological processes, and how signs express complex meanings. In each case we are concerned with what we can learn in general about ASL as a language, and how the structure and the processes of this language compare with what we know about spoken languages. Much of this work is discussed in greater detail in *The Signs of Language* (Klima & Bellugi, 1979) and in two other articles (Bellugi & Klima, 1979; Bellugi & Newkirk, in press).

Signing vs. Speaking

ASL differs dramatically from English and other spoken languages in its *mechanisms* for modifying its lexical units (signs). The way in which the language developed appears to make a crucial difference to its morphological processes: the processes by which individual units of meaning (morphemes) combine to make words or signs that have complex meanings. In spoken languages, the most widespread morphological device for modification of meaning is probably affixation: the addition of sound segments at the beginning, within, or at the end of the word. Other devices include vowel and consonant changes, reduplication (repetition of part or all of a word, and changes in stress or tone.

In ASL there appears to be a strong resistance to sequential segmentation as an inflectional device and hence a resistance to the morphological device frequently used by English and a great many other spoken languages: affixation. ASL signs are made by moving the hands in space; the language uses dimensions of space and movement for its grammatical processes. Rather than adding parts to signs that are like spoken language affixes, most inflections or modifications in ASL involve spatial and temporal patterns which are overlaid on the movement of basic signs.

Inflectional Processes

The semantic (meaning) distinctions expressed in ASL are commonly expressed in many spoken languages as well (though often not in English). Inflectional processes in ASL express distinctions within the grammatical categories of *referential indexing, reciprocity, number, distributional aspect, temporal aspect and focus, manner,* and *degree.*

1. *Referential Indexing*

The structured use of space is seen in how verbs indicate the principal actors in a sentence—the way they indicate indexic references. ASL verb signs that can change in space move toward different spatial target points. Figure 1 shows indexic inflections on the signs ASK and INFORM, indicating "me to you," "me to him," "you to me."

2. *Reciprocity*

ASL has a reciprocal inflection, which operates on verbs to indicate mutual relations or actions. This inflectional process expresses the grammatical notion of mutual action or mutual relation in a direct and visibly appropriate way. The verb sign is doubled: it is made with two hands rather than one in simultaneous movement, and the hands are either directed or oriented toward or away from each other. This inflection expresses the meaning "to do (something) to each other," as illustrated in Figure 2 with the verb PREACH.

3. *Grammatical Number*

Verbs in ASL are inflected for several kinds of plural distinctions. Such distinctions as whether the object or subject of the verb is *dual, trial,* or *multiple* result in internal changes in the form of the verb. For example:

Dual inflection indicates an action with two recipients or agents, meaning "to both of them." There is also a *trial* form, meaning "to three of them."

Multiple inflection is the general form used when the object or subject of a verb numbers more than three.

4. *Distributional Aspect*

Several inflections focus not only on grammatical number, but also on differentiating the actions of the verb, to distinguish: (a) whether a specific act presents itself as an indivisible whole or as several separate actions, (b) whether the actions occur at distinct points in time, (c) whether the actions have a specific order of occurrence, and

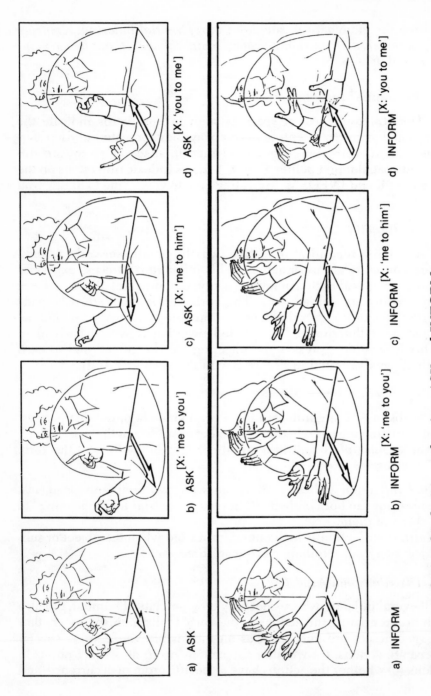

Figure 1. Referential indexing on the signs ASK and INFORM.

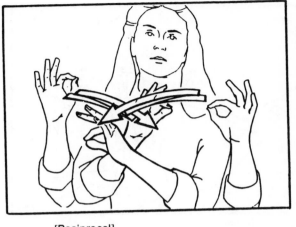

PREACH [Reciprocal]
'preach to each other'

Figure 2.   Inflection for reciprocity

(d) how the actions occur in relation to individuals participating in the action—an action for each one, or actions for certain onces, certain groups, or just anyone. These and other distinctions are made by inflections for the grammatical category of *distributional aspect* on ASL verbs. A few of the distributive inflections we have identified are as follows:

Exhaustive inflection: actions distributed to each individual in a group, when the actions are viewed as a single event (in a single time frame), meaning "to do (something) to each of them."

Allocative Determinate inflection: actions distributed to specified individuals at distinct points in time, meaning "to do (something) to certain ones at different times."

Allocative Indeterminate inflection: actions distributed to unspecified individuals over time, meaning "to do (something) to any at different times."

See Figure 4 for an illustration of these three modulations for distributional aspect with the sign PREACH.

5. *Temporal Aspect and Focus*

Verb signs in ASL are also inflected for "temporal aspect" and "temporal focus." That is, there is a wide array of inflectional forms

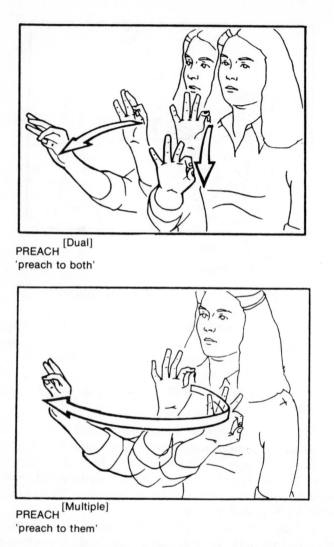

PREACH [Dual]
'preach to both'

PREACH [Multiple]
'preach to them'

Figure 3.   Inflections for number

which indicate meanings like "uninterruptedly," "over time," "regularly," "for a long time," "over and over again," "from time to
time," "characteristically," and so on.

For example, the sign LOOK-AT has a variety of inflections for
temporal aspect and focus (see Figure 5). LOOK-AT has both a *punc-
tual* (point in time) stem that has a short directional-path movement

PREACH[Exhaustive]
'preach to each of them'

PREACH[Allocative Determinate]
'preach to selected ones at different times'

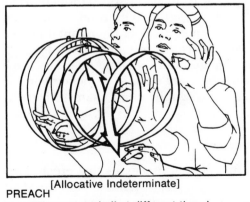

PREACH[Allocative Indeterminate]
'preach to any and all at different times'

Figure 4.   Inflections for distributional aspect

(5a) and a *durative* (extended time) stem without directional-path movement (not shown).

A *protractive* form of the sign LOOK-AT is made with a long tense hold and without motion and translates roughly as "to stare at uninterruptedly" (5b). A parallel form is made with short tense, repeated movement (5c); the meaning involves *incessant* acts, roughly, "to look at so frequently that it seems without interruption."

Another inflected form has smooth, circular, repeated movement; it focuses on the verb's *durational* characteristics, and the meaning is roughly "to gaze at over time" (5d). A parallel form has rapid non-tense repetitions; the meaning is *habitual* action: "to watch regularly" (5e).

The *continuative* inflected form is made with a tense fast movement continuing in a slow elongated return; the meaning is "to look at for a long time" (5f). A parallel form of the verb, the *iterative* inflection, is made with a tense fast movement ending in a stop, and then a slow elongated return. The meaning is "to look at again and again" (5g).

6. *Manner and Degree*

Verbs are also inflected to express distinctions of manner (meanings such as "with ease," "readily," "with mental pre-occupation") and to express distinctions of degree ("a little," "very," "sort of," "excessively").

The broader differences in meanings that distinguish different grammatical categories are related to general differences in form. The most salient physical characteristic of inflections for number and distributional aspect is *spatial* patterning: the signs move along lines, arcs, and circles in vertical and horizontal planes. By contrast, inflections for temporal aspect rely heavily on *temporal* patterning, so that the signs change their dynamic qualities, such as rate, tension, evenness, duration, and manner of movement. Various types of multiple articulations (reduplication) characterize some inflections for both groups.

Derivational Processes

In addition to inflectional processes that create large numbers of signs with complex meanings, ASL has a wide variety of devices that expand the vocabulary by regular systematic changes in lexical roots and result in the formation of related lexical items: basic verbs can be

(a) LOOK-AT

(b) LOOK-AT [Protractive]
    'stare'

(c) LOOK-AT [Incessant]
    'look at incessantly'

(d) LOOK-AT [Durational]
    'look continuously'

(e) LOOK-AT [Habitual]
    'look at regularly'

(f) LOOK-AT [Continuative]
    'look for a long time'

(g) LOOK-AT [Iterative]
    'look at over and over'

Figure 5.   Inflections for Temporal aspect.

changed into nouns or adjectives; basic adjectives can become verbs or nouns, etc. Traditionally these are called "derivational processes," although, as in spoken languages, the distinctions between inflectional and derivational processes in ASL are not easy to draw.

1. *Derivation of nouns from verbs*

One very widespread process derives nouns from certain verbs. Supalla and Newport (1978) have described 100 activity verbs and their formationally related concrete nouns. They have shown that these noun-verb pairs differ systematically in the way they are made, in particular the frequency of their repetition and the manner of their final movement. Verbs may vary in quality of movement, number of repetitions, and manner of movement. Typically the related nouns are made with a restrained repeated movement which is abbreviated. Thus, where handbooks and dictionaries of signs indicate that one sign form is used for both "sit" and "chair," in fact the two signs have different movements. The sign SIT-DOWN is made with one movement before final contact; CHAIR has a smaller, repeated and restrained movement (see Figure 6a). The movement of CHAIR is typical of noun forms that are derivationally related to verbs: repeated smaller movements with restrained manner. But these verb-noun distinctions are not limited to activity verbs and their related concrete nouns. The sign COMPARE is a verb that has repeated
                                                                    [D: noun]
movement. From the verb sign, a noun form COMPARE
can be derived, which means "comparison" and is made with a smaller movement and restrained manner (see Figure 6b). The process of deriving nouns from verbs is widespread in the language and extends to new forms.

At the Salk Institute, as we discovered more and more derivational processes, we discussed *derivations* in ASL in our daily conversations but had no commonly used sign for this concept. A deaf researcher coined an appropriate sign for the concept "derivation": from the ASL verb DERIVE (related to the sign QUOTE), she created a noun meaning "derivation," made with the repeated movement and restrained manner that is characteristic of derived nouns in ASL (see Figure 6c).

2. *Derivation of predicates from nouns*

Certain nouns can form predicates (which act like verbs or adjectives) by a derivational process which also changes the movement. In

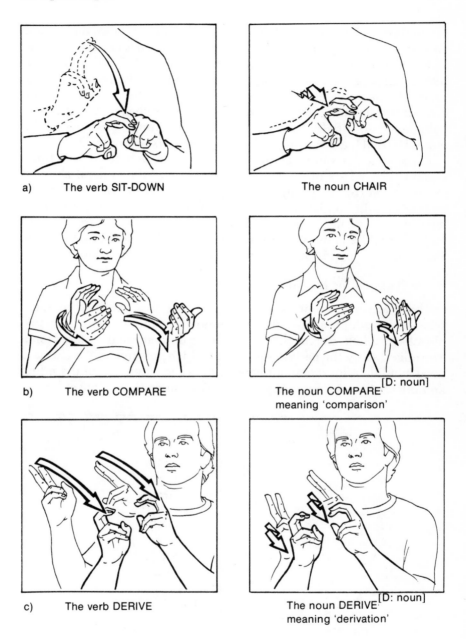

a)   The verb SIT-DOWN   The noun CHAIR

b)   The verb COMPARE   The noun COMPARE[D: noun]
meaning 'comparison'

c)   The verb DERIVE   The noun DERIVE[D: noun]
meaning 'derivation'

Figure 6.   Derivationally related verbs and nouns.

the derived form, the movement of the sign is made once and is fast and tense, with a restrained beginning. This process changes a noun to a predicate that means "to act like _____," or "to appear like _____." Thus the sign CHINA can be changed to form a predicate meaning "to seem Chinese"; GIRL can be changed to form a predicate meaning "effeminate"; BABY, a predicate "to act like a baby(babyish)"; BUSINESS, a predicate meaning "business-like"; and CHURCH, a predicate meaning "pious" (see Figure 7).

There is a derivational process that derives activity nouns from certain verbs. This process adds the meaning "the general activity of" to the verb, for example, changing WRITE to "the activity of writing" (as in "authoring books"), MEASURE to "the activity of measuring" (as in "engineering a building") (see Figure 8), IM-PROVE to "the activity of improving" (as in "improving a house"). These activity nouns often serve as the names of professions.

3. *Derivations for Extended Meanings*

There are other morphological processes that seem to operate when a sign adopts a figurative or extended meaning. There are pairs of well-established signs that appear to be derivationally related (and are judged so by the native signers), in which one sign of the pair is a good candidate for metaphorical or figurative extension of the other and differs from it minimally in quality of movement (tense, lax, or

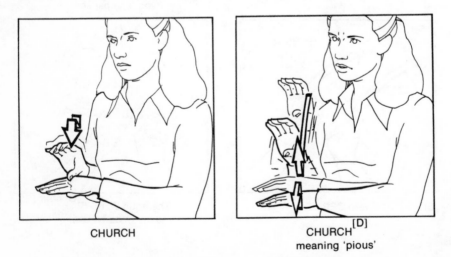

CHURCH   CHURCH[D]
                               meaning 'pious'

Figure 7. The sign CHURCH and a derived form.

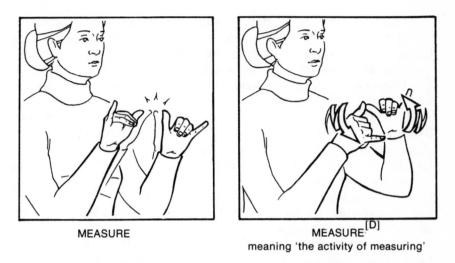

MEASURE   MEASURE[D]
                       meaning 'the activity of measuring'

Figure 8. The sign MEASURE and a derived form.

accelerated): a form of "horny" differing from HUNGRY; a sign meaning "have a hunch" differing from FEEL; a sign meaning "acquiesce" from QUIET. Even in the case of metaphorical extensions that may have been based originally on extensions found in English (the English word *blue* with its extended meaning "to feel blue" or "sad" [see Figure 9]; *chicken* in its meaning "cowardly"), the sign forms with the figurative meanings differ in quality of movement from the signs BLUE (the color) and CHICKEN (the fowl).

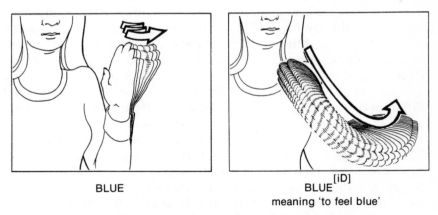

BLUE   BLUE[iD]
                       meaning 'to feel blue'

Figure 9. The sign BLUE and an idiomatic derivative.

Though words of many spoken languages can be used figuratively without any change in phonological shape, it seems that in ASL, figurative extensions of meaning are usually accompanied by minimal changes in movement. There appears to be a strong tendency in this language for shifts in meaning to operate in concert with shifts in movement.

The derivational processes described in this section are productive ways of extending the lexicon of ASL. We have found many new signs coined in this way: a sign for "acquisition" from the verb sign LEARN; a sign for "drive-in" from the sign PARK-CAR; a sign for "iconicity" from the sign PICTURE; a sign for "grammatical aspect" from the sign PART; a sign for "speed-reading" from the sign meaning "to have one's nose in a book"; a sign for "simulate" from the sign MAKE, and so forth.

In each of these instances, the derived sign differs from the basic form of the sign according to regular, derivational processes that involve specific changes in movement. In a similar manner, many other new concepts are expressed by changes in the movement of commonly known signs. These derivational processes, in which signs adopt new and extended meanings, are typical ways of enlarging the vocabulary of ASL.

Productivity Through Compounding

Compounding is a productive device that some (but not all) spoken languages use to create a new word from two or more existing words. The newly created compound word then functions like a single lexical item in the language. These compound words take on special meanings that are different from the meanings of the same two words used as a phrase. A compound would be entered as a separate lexical item in the dictionary of the language, but the same two words as a syntactic phrase are not listed in this way. Although there are several different types of compounds, the following discussion includes only a few examples of the simplest kinds of compounds.

One compound in ASL is formed with the signs GOOD and ENOUGH. As a phrase, GOOD ENOUGH means "adequate," but as a compound, GOOD ENOUGH means "just *barely* adequate." Notice the shift in meaning in the compound: it no longer means "well enough," but now means "hardly at all," or sometimes "with just a lick and a promise."

1) (SHE) CLEAN HOUSE GOOD ENOUGH
   "She cleaned the house adequately."
2) (SHE) CLEAN HOUSE GOOD͡ ENOUGH
   "She cleaned the house just barely adequately."

The phrase and compound in sentences (1) and (2) have a different rhythm (see Figure 10). When the phrase GOOD ENOUGH is compared with the compound GOOD͡ ENOUGH, we see that the first sign in the compound is drastically reduced; that the transition between the parts is abbreviated; and that the compound as a whole takes far less time to make than the same two individual signs. It is

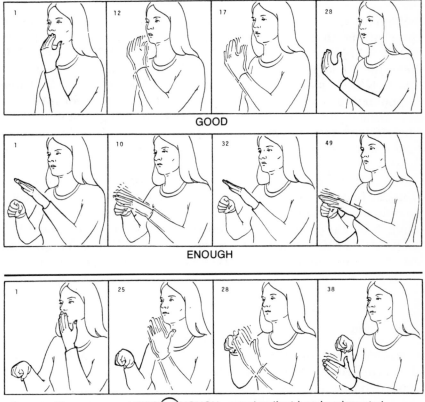

GOOD

ENOUGH

The compound GOOD͡ ENOUGH, meaning 'just barely adequate.'

Figure 10.   Temporal properties of two separate signs and the same signs as a compound. (Numbers represent field numbers from videotape.)

almost as if the compression of meaning into a single sign unit is accompanied by a compression of the sign as well.

As we have just shown, compounds in ASL are usually produced differently from phrases with the same signs. As in English compounds, there is typically an overall temporal compression. However, unlike similar English compounds, which have heavier *stress* on their first elements, there is invariably a *reduction* and *weakening* of the first element in a compound in ASL. Thus, ASL has its own structural rules for compounds. Figure 11 illustrates the difference between two signs as a phrase and then as a compound, showing the phrase BLUE SPOT and the compound BLUE SPOT, meaning "a bruise."

We have recorded more than a thousand established, lexicalized compounds that are commonly used in ASL: for example, TIME SAME meaning "simultaneously," MONEY BEHIND meaning "emergency money," EAT NOON meaning "lunch," TALK NAME meaning "to mention." Furthermore, we find that compounding is a commonly used productive process for inventing new names: for example, PILL QUIET meaning "tranquilizer," MEDICINE HELP "medicare," HEREDITY CHANGE meaning "genetic engineering," FALSE HEART meaning "heart transplant."

Notice that these ASL compounds are not based on English compounds. In fact, ASL and English frequently have different compounds for the same concept. For example, the concept which in English is 'zip code' is expressed in ASL by the compound LETTER NUMBER; the concept expressed in English as 'credit card' may be expressed in ASL by SIGNATURE RECTANGULAR.

Conclusion

It is clear from this brief survey of ASL morphological devices that the vocabulary of ASL is far richer than people have claimed. It is expanded by a number of active processes that create new signs from existing signs. It is strikingly clear from these studies that the visual-gestural communication system of deaf people has been shaped into an independent language with its own grammatical rules. It is also strikingly clear that the human capacity for building complex linguistic systems is the same—whether we speak or sign.

a) BLUE   b) SPOT

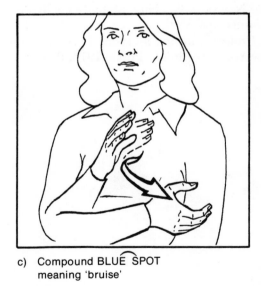

c) Compound BLUE͡ SPOT
    meaning 'bruise'

Figure 11. The signs BLUE (a) and SPOT (b), and the compound BLUE͡ SPOT (c) meaning 'bruise.'

References

Bellugi, U. and Klima, E. S. "Language: Perspectives from Another Modality." In *Brain and Mind (Ciba Foundation Symposium 69) Excerpta Medica,* Amsterdam, 1979, 99–117.

Bellugi, U. and Newkirk, D. "Formal Devices for Creating New Signs in American Sign Language." In *Proceedings of the Second National Symposium on Sign Language Research and Teaching,* in press.

Cohen, E., Namir, L., and Schlesinger, I. M. *A New Dictionary of Sign Language.* The Hague: Mouton, 1977.

Klima, E. S. and Bellugi, U. *The Signs of Language.* Cambridge, Mass.: Harvard University Press, 1979.

Stokoe, W.C. "Sign Language Structure." *Studies in Linguistics: Occasional Papers 8.* Buffalo: University of Buffalo Press, 1960. [Reprinted 1978, Silver Spring, MD: Linstok Press]

Stokoe, W. C., Casterline, D. and Croneberg, C. G. *A Dictionary of American Sign Language.* Washington, D.C.: Gallaudet College Press, 1965. [Reprinted 1976, Silver Spring, MD: Linstok Press]

Supalla, T. and Newport, E. "How Many Seats in a Chair? The Derivation of Nouns and Verbs in American Sign Language." In P. Siple (Ed.), *Understanding Language Through Sign Language Research.* New York: Academic Press, 1978, 91–132.

Sentences in American Sign Language

by Charlotte Baker

I first met Bill Stokoe in the summer of 1974, after my first year of graduate work in linguistics at the University of California at Berkeley. At that time I was preparing to do some research on the relationship between language and culture, and I was exploring the possibility of including Deaf people and their language as one of the four linguistic groups I would study. Part of the research involved the examination of eye movements—a subject that intrigued me and one that evoked a strongly respondent chord in Bill. Despite my near total ignorance of what I was getting into, Bill's encouragement was warm, and he freely provided me with helpful information, advice and his time—as he has done for literally hundreds of people like me.

That interaction with Bill sparked my interest in Sign Language and by the summer of 1975, I was working with him in the Linguis-

Charlotte Baker is presently a Research Associate in the Linguistics Research Lab at Gallaudet College where she is writing her dissertation on American Sign Language for her Ph.D. in Linguistics from the University of California, Berkeley. She received her B.S. in Psychology from Clark University in 1972 and her M.A. in Linguistics from UCB in 1975. At Gallaudet, she teaches courses on the structure of American Sign Language for faculty, staff, and undergraduates. With Dennis Cokely, she has co-authored two texts for Sign Language teachers: American Sign Language: a teacher's resource text on grammar and culture (1980) and American Sign Language: a teacher's resource text on curriculum, methods, and evaluation (1980), and will soon publish three student texts with accompanying videotapes. Her current research focuses on the linguistic functions of eye, face, head, and body movements in ASL.

75

tics Research Lab, taking advantage of every available summer and Christmas vacation. In 1977, I left Berkeley to take a full-time position in the Lab.

That first meeting in 1974 showed me something very important about Bill Stokoe: despite the tremendous significance of his work and the respect it has brought him from scholars around the world, Bill continues to be one of those rare individuals who, in Kipling's words, can "walk with kings and not lose the common touch." He always has time to be encouraging and helpful to students, professionals, and those who are "just curious." During the past five years, I've also found that Bill Stokoe is a man who is not afraid to speak out against any form of oppression, no matter what the status or power of the oppressor. He is a sure advocate of the human rights of all individuals—deaf and hearing—and a man who respects the dignity of each person. I am grateful for the privilege of knowing Bill, learning from him, and sharing the work he began.

Introduction

Among the many surprisingly "prophetic" statements of William Stokoe in his 1960 publication of *Sign Language Structure* was the assertion that the facial activity of ASL signers "needs much more investigation; for it is the key to syntactical structure" (p. 63). Bill meant that in order to understand how sentences and sentence parts are formed in ASL, one would have to study not just what signers are doing with their hands, but what they are also doing in the facial area of their body. Now, twenty years later, researchers are finding that Bill's early observations and intuitions were right on target once again.

What Bill saw was that often the same signs would occur in sentences that had different meanings. For example, the same signed sentence might be a statement like 'I remember', or a question like 'Do you remember?', or have a negative meaning like 'I don't remember'. If the same manual signs were used in all of these sentences, then something else had to be different in order to communicate these different meanings. Bill saw that these differences concerned the "non-manual" aspect of signing—meaning the movements of the signer's eyes, face, head, and body.

However, not much attention was given to Bill's strong assertion about the importance of eye, face, head and body movements in ASL until about a dozen years later. Then some linguists began to see that these "nonmanual behaviors" had a variety of linguistic functions in ASL and were not simply used to "express emotions," as many people had thought. They found that a few signs in ASL are made only with facial and other non-manual movements, that facial expressions, etc., are actually a part of some signs, and that movements of the eyes, face, and head often function as adverbs, adjectives, and pronouns.

For example, Liddell (1977) described an adverb in ASL that means "close in time or space"; it is made by raising and moving forward the shoulder on the side of the signing hand, tilting the head toward that shoulder, and raising the cheek and side of mouth toward that shoulder. When this adverb is made with a sign like NOW (Fig. 1), the meaning is "right now" or "just now." If the adverb is made with a verb like ARRIVE-AT, the meaning is "just arrived" (Fig. 2). Another non-manual adverb means something like "normally" or "regularly"; it is made by pushing the lips out, with the head slightly back and tilted to one side. When this adverb is made with the verb DRIVE, the meaning is something like "driving along in the usual way" (Fig. 3). However, when a different non-manual adverb is used with the same sign, like the one that means "carelessly" or "without paying attention", the meaning changes to "driving along without paying attention" (Fig. 4). These few examples illustrate how non-manual behaviors are important for understanding the *morphology* of ASL signs, the level of linguistic analysis that Ursula Bellugi describes in this volume.

Figure 1   **Figure 2**

Figure 3   **Figure 4**

However, continuing research on the role of eye, face, head, and body movements in ASL has shown that they are even more important at the level of whole sentences. These non-manual behaviors are important for binding signs together into clauses and sentences, and for indicating what kind of clause or sentence the signer is using. For example, is the sentence a question or a statement? Is the sentence a conditional statement (like 'If the woman left her book, then she will have to buy a new one'), or a statement describing two events that occurred in the past (like 'The woman left her book and had to buy a new one')? Linguists have found that in order to understand these differences in the role and meaning of ASL sentences, they must look at what signers are doing with their eyes, face, head, and body. This type of research on the *syntax* of ASL is fairly new, and we have much to learn about the types of sentences used in ASL and how they are formed. The rest of this paper will describe some of what we have learned about sentences in ASL.

Sentences in ASL

Linguists have observed that certain non-manual behaviors function as *grammatical signals* in ASL, indicating what type of sentence is being used. For example, the grammatical signal that we write as 'q' involves specific face, eye, and head behaviors which indicate that a particular sentence or utterance is a question. The period of time during which a non-manual grammatical signal occurs is shown on paper by drawing a line over the manual sign or signs that occur with that signal. This is illustrated below:

$$\overline{\text{Signed Sentence A, Signed Sentence B}}^{\,q}$$

for example:

$$\overline{\text{(1) ME HUNGRY, WANT EAT YOU}}^{\,q}$$

(1) ME HUNGRY, WANT EAT YOU
  'I'm hungry. You want to get something to eat?'

The line drawn over Sentence B with the superscript 'q' shows that Sentence B is a question, as illustrated in the first example. It also indicates that the non-manual behaviors which comprise the grammatical signal 'q' occurred continuously during the production of all of the signs below the line. As shown in example (1), *glosses* (i.e. English words used to transcribe signs on paper) are written in capital letters. The comma after the first sentence indicates that there was a pause after the first sentence, before the second sentence was signed.

Now suppose an ASL signer is conversing with someone about a woman and the book she brought to their class yesterday, and the signer uses the following three signs in the order written below.*

(2) WOMAN   LEAVE   BOOK

Is this sentence a *statement*? ('The woman left her book.')
Is this sentence a *question*? ('Did the woman leave her book?')
Is this sentence a *negated statement*? ('The woman didn't leave her book.')
Is this sentence an *asserted statement*? ('Yes, the woman *did* leave her book.')
Is this sentence a *negated question*? ('Didn't the woman leave her book?')
Does this sentence *question an assertion*? ('The woman *did* leave her book?')

*The verb glossed here as LEAVE is made with two hands (open with fingers together) and means "to leave something."

In ASL, it is possible to form all of these different types of sentences using the same manual signs. Of course, the context in which the sentence occurs will help the addressee understand the meaning of the sentence. However, the signer also clearly indicates which type of sentence it is by using a specific, non-manual grammatical signal with the sentence.

For example, if the sentence is a *question*, the signer will use the grammatical signal 'q'—composed of a brow raise, widened eyes, and frequently, a tilting of the head or the whole body forward. This signal will show that the sentence is a question meaning "Did the woman leave her book?." We would write this as:

$$\overline{\hspace{4cm}}^{\text{q}}$$
(3)   WOMAN   LEAVE   BOOK

If the sentence is a *negated statement,* the signer will use the grammatical signal that we write as 'neg'—composed of a side-to-side headshake, frequently accompanied by a frown, and sometimes a brow squint (brows drawn together and/or lowered), wrinkled nose, and raised upper lip. This signal will show that the sentence is a negated statement meaning "The woman didn't leave her book." We would write this as:

$$\overline{\hspace{4cm}}^{\text{neg}}$$
(4)   WOMAN   LEAVE   BOOK

If the sentence is an *asserted statement,* the signer will use a type of head nodding that will probably begin before any of the manual signs are made and continue throughout the sentence. There may be other non-manual behaviors that accompany this nodding, but no one has yet done enough research on this type of sentence to know if other behaviors regularly occur. This 'nodding' signal will show that the sentence is an asserted statement meaning "Yes, the woman *did* leave her book." We would write this as:

$$\overline{\hspace{4cm}}^{\text{nodding}}$$
(5)   WOMAN   LEAVE   BOOK

If the sentence is a *negated question,* the signer will use both the grammatical signal 'q' and the grammatical signal 'neg'. This means drawing the brows together and raising them, widening the eyes, and tilting the head forward while shaking it from side-to-side. This combined signal will show that the sentence is a negated question meaning "Didn't the woman leave her book?." We would write this as:

$$\overline{\text{WOMAN \quad LEAVE \quad BOOK}}^{\text{neg +q}}$$

(6) WOMAN   LEAVE   BOOK

If the sentence is a *question about an assertion,* the signer will use both the grammatical signal 'q' and the signal 'nodding'. This means raising the brows, widening the eyes, and tilting the head forward while nodding it up and down. This combined signal will show that the sentence is a question about an assertion, meaning "(Is it true that) the woman *did* leave her book?." We would write this as:

(7) WOMAN   LEAVE   BOOK

We have just seen that there are specific grammatical signals in ASL for questions, negated statements, asserted statements, negated questions, and questions about assertions. However, in the case of simple statements (for example, meaning "The woman left her book"), there does not seem to be any specific signal accompanying all of the signs in the sentence. Instead, the *absence* of any special signal seems to indicate that the sentence is a simple statement. Because of this, it may be useful to think of the simple declarative sentence as the most basic type of sentence in ASL—to which other signals are added to indicate other types of sentences.

There are other types of statements and questions in ASL that use non-manual grammatical signals. For example, the signal that we write as 'cond' is used to indicate a *conditional sentence.* This type of sentence has two parts: a part that states a *condition,* and a part that concerns the *result* of that condition. The second part can be a statement, a question, or a command. For example, the sentence 'If the woman left her book, then she will have to buy a new one' is a *conditional statement.* The sentence 'If the woman left her book, will she have to buy a new one?' is a *conditional question.*

In ASL, the *condition* is usually signed first and is accompanied by the non-manual grammatical signal that we write as 'cond'. This signal is composed of a brow raise, usually with the head tilted in one direction and sometimes, the body slightly tilted in that direction. At the pause between the *condition* and the *result* segment, several of the non-manual behaviors will change. If the result segment is a statement, the brows return to normal position and the head and/or body will shift in a different direction than that which occurred during the first segment.

$$\overline{\qquad\qquad\text{cond}\qquad\qquad}$$
Signed 'Condition',   Signed 'Result'

If the result segment is a question (like the one described earlier), the brows are usually raised higher, the head is tilted toward the addressee, and the signer looks directly at the addressee.

$$\overline{\qquad\quad\text{cond}\qquad}\qquad\overline{\qquad\qquad\text{q}}$$
Signed 'Condition',   Signed 'Result'

The conditional statement and conditional question mentioned above would then be written as:

$$\overline{\qquad\qquad\qquad\qquad\text{cond}}\qquad\overline{\qquad\qquad\text{nodding}}$$
(8) WOMAN   LEAVE   BOOK,   MUST   BUY   NEW

'If the woman left her book, she will have to buy a new one.'

$$\overline{\qquad\qquad\qquad\qquad\text{cond}}\qquad\overline{\qquad\qquad\qquad\text{q}}$$
(9) WOMAN   LEAVE   BOOK,   MUST   BUY   NEW

'If the woman left her book, will she have to buy a new one?'

If the signer wants to describe two events that happened in the past and say 'The woman left her book and had to buy a new one', then the first segment would be signed as a simple statement (not a conditional).

$$\overline{\qquad\qquad\qquad\quad\text{slight nodding}}$$
(10) WOMAN   LEAVE   BOOK,   MUST   BUY   NEW

'The woman left her book and had to buy a new one.'

Another non-manual grammatical signal in ASL is used to show that a particular segment is a *restrictive relative clause*. Relative clauses help identify a specific person or thing that a speaker or signer wants to talk about. For example, in the sentence 'The woman *who left her book* had to buy a new one', the words in italics form a restrictive relative clause that helps to identify *which* woman had to buy a new book.

Relative clauses seem to be used less frequently in ASL than the other types of sentences described above, but they have been observed in the signing of some native ASL users across the country. Liddell (1977) has described the non-manual behaviors that form the grammatical signal that we write as 'rel.cl' (Liddell uses 'r'). He says that the signal is composed of a brow raise, cheek and upper lip raise, and backward tilt of the head. The sentence given above would then be written as:

$$\overline{\hspace{3.2cm}\text{rel.cl}\hspace{3.2cm}}$$
(11) WOMAN   LEAVE   BOOK   MUST   BUY   NEW

'The woman who left her book must buy a new one.'

A very common type of sentence in ASL is one in which a segment has been *topicalized*. Basically, in this type of sentence, the thing the signer wants to talk about (the *topic*) is signed first and is accompanied by the grammatical signal that we write as 't'. This grammatical signal 't' is composed of a brow raise, head tilt, and fairly constant eye gaze on the addressee (except where the signer's eye gaze is needed for other linguistic purposes). The last sign in the topic segment is held longer than usual, resulting in a pause. After the topic is signed, followed by the pause, the signer *comments* on the topic and will change his or her brows, eye gaze, and head position in various ways depending on the type of comment that follows—e.g. negated statement, question, etc. (For more information, see Liddell, 1977; Baker & Cokely, 1980.) Below are three examples of sentences in ASL with topicalized segments.

$$\overline{\hspace{1.6cm}\text{t}\hspace{1.6cm}}$$
(12) WOMAN,   LEAVE   BOOK

'That woman, she left her book.'
(or) 'That woman left her book.'

$$\overline{\quad\;\text{t}\quad\;}$$
(13) BOOK,   WOMAN   LEAVE

'That book, the woman left it.'
(or) 'As for the book, the woman left it.'

$$\overline{\qquad\qquad\qquad\qquad\text{t}\quad}$$
(14) YESTERDAY   MEETING,   BORING

'That meeting yesterday, it was boring.'
(or) 'Yesterday's meeting was boring.'

There are also other types of questions that are different from the type described in the beginning of this section. The question sig-naled with 'q' is what we call a *"yes-no" question* because it can be answered by saying 'yes' or 'no'. That is, if someone asks 'Did the woman leave her book?', the addressee can respond 'yes' or 'no'. However, if someone asks 'What did the woman leave?', the answer cannot be 'yes' or 'no', but instead must be something like 'her book'.

We refer to this second type of question as a *"wh-word" question* because these sentences usually include an interrogative form (word or sign) that often begins with the letters 'wh' in English (e.g. who, what, where, when, which, why). In ASL, "wh-word" questions are accompanied by the non-manual signal that we write as 'wh-q'— composed of a brow squint (although the brows are sometimes raised as well as drawn together), frequently a tilting of the head, and some-times a raising of the shoulders and a forward body shift.

Below is an example of a "wh-word" question followed by a "yes-no" question. The sign glossed as "WHAT" is made with an open hand (fingers spread apart), with the palm facing upward, and may be made with two hands.

$$\overline{\qquad\qquad\qquad\qquad\text{wh-q}\quad}\quad\overline{\;\;\text{q}\;\;}$$
(15) WOMAN   LEAVE   "WHAT",   BOOK

'What did the woman leave? Her book?'

Another related type of question which is frequently used in ASL is called a *rhetorical question*. Rhetorical questions are not "true" questions since the addressee is not expected to respond. Instead, they are used to introduce the information that the signer will then supply. For example, one could say 'The woman remembered to pick up her newspaper, her pencils, and her ruler. But what did she leave behind? Her book'. In effect, the speaker is posing a question and then responding to it herself. Rhetorical questions ('rhet.q') in ASL usually include a "wh-word" interrogative sign (like WHO, "WHAT", WHERE, WHY), but in this type of question the brows are raised. Below are two examples of rhetorical questions.

$$\overline{\quad\quad t\quad\quad}\quad\quad\quad\quad\quad\quad\quad\quad\overline{\quad\quad\quad rhet.q\quad\quad\quad}$$
(16) WOMAN, REMEMBER...., LEAVE "WHAT", BOOK

'That woman, she remembered .... What did she leave behind? Her book.'

$$\quad\quad\quad\quad\quad\quad\overline{\quad\quad\quad\quad t\quad\quad\quad\quad}\quad\quad\quad\quad\overline{\quad rhet.q\quad}$$
(17) LAST-WEEK FRIDAY, WOMAN DIE, WHY, REFUSE EAT

'Last week on Friday, a woman died. Why? She refused to eat.' (or) 'A woman died last Friday because she refused to eat.'

Summary

This paper has described 13 different types of sentences in ASL. As we have seen, non-manual signals are important indicators of the structure and meaning of each of these sentences. This analysis of the structure of sentences in ASL is still fairly new. We expect to find that movements of the signer's eyes, face, head, and body have many more syntactic functions, in addition to those described in this paper. Twenty years ago, Bill Stokoe predicted what we have now found to be true: that these non-manual behaviors *are* "the key to [the] syntactical structure" of American Sign Language.

References

Baker, C. & Cokely, D. *American Sign Language: a teacher's resource text on grammar and culture*. Silver Spring, Maryland: T. J. Publishers, Inc., 1980.

Liddell, S. An Investigation into the Syntactic Structure of American
    Sign Language. Unpublished doctoral dissertation, University of
    California at San Diego, 1977.
Stokoe, W. *Sign Language Structure: An Outline of the Visual
    Communication System of the American Deaf.* University of Buf-
    falo, Occasional Paper 8, 1960. [Reprinted 1976, Silver Spring,
    MD: Linstok Press]

III
THE DEAF
COMMUNITY

The Deaf Community and the Culture of Deaf People

by Carol Padden

I was eighteen, and quite determined. I wrote Bill Stokoe a letter explaining that I wanted to begin a career in Linguistics and I thought that working at the Linguistics Research Lab at Gallaudet College under his direction would be a good way to get the training I needed. In a few weeks he answered my letter and I was hired as a research assistant.

But my case is not unusual; Bill has always supported young students looking for a place and an opportunity to develop their skills. I remained at the LRL for four years, and I can truly say that my experience there was invaluable in giving me the background in research skills and linguistics that I wanted. I appreciate Bill Stokoe being there at what became a turning point in my career.

Carol Padden is presently a Research Assistant at the Laboratory for Language and Cognitive Studies at the Salk Institute and is working toward a doctorate in Linguistics at the University of California, San Diego. She received a B.S. degree in Linguistics from Georgetown University in 1978, and an M.A. in Theoretical Linguistics from U.C.S.D. Carol previously worked as a Research Assistant at the Linguistics Research Lab at Gallaudet College and as Assistant Director of the Communicative Skills Program, National Association of the Deaf.

"Deaf Community and the Culture of Deaf People" draws from her earlier work with Harry Markowicz on cultural boundaries within the Deaf community, as well as from her own experiences as a Deaf child of Deaf parents. Her current research interests lie in the area of ASL syntax. With Charlotte Baker, she co-authored American Sign Language: a look at its history, structure, and community *(1978).*

The *Dictionary of American Sign Language*, published in 1965 by Bill Stokoe, Carl Croneberg, and Dorothy Casterline, was unique for at least two reasons. First, it offered a new description of Sign Language based on linguistic principles. Second, it devoted a section to the description of the "social" and "cultural" characteristics of Deaf* people who use American Sign Language.

It was indeed unique to describe Deaf people as constituting a "cultural group." Professionals in the physical sciences and education of deaf people typically describe deaf people in terms of their pathological condition: hearing loss. There are numerous studies which list statistics about the types, ranges, and etiologies of hearing loss and how these physical deficiencies may subsequently affect the behavior of deaf people. But rarely had these professionals seriously attended to other equally important aspects of Deaf people: the fact that Deaf people form groups in which the members do not experience "deficiencies" and in which the basic needs of the individual members are met, as in any other culture of human beings.

Deaf people have long recognized that their groups are different from those of hearing people; in the "Deaf world", certain behaviors are accepted while others are discouraged. The discussion of the "linguistic community" of Deaf people in the *Dictionary of ASL* represented a break from a long tradition of "pathologizing" Deaf people. In a sense, the book brought official and public recognition of a deeper aspect of Deaf people's lives: their culture.

When I re-read the book, as I do from time to time, I am always appreciative of the many insights that I find about the structure of American Sign Language and the culture of Deaf people.

The Deaf Community

We commonly hear references to the "deaf community".† The term has demographic, linguistic, political and social implications. There is a national "community" of deaf people who share certain

---

*I will use here a convention adopted by a number of researchers where the capitalized "Deaf" is used when referring to cultural aspects, as in the culture of *Deaf* people. The lower-case "deaf," on the other hand, refers to non-cultural aspects such as the audiological condition of deafness.

†As will be explained in a later section, the "deaf community" as described here is not a cultural entity; thus, the capitalized *Deaf* adjective will not be used to describe it. This differs from earlier treatments of the deaf community such as those found in Markowicz & Woodward (1975), Padden & Markowicz (1976), and Baker & Padden (1978).

characteristics and react to events around them as a group. In addition to a national community of deaf people, in almost every city or town in the U.S. there are smaller deaf communities. But what is a "deaf community?" More precisely, who are the members of a deaf community and what are the identifying characteristics of such a community?

To answer these questions, we need first to look at a definition of *community*. Unfortunately, there is much disagreement among anthropologists and sociologists about what constitutes a "community".

George Hillery, a sociologist, evaluated 94 different definitions of "community" proposed by various researchers who have studied communities of people. In search of a definition, he singled out common features from the majority of the 94 definitions of local communities. Other sociologists such as Allan Edwards and Dennis Poplin have come to the same definition which Hillery proposes. Hillery's definition of "community" is as follows:

> 1. A community is a group of people who *share common goals* and cooperate in achieving these goals. Each community has its own goals. A goal may be equal employment opportunities, greater political participation, or better community services.
>
> 2. A community occupies a *particular geographic location*. The geography of a community determines the ways in which the community functions.
>
> 3. A community has some degree of *freedom to organize the social life and responsibilities of its members*. Institutions such as prisons and mental hospitals bring together groups of people in one locality, but the people have no power to make decisions about their daily lives and routines. Thus, we can not call these types of groups "communities."

Communities may be small and closed, such as those we find in villages and tribes; but in large, industrialized societies, communities tend to be more mixed and are composed of several smaller groups of people. Consequently, while members of a community may cooperate with each other to carry out the goals of the community, there may also be conflicts and antagonism between various groups of people within the community. The conflicts are greater when any group within a community has low status or lacks power because it is a minority group. A good case is a borough of New York City that has Black, Puerto Rican, Jewish, and Protestant residents. The members of this community may unite over common concerns such as housing, but at the same time, they may conflict over other concerns that may benefit one group, but not another.

But how do we distinguish between *community* and *culture?*

A *culture* is a set of learned behaviors of a group of people who have their own language, values, rules for behavior, and traditions. A person may be born into a culture; he is brought up according to the values of the culture and his personality and behavior are shaped by his cultural values. Or, a person may grow up in one culture and later learn the language, values, and practices of a different culture and become 'enculturated' into that culture.

A *community,* on the other hand, is a general social system in which a group of people live together, share common goals, and carry out certain responsibilities to each other. For example, the culture of a community of people living in a small New England town is the same as that of the larger society in which they participate. And my example earlier of a New York borough is one where a community may be composed of a number of different cultural groups. A Puerto Rican person has the beliefs and the behaviors of his cultural group, but he lives in a larger community of people where he works and, to some degree, socializes with other people who are not Puerto Rican. Thus, a person's beliefs and actions are mainly influenced by his *culture*, but his work and many social activities are carried out within his *community*.

With this background, we can now begin to define "deaf community." The term has been used in two restricted ways—either meaning only those persons who are audiologically deaf, or those persons who are a part of the culture of Deaf people. But it is clear that Deaf people work with and interact with other people who are not Deaf, and who share the goals of Deaf people and work with them in various social and political activities. Earlier definitions of "deaf community," such as Schein's study of the Washington, D.C. deaf community in 1968, included only those persons who are audiologically hearing impaired. I propose a definition which differs from earlier ones:

> A deaf community is a group of people who live in a particular location, share the common goals of its members, and in various ways, work toward achieving these goals. A deaf community may include persons who are not themselves Deaf, but who actively support the goals of the community and work with Deaf people to achieve them.

The definition I have proposed here fits well with the way Hillery defined "community." A community in New York City may be composed of different cultural groups; likewise, a deaf community has not only Deaf members, but also hearing and deaf people who are not culturally Deaf, and who interact on a daily basis with Deaf people and see themselves as working with Deaf people in various common concerns.

The culture of Deaf people, however, is more closed than the deaf community. Members of the Deaf culture behave as Deaf people do, use the language of Deaf people, and share the beliefs of Deaf people toward themselves and other people who are not Deaf.

I will now discuss some characteristics of the deaf community and then turn to describing certain aspects of the American Deaf culture.

Characteristics of Deaf Communities

Location Each deaf community in the United States is uniquely affected by its location. For example, the identity of the Washington, D.C. community is undeniably influenced by the political and educational institutions in Washington, D.C. The Los Angeles deaf community is shaped by the fact that it is located in one of the largest urban areas in the United States. A great number of deaf people are employed in this area, and thus they make up a very large and powerful community.

Other deaf communities, smaller in size than the Washington, D.C. or Los Angeles communities, may be more closed, and some have less participation of non-Deaf people in their affairs.

Deaf people can move from one geographical location to another and enter into a new community with relative ease. They carry with them the knowledge of their culture to help them establish new community ties and learn the specific issues and operations of the new community. Thus, there are many different deaf communities across the United States, but there is a single American Deaf culture with members who live in different communities.

Language use Since a deaf community is composed of people from different cultural groups, language use within the community is different from language use within the particular cultural group. As will be discussed in more detail in a later section, the language of the *culture* of Deaf people is American Sign Language (ASL). The use of ASL by Deaf people in *community* affairs is tolerated to some degree by community members. For example, some Deaf people prefer to use ASL in public speaking situations, and sign-to-voice interpreting is provided for them. At the same time, when Deaf people are involved in community activities which include hearing people who use English, they may choose to use a variety of Sign English. Language use at the community level is rather flexible, but within the cultural group, language use is more restricted.

The distinction between *community* and *culture* allows us to explain how some Deaf people may accept, respect, and in community activities, even use the language of the majority group—English—but at the same time, they can prefer the language of their cultural group. Deaf people feel a strong identification with ASL since it is a part of their cultural background, but when they are involved in community activities, the use of another language allows them to interact with other persons who are not Deaf.

Goals A community is a group of people in a certain geographical location who share common goals. What are the goals of deaf communities?

A primary goal of the national deaf community is to achieve public acceptance of deaf people as equals—equals in employment, in political representation, and in the control of institutions that involve deaf people, such as schools and service organizations. An equally important goal is the acceptance and recognition of their history and their use of signing as a means of communication. As an example, the National Association of the Deaf prints on its envelopes, the message, "Hire the Deaf—They're Good Workers!" The message is a public exhortation of an important goal of the community: to convince the public that deaf workers are not a liability, and should be given equal employment opportunities. Many deaf communities have been pushing for media exposure of Sign Language in television programs and newspaper articles as a means of accomplishing another important goal: public recognition and acceptance of the use of signs to communicate.

The goals of deaf communities are derived primarily from the values of Deaf and hearing people in America. The *values* of a cultural group are represented in those attitudes and behaviors that the group considers most respected and important. Values can be positive: they can show what a group admires and respects. But values can also be negative: members of a cultural group may reject or be suspicious of certain attitudes and behaviors which they consider to be in conflict with their beliefs.

The Culture of American Deaf People

I will turn now to a discussion of some identifying characteristics of the American Deaf culture. My descriptions here are based first on intuition—my own understanding of how I grew up as a child of Deaf parents and how I interact with other Deaf people. I also consulted a number of books and articles written by Deaf people and have found several ideas and concerns repeated throughout these writings. I have picked out some of the more frequently occurring comments Deaf people make about themselves or their lives and have placed them in a framework of culture and cultural values. Some of the books I found helpful in explaining concerns of Deaf people are: Leo Jacobs' *A Deaf Adult Speaks Out* and W. H. Woods' *The Forgotten People*. The *Deaf American* magazine is another good source of information about issues that concern Deaf people.

Deaf people

What does it mean to be Deaf? Who are Deaf people?

Deaf people can be born into the culture, as in the case of children of Deaf parents. They begin learning the language of their parents from birth and thus acquire *native competence* in that language. They also learn the beliefs and behaviors of their parents' cultural group. When they enter schools, they serve as cultural and linguistic models for the larger number of deaf children who do not have Deaf parents and who become a part of the culture later in life.

Being Deaf usually means the person has some degree of hearing loss. However, the type of degree of hearing loss is not a criterion for being Deaf. Rather, the criterion is whether a person identifies with other Deaf people, and behaves as a Deaf person. Deaf people are often unaware of the details of their Deaf friends' hearing loss, and for example, may be surprised to learn that some of their friends can hear well enough to use the telephone.

But the most striking characteristic of the culture of Deaf people is their cultural values—these values shape how Deaf people behave and what they believe in.

Cultural values

What are some examples of values held by Deaf people?

a. Language—Certainly an all-important value of the culture is respect for one of its major identifying features: American Sign Language. Not all Deaf individuals have native competence in ASL; that is, not all Deaf individuals have learned ASL from their parents as a first language. There are many individuals who become enculturated as Deaf persons and who bring with them a knowledge of some other language, usually English. While not all Deaf people are equally competent in ASL, many of them respect and accept ASL, and more now than before, Deaf people are beginning to promote its use. For Deaf people who prefer to use ASL, the language serves as a visible means of displaying one of their unique characteristics. While use of ASL sets the Deaf person apart from the majority English-speaking culture, it also belongs to Deaf people and allows them to take advantage of their capabilities as normal language-using human beings.

Because Sign Language uses the hands, there is a "sacredness" attached to how the hands can be used to communicate. Hands are used for daily manual activities, gestures, and Sign Language, but not for other forms of communication that are *not* Sign Language. Deaf people believe firmly that hand gestures must convey some kind of visual meaning and have strongly resisted what appear to be "nonsense" use of hands—one such example is Cued Speech.

Deaf people frequently explain signs in terms of the "pictures" they depict. While some signs visually represent the object in some way—for example, the sign HOUSE outlines the shape of a typical house—other signs have a less clear pantomimic origin. The sign WHITE supposedly refers to the white ruffles on shirts that men used to wear. Whether the sign actually had that origin is not the point, but that the signer believes strongly that there must be "reason and rhyme" behind a sign.

b. Speaking—There is a general disassociation from speech in the Deaf culture. Some Deaf people may choose to use speech in community activities that involve non-Deaf people, such as mixed parties, parent education programs, or while representing the community in some larger public function. But on the cultural level, speaking is not considered appropriate behavior. Children who are brought up in Deaf culture are often trained to limit their mouth movement to only those movements that are a part of their language. Exaggerated speaking behavior is thought of as "undignified" and sometimes can be interpreted as making fun of other Deaf people.

Before the 1960's and the advent of "total communication" and "simultaneous communication," many Deaf people preferred to sign with the mouth completely closed. This type of signing was considered "proper" and aesthetically pleasing. Now, usually only older Deaf people continue to sign in this way. Although more mouth movement is permitted now, exaggerated mouth movement while signing is still not acceptable to Deaf people.

Mouthing and the use of speech represents many things to Deaf people. Since speech has traditionally been forced on Deaf people as a substitute for their language, it has come to represent confinement and denial of the most fundamental need of Deaf people: to communicate deeply and comfortably in their own language. Deaf people often distrust speech communication for this reason. In speaking, the Deaf person feels she will always be at a disadvantage and can never become fully equal to hearing people who, from the viewpoint of the Deaf person, are always the more accurate models of speaking.

c. Social relations—As with any minority group, there is strong emphasis on social and family ties when family members are of the same culture or community. Carl Croneberg commented on this fact in the *Dictionary of ASL*. Deaf people consider social activities an important way of maintaining contact with other Deaf people. It has frequently been observed that Deaf people often remain in groups talking late, long after the party has ended, or after the restaurant has emptied of people. One reason is certainly that Deaf people enjoy the company of other like-minded Deaf people. They feel they gain support and trusting companionship from other Deaf people who share the same cultural beliefs and attitudes.

Additionally, in some cases, access to other culture members may be limited to parties, club meetings, or other social activities. This is often the case with Deaf people who work in a place that has no other Deaf employees. Thus, because the time that Deaf people spend together in a comfortable social atmosphere may be limited, they like to take advantage of social occasions where they are likely to meet their friends.

d. Stories and literature of the culture—The cultural values described in this paper are never explicitly stated; there are no books that Deaf children read to learn these values. Deaf children learn them through the process of training in which other Deaf people either reinforce or discourage their comments and actions. And these values are found among the symbols used in the literature of the culture. The play, *Sign me Alice* by Gil Eastman is a good example, or the poetry of Dot Miles in *Gestures: Poetry in Sign Language*, and many other unrecorded stories or games. Among the stories that Deaf people tell are the famous "success stories." A typical story may go like this: a *d*eaf person grows up in an oral environment, never having met or talked with *D*eaf people. Later in life, this *d*eaf person meets a *D*eaf person who brings him to parties, teaches him Sign

Language and instructs him in the way of *D*eaf people's lives. This person becomes more and more involved, and leaves behind his past as he joins other *D*eaf people.

In much the same way that Americans support and propagate the "American Dream," these success stories reinforce the strong belief and pride Deaf people have in their way of life: that it is good and right to be *D*eaf.

Entering into the culture of Deaf people

An interesting perspective on being *D*eaf comes from deaf people who are going through a process of becoming *D*eaf and are beginning to assimilate the values of Deaf people. In a study that Harry Markowicz and I did several years ago, we described the conflicts that these people experience. For many people who grow up as part of the culture of Hearing people, they think of themselves as hearing people with a hearing loss. But when they encounter the new and different culture of Deaf people, they find that not all of their beliefs and values will be accepted. They experience a conflict between what they have always believed and what they must accept when they are with other Deaf people. Their success in becoming full members of the culture of Deaf people depends on how they are able to resolve the conflicts they experience.

As an example of a conflict, a deaf person may value her speaking ability and may have always spoken when communicating with other people. But now she learns that speaking does not have the same positive value with Deaf people that it has with hearing people. Even though some Deaf people can hear some speech, and some speak well themselves, speaking is not considered usual or acceptable behavior within the cultural group. The deaf person finds that she must change the behavior that she has always considered normal, acceptable, and positive.

Another example of conflict between old and new behavior concerns how the eyes are used. In the American hearing culture, people are taught that staring is inappropriate, and many deaf people have learned to watch hearing people's faces for short periods of time, then look away quickly in order to avoid being thought as "stupid" or "making improper advances." But in ASL conversations, the listener is expected to watch the face of the signer throughout the conversation. Breaking eye contact between signer and "listener" too soon may be interpreted by Deaf people as "rude," "disinterested," or "trying to act hearing." There is a full range of rules about how to use the eyes in ASL conversations; Charlotte Baker discusses this in more detail in her 1977 article.

In learning the language of Deaf people, the deaf person needs to overcome her own cultural training in how the face is used. Facial expression among hearing people is typically quite restrained when compared with Deaf signers. However, movements of the eyes, face, and head are an important part of ASL—they are used as a part of its grammar, and used to convey information necessary to control conversations between signers as well as to convey information about the emotion of the signer. Thus, the deaf person may experience a conflict between her upbringing, in which she is taught to limit the movements of her body and face, and her attempt to learn a new language in which she must "exaggerate" these behaviors.

Possibly the very first indication that another person is not a member of Deaf culture occurs during the ritual of introduction and exchanging names. Hearing people often introduce themselves by their first names only, and deaf people may do the same. However, Deaf people normally introduce themselves by their full names, and it is not unusual to also add which city or state they are from. This information is important to Deaf people because the cultural group is small, and maintaining ties with all members is a means of preserving group cohesiveness. In the same way that children long ago received names such as 'John's son' or 'Johnson', giving last names allows Deaf people to check the family background of the person being introduced and have additional information about that person. And when the deaf person is asked where he is "from," he may mistakenly give the city or state where he is currently living; a Deaf person would state where she went to school, or spent most of her childhood. It is important to Deaf people to ask for and give each other information about where they were raised and which schools—usually residential schools—they attended. This information allows Deaf people to identify themselves to other Deaf people in their cultural group.

Finally, an important behavior to learn is what to call yourself. In hearing culture, it is desirable to distinguish between degrees of hearing loss. "Hard-of-hearing" is more valued and indicates that the person is closer to being hearing and is more capable of interacting on an equal basis with other hearing people. However, "deaf" is viewed more negatively and usually carries the implication that the person is difficult to communicate with, or may not speak at all.

Thus, a deaf person is more likely to be avoided if he calls himself "deaf." But, among Deaf people, the distinctions between hearing loss are not considered important for group relations. "Deaf" is not a label of deafness as much as a label of identity with other Deaf people. A person learning to interact with other Deaf people will quickly learn that there is one name for all members of the cultural group, regardless of the degree of hearing loss: Deaf. In fact, the sign DEAF can be used in an ASL sentence to mean "my friends," which conveys the cultural meaning of "Deaf." Although Deaf people recognize and accept members that are audiologically hard-of-hearing, calling oneself "hard-of-hearing" rather than by the group name is interpreted by some Deaf people as "putting on airs," because it appears to draw undue attention to hearing loss.

The existence of conflict brings out those aspects of the culture of Deaf people that are unique and separate from other cultural groups. It also shows that the group of Deaf people is not merely a group of like-minded people, as with a bridge club, but a group of people who share a code of behaviors and values that are learned and passed on from one generation of Deaf people to the next. Entering into Deaf culture and becoming *Deaf* means learning all the appropriate ways to behave like a Deaf person.

Hearing children of Deaf parents

As mentioned earlier, being Deaf usually means the person has a hearing loss. But there are hearing children of Deaf parents who have grown up with their parents' culture and feel a strong personal affiliation with other Deaf people. They are like other Deaf people in that they actively participate in various cultural affairs and consider themselves a part of the cultural group. However, the fact that they have an "extra sense," like the "sighted man in a country of the blind," is often a source of conflict for these hearing children of Deaf parents.

They may find themselves cast in the demanding role of being "links" between their families and the majority culture. At a very young age, they may learn to interpret for their families and make contact with other hearing people on behalf of the family. Even after they have left the family, they may still maintain the role of a "go-between," perhaps as professional interpreters, or as part of a Deaf organization that makes contact with hearing people.

Hearing children of Deaf parents are usually given greater access to the culture of Deaf people than other hearing children who do not have Deaf parents. Since they often have been brought up to share the cherished values of Deaf people, Deaf people perceive them as less likely to threaten or try to change the structure of the cultural group, and thus, will allow them to interact more fully with Deaf people. An equally important factor in their being able to become members of the cultural group is their knowledge of the group's language. Hearing children of Deaf parents may acquire native competence in ASL to the point where Deaf people will say, "he signs like Deaf people."

Some hearing children of Deaf parents are acutely aware that the behaviors they must use when they interact with a group of Deaf people are different from the behaviors they must use with a group of hearing people. When they are with Deaf people, they find that they must change many aspects of their behavior: the language they use, the kind of jokes they tell, or how they use their eyes. On the other hand, there are other hearing children of Deaf parents who do not seem to be as aware of conflicts between hearing and Deaf cultures. These children say that when interacting with Deaf people, they behave a certain way, but when with hearing people, they find that they switch behaviors unconsciously.

We need to study more deeply and carefully the experiences of hearing children of Deaf parents. Their varied experiences raise many questions about the characteristics of the culture of Deaf people. For one thing, their experiences will help us understand the role hearing loss plays in shaping the culture of Deaf people.

Summary

The term "deaf community" is used in many different ways. The fact that the word "community" has had different definitions has probably contributed to the variety of definitions that have been used for "deaf community." I follow the definition of community proposed by Hillery, and the term "deaf community" is used here in a more general sense than has been used before: to describe the group of people who interact and contribute to the goals of the community. These people can be members of different cultural groups, and are joined together to the extent that they share in the goals of the community as a whole.

While there is general consensus on the goals of the community, there may also be conflicts over various issues that arise in the community, resulting from the different values of each cultural group.

The culture of Deaf people has not yet been studied in much depth. One reason is that, until recently, it was rare to describe Deaf people as having a *culture*, although it has often been remarked that deaf people tend to seek out other deaf people for companionship. Descriptions of Deaf people have often focused on details of their deficiency, and not on the normal aspects of their lives: that they, like other human beings, are members of communities and cultural groups.

Values of Deaf people reflect the beliefs and ways in which Deaf people react to their social environment. These values are often different from those of the majority culture and need to be learned by incoming deaf people; this is reflected in the problems experienced by deaf people who first grow up as hearing people.

Bill Stokoe's perspective on the language and culture of Deaf people shows his attempt to describe Deaf people not as abnormal, pathological cases, but as individuals who have a cultural and linguistic identity. His work hopefully has begun an age in which facts about Deaf people are not hidden or ignored, but are brought out to help us reach a new stage of awareness and acceptance of Deaf people. It is only then that Deaf people can achieve the kind of equality they have long sought.

References

Baker, Charlotte. Regulators and turn-taking in ASL discourse. In Friedman, L. (Ed.), *On the Other Hand: New Perspectives on American Sign Language.* New York: Academic Press, 1977.

Baker, Charlotte & Padden, C. *ASL: A Look at its History, Structure, and Community.* Silver Spring, MD: TJ Publishers, Inc., 1978.

Bell, Colin and Newby, H. *Community Studies.* London: George Allen & Unwin, Ltd., 1971.

Deaf American, Silver Spring, MD: National Association of the Deaf.

Eastman, Gilbert. *Sign Me Alice: A Play in Sign Language.* Washington, D.C.: Gallaudet College, 1974.

Edwards, Allan and Jones, D. *Community and Community Development.* The Hague, Netherlands: Mouton & Co., 1976.

Hillery, George. *Communal Organizations.* Chicago: Chicago University Press, 1974.

Jacobs, Leo. *A Deaf Adult Speaks Out.* Washington, D.C.: Gallaudet College Press, 1969.

Markowicz, Harry and Woodward, James. Language and the maintenance of ethnic boundaries in the Deaf Community. Paper presented at the Conference on Culture and Communication held at Temple University, March 13–15, 1975.

Meadow, Kay. The deaf subculture. *Hearing and Speech Action*, July-August 1975.

Miles, Dot. *Gestures: Poetry in Sign Language*. Northridge, CA: Joyce Publishers, Inc., 1976.

Mow, Shanny. How do you dance without music? In Little, J. (Ed.), *Answers*. Sante Fe: New Mexico School for the Deaf, 1970.

Padden, Carol and Markowicz, H. Cultural conflicts between hearing and Deaf communities. In *Proceedings of the Seventh World Congress of the World Federation of the Deaf*. Silver Spring, MD: National Association of the Deaf, 1976.

Poplin, Dennis. *Communities: A Survey of Theories and Methods of Research*. New York: Macmillan, 1972.

Schein, Jerome. *The Deaf Community*. Washington, D.C.: Gallaudet College Press, 1968.

Stokoe, William C., Croneberg, C. and Casterline, D. *Dictionary of American Sign Language*. Washington, D.C.: Gallaudet College Press, 1965; Second publication, Silver Spring, MD: Linstok Press, 1976.

Switzer, Mary and Williams, B. Life problems of deaf people. *Archives of Environmental Health, 15*, August 1967.

Woods, W. H. *The Forgotten People*. St. Petersburg, Fla.: Dixie Press, 1973.

Wright, David. *Deafness*. New York: Stein & Day, 1969.

Personal Awareness and Advocacy in the Deaf Community

by Barbara Kannapell

Introduction

I feel honored to contribute an article in honor of Dr. William Stokoe. During my five years at Gallaudet as a student, all I knew about him was that he was a good friend of Dr. Detmold, who was the Dean of the College. Also, Dr. Stokoe practiced the bagpipe with some friends on the campus. He thought it was logical to practice on our campus because the students were deaf! I never associated his name with research on American Sign Language until much later, when I was working as a research assistant to Dr. Harry Bornstein, the Director of the Office of Institutional Research. As the chairman

Barbara Kannapell is presently a Linguistics Specialist with a group of instructional materials developers at Gallaudet College. She received her B.S. in Education from Gallaudet in 1961, her M.A. in Educational Technology from Catholic University in 1970, and currently is a Ph.D. candidate in Sociolinguistics at Georgetown University.

From 1962 to 1972, she worked at Gallaudet College as a research assistant in the Office of Institutional Research. She conducted research on how to improve the educational and communication techniques of deaf persons. This project included developing new signs that were published in a text Signs for Instructional Purposes, *which she co-authored with Harry Bornstein and Lillian Hamilton in 1969. Barbara was born deaf into a deaf family. She is the president of Deafpride, a non-profit organization that she helped establish in 1972. Deafpride advocates human rights among deaf persons and their families and promotes bilingual education for deaf children. Barbara also teaches American Sign Language and Orientation to Deafness at the University of Maryland.*

of the English Department, Dr. Stokoe had a contract with our office to investigate a new method of teaching English to deaf students. That's how I began to know him. Although I interacted professionally with Dr. Stokoe, it was other people who introduced me to his works on ASL. Now, almost 20 years later, I can see how Dr. Stokoe's research and writings have influenced my own interest in studying ASL and the community of deaf persons.

Through my work with Deafpride, Inc., I have seen the need to work for the human rights of deaf persons and the important role of language in that struggle. With this knowledge, I began my studies in sociolinguistics to strengthen my advocacy work. I was convinced that "my language is me" and that the best way for me to be an advocate would be to understand my own language and identity as a deaf person and to teach, explain, and share this with other deaf persons.

In this paper, I will first talk about how I became aware as a deaf person and aware of ASL as my native language. Although I will speak from personal experiences, I am sure that much of my story is true for a large number of deaf people. Then I will show how the study of sociolinguistics contributes to a better understanding of the community of deaf people and of the education of deaf children.

Confessions of a Deaf Advocate

To explain where I am today and who I am today, I need to go back to the past, when I accepted all those negative labels that hearing people placed on me directly or indirectly, such as "oral failure." There were other labels, all part of the well-known "can't" syndrome. I do not mean to include all hearing people in this group. I refer to those who were involved in educating deaf children like myself, and who affected our personal awareness and self-concept. None of these hearing professionals looked at me as a person or as a friend. Indirectly they communicated to me that if I wanted to succeed in a hearing world, I must talk well or at least write English well. I know that I was an "oral failure" in the eyes of those people.

I did not feel good about my speech and my English skills, but I tried hard to communicate with hearing people on their terms. I limited my facial expressions and body movements, was worried about using correct English, tried to use my voice, and was anxious to end conversations with them. Hearing people in general were always interested in how well I talked or heard or wrote English.

They didn't seem to be interested in making friends with me. The teachers always corrected the errors I made in writing or talking and the supervisors always said, "Don't do this," or "Don't do that." They never sat down for a moment to chat with me or other students as friends. This is why I socialized only with deaf people for a long time.

I think these personal reflections are very important when we study deaf children's view of hearing people, and how this affects their self-concept. For me personally, I had a tremendous conflict in my self-concept—my perceptions of myself were positive within the community of deaf persons, but negative within the hearing community. Although I was born deaf to deaf parents and although I grew up learning ASL as my native language, it took me many years to recognize exactly how this early language experience affected my identity as a person. All my life I was not aware that American Sign Language was my first language and English my second language. I always felt inferior when I wanted to communicate with hearing people with my English, but I noticed that I felt comfortable communicating with deaf people.

One year after graduating from Gallaudet College in 1961, I got a job at Gallaudet. My hearing colleagues treated me not only as a professional, but also as a friend, but I did not believe they wanted me to be their friend. I did not realize until much later that I had built a wall between them and me, based on my old definitions or labels of hearing people. Those feelings and experiences continued through college years and the first ten years of working at Gallaudet.

I began to learn things. After several years of working at Gallaudet, I remembered asking Merv Garretson, a professor in the Graduate School, if it was true that Sign Language was a language. He told me it was, because Sign Language had sentence patterns. Also during that time, I taught what we would now call Pidgin Sign English in the Sign Language Program at Gallaudet. I was not aware at that time that there were different sign systems, because the terms ASL, Pidgin Sign English (PSE) and Manual English were not yet in general use. I used the term "sign language" to refer to all kinds of sign systems.

Starting in the summer of 1966, I worked on a three-year project with Dr. Harry Bornstein and Lillian Hamilton to invent new signs for technical words that were vital in college classrooms. I earned a reputation for being an expert on inventing new signs as well as compiling signs from other sources. In the summer of 1967, I was invited to the workshop on "Better Techniques of Communication For Severely Language-Handicapped Deaf People' in Knoxville, Tennessee to assist the participants in inventing new signs for the most common English words which had no signs.

The term paper I wrote in 1968 for a graduate course at Catholic University illustrates how I felt about Sign Language at that time. I said there had been controversy between manualism and oralism in educational systems for deaf people for about 90 years. I thought now was the time to change the philosophy of the education of the deaf. We deaf people knew that Sign Language should be used as a medium of instruction to teach young deaf children, but according to Dr. Stokoe's *Dictionary of ASL*, Sign Language had only 2000 signs and lacked specific signs to convey the meanings of English words. This misconception was a part of a rationale to explain why the invention of new signs for instructional purposes was necessary. In the final report of *New Signs for Instructional Purposes*, Dr. Bornstein and I wrote in the introduction:

> However, manual communication has a serious shortcoming for lectures on complex materials. Because the sign language is limited in size, much of the lecture must be fingerspelled.

The footnote under this statement says, "The most comprehensive published dictionary on the Sign Language, the *Dictionary of ASL* by Stokoe *et al* . . . has an index of approximately 2000 signs." I used this statement to support my paper.

In that paper I wrote about how Max Mossel and David Anthony, in their separate ways, devised a system of signs corresponding to English words by incorporating the first letter of the word into the sign (with fingerspelling handshape) or by inventing a new sign. This system was known as Signing Exact English (SEE I), developed by Anthony. Max Mossel proposed this kind of system of new signs in a series of articles entitled, "Manually Speaking . . . " in *The Silent Worker* (presently *The Deaf American*) in the years 1956–57. I believed in it at the time, and thought it would solve the problem of using Sign Language to teach English to deaf children. This supported my reason for inventing new signs for instructional purposes. That project was successful, and led to a book, *Signs for Instructional Purposes* (Kannapell, Hamilton & Bornstein, 1969). We also produced a series of Signed English books for deaf children.

At that time, at one level it seemed appropriate to me to change Sign Language to Manual English to fit into the hearing world. At another level, inside me, I felt something was wrong. I could not explain this feeling in words, or even in signs, until later.

In 1971 I met Eileen Paul, a hearing person who loves to learn languages. She wanted to be friends with deaf people, and said, "I want to learn your language—the way deaf people sign to each other." I told her it was impossible for hearing people to learn how to sign like a deaf person. I suggested that she go to a Sign Language class and learn the "500 basic signs." She said she did not want the 500 basic signs—she wanted the signs deaf people used with each other. Reluctantly, she went to a Sign Language class but soon dropped out, complaining that she wasn't learning any ASL. (About that time we began to use the term "Ameslan" or "ASL" to distinguish it from the term "Manual English.") She kept insisting that she wanted to learn my language, and I did not understand what she meant. Eventually, Eileen changed my view of Sign Language and of hearing people. Using Eileen's previous experience with teaching other languages, we began to develop videotapes to teach ASL as a language. We videotaped our deaf friends to try to understand how ASL worked in everyday use.

At that time, there were virtually no materials for teaching ASL as a language. The only materials that were relevant at that time were the *Dictionary of ASL*, the draft copy of *Ameslan* by Lou Fant, and a paper entitled, "Some Sociolinguistic Considerations of ASL" by Harry Markowicz. I wanted to try my hand at teaching ASL to hearing people so I applied for teaching a Sign Language course at Gallaudet. I got a job to teach Sign Language to new faculty members at the intermediate level. There were many ASL signs in the third part of a book, *Conversational Sign Language II* by Willard Madsen. These signs were called Sign Language "idioms." I found teaching ASL to hearing people very difficult. Everytime I wanted to teach ASL to hearing people, I found myself teaching them Pidgin Sign English (a mixture of ASL and English, using certain types of ASL signs in English word order). I thought it might be due to my habit of signing in English with hearing people, and in ASL with deaf people. I was wondering if I would ever be able to teach ASL to hearing people.

The years 1971 and 1972 were a threshold for my understanding of ASL as a true language and as my first language. From that time to today, I have been in the process of discovering myself as a deaf person. Several milestones happened about the same time during that year. Here I will mention two: one was the founding of Deafpride, Inc.; the other was taking courses in linguistics in the Ph.D. Sociolinguistics program at Georgetown University.

Deafpride was established in the Fall of 1972. At a Sign Language class, Eileen Paul met Ann Wilson, a mother of four children whose oldest son is deaf, and introduced her to me. After a series of meetings, we concluded that hearing community workers, parents of deaf children, and deaf adults needed to work together to promote the human rights of deaf persons; thus we decided to work together and founded Deafpride, Inc. Our activities continue to the present. We encourage deaf people to develop self-pride and pride in their language—ASL. We give lectures and workshops to various groups, explaining the organization itself, my awareness as a deaf person, ASL from linguistic and sociolinguistic perspectives, and the impact of deafness on the family. Also, since 1976, Eileen and I have been developing ASL materials to teach undergraduates at the University of Maryland. We not only teach ASL as a second language, but also teach deaf culture and the impact of deafness on the family.

One of my activities in Deafpride, Inc. has involved teaching ASL to hearing parents of deaf children. This has been both a rewarding and a saddening experience for me. It is so important to teach ASL to those parents so that they are able to understand their own children's use of ASL. For so many years, deaf children have been cut off from participating in the family as a unit. Even though educators know that deaf children use ASL all the time, they refuse to teach the children or their parents this language. Over the last ten years, the schools have begun to teach hearing parents to sign, but what kind of signing? Manually-coded English. Once again, the deaf child is cut off from the family. Or, if the child uses Manual English, she or he is cut off from the greater deaf community.

Through working with the parents, I have seen them change their attitudes toward ASL, and accept their children as they are, and that has been rewarding. But it has been sad to see the Manual English signs the parents bring to my class. I explain to them that deaf people do not use those signs, and also explain that some of the Manual English signs violate linguistic principles. Some of the signs the parents had learned were actually obscene. That's why I am very much in favor of both groups—parents and deaf adults—interacting with each other.

The other milestone was taking two courses on ASL linguistic principles taught by Dr. James Woodward at Gallaudet College. My first term paper proposed bilingual education for deaf children. The expanded version of that paper, "Bilingualism: New Directions for the Education of the Deaf," was published in *The Deaf American* in June 1974.

Throughout the Ph.D. program in Sociolinguistics at Georgetown University, studying has constantly reinforced my thoughts about the need for bilingual education of deaf children. Also, I can see that the field of sociolinguistics, the study of language in its social context, can contribute so much to a better understanding of the community of deaf persons and their use of the language. One of the first concepts I learned from my first class in Sociolinguistics was "group reference." It means that a child is less motivated to learn one language because he or she wants to learn another language that the peers use. The language the peers use could be slightly or very different from the language used in the classrooms. I was able to understand why I was not comfortable using new signs of Manual English when I worked on a series of Signed English books for Deaf Children. The first reason is that if I tried to use SEE signs with hearing people, I was afraid that my deaf friends would reject me. I wanted them to accept me as part of their group. They were my group identity, my group reference. I belong to them and wanted to be identified with them. The second reason is that when I used SEE, I was not really myself. It was not really part of me as an individual. I could not identify SEE with myself. So it was also a question of individual identity. One other thing I learned in my classes was "language choice." It means a person will choose which language or variety of a language to use depending on with whom and in which situation. It is also identity choice. For example, deaf people choose ASL or English depending on the identity the system wants for them. They have learned that they are not supposed to sign to hearing people in ASL, and so they try to sign in English and speak also. When they are with other deaf people, they feel comfortable using ASL, and experience a strong sense of group identity.

One more thing in relation to language identity: the study of sociolinguistics made me realize that in order to study a language one must understand the people who use it. What gives me special insight as a sociolinguist is the fact I was born into, and grew up as a member of the community of deaf people. So I know that a critical factor in understanding ASL is understanding that ASL is very much a part of a deaf person. If you want to change ASL, or take ASL away from the person, you are trying to take his or her identity away. I believe "my language is me." To reject a language is to reject the person herself or himself. Thus, to reject ASL is to reject the deaf person. Remember ASL is a personal creation of deaf persons as a group. Perhaps those hearing or deaf people who can not deal with ASL are really saying they can not deal with or accept the deaf person.

Also, in sociolinguistics, I have learned that language can serve many functions. Garvin and Mathiot (1976) described two symbolic functions of language in their paper, *Functions of a Standard Language*. They discuss the unifying and separatist functions of language in relation to French Canadians in Quebec. I will apply their insights to the use of American Sign Language by deaf people.

ASL has a unifying function, since deaf people are unified by their common language. But the use of ASL simultaneously separates deaf people from the hearing world. So the two functions are different perspectives on the same reality—one from inside the group which is unified, and the other from outside. The group is separated from the hearing world. This separatist function is a protection for deaf people. For example, we can talk about anything we want, right in the middle of a crowd of hearing people. They are not supposed to understand us.

It is important to understand that ASL is the only thing we have that belongs to deaf people completely. It is the only thing that has grown out of the deaf group. Maybe we are afraid to share our language with hearing people. Maybe our group identity will disappear once hearing people know ASL.

The explanation of these functions helped me understand why it was so difficult for me to teach ASL to hearing people. As I said before, I have taught Sign Language to hearing people three different times. The first time, I taught Pidgin Sign English (PSE). The second time I accepted ASL as a language on an intellectual level, but it was still difficult to teach ASL to hearing people. The third time around, my acceptance of ASL had reached a gut level. Now I am much more comfortable teaching ASL to hearing people. This change has something to do with my understanding of identity and language.

Once I learned that ASL is my native language, I developed a strong sense of identity as a deaf person and a more positive self-image. Once I accepted ASL as my native language I became eager to improve my English because I was then able to accept hearing people as equals. I found myself enjoying teaching hearing people

ASL as their second language. And I liked having hearing people teach me English as a second language.

This part gives you a general idea of where I am today and who I am today. As a result of my personal and professional experiences, I am now convinced that we must base our research and studies on a positive definition of the community of deaf persons, rather than basing them on negative labels like "communication disorder, language deficiency, culturally deprived," etc. I believe we can learn from anthropologists and sociolinguists how to accurately describe the reality of the community of deaf persons as well as the education of deaf children.

Bilingual Education for Deaf Children

The traditional educational systems for deaf children essentially teach them English through English. They do not encourage them to explore the possibilities of a variety of ASL meanings corresponding to a variety of English meanings. Neither do they help the students learn the difference between formal and informal English usage. From the perspective of sociolinguistics, this means they do not accept that deaf children may be bilinguals to varying degrees (Kannapell, 1979).

A bilingual is a person who understands and is able to use two languages to some degree. There are several types of bilinguals. One is a person who is fully competent in both languages and is considered a "balanced" bilingual (Lambert, Havelka & Gardner, 1959). Another is a person who is more fluent and more comfortable with his "dominant," or first, language than with his second language. There are also people who can understand the second language, even though they, themselves, never use it. As Peter Hornby (1977) points out: "Bilingual individuals differ considerably in terms of their degree of competence in their two languages (balanced versus dominant), in the linguistic relationship between the two speech varieties (distinct languages versus stylistic variations), in the degree of cultural duality involved (bilingualism versus biculturalism), and in the socio-cultural significance or function of the languages involved, as well as other possible sources of variation."

Bilinguals can be classified in another way as "coordinate" or "compound" bilinguals. According to Weinriech (1953): "A coordinate bilingual has two separate (and different) semantic systems. A compound bilingual is taken to have two distinct modes of expression (the two languages) for an underlying semantic network."

How does this relate to deaf people as bilinguals? I would say that ideally a deaf bilingual is fluent in using and understanding two languages—American Sign Language and English. By this I mean that a deaf person is able to read and write English and use Pidgin Sign English and ASL. The ability to speak English should be also considered for those deaf people who can talk, but it is not required by this definition: a person can *know* and *use* English without being able to *speak* it.

So far, there has been no research attempting to measure the degree of bilingualism among deaf people. Measurement of language skills of deaf people has been done only in terms of English, and usually focuses on speaking, lipreading, reading and writing skills. In focusing on English, research overlooks the rich social reality of the deaf community where there is a diversity of communication modes.

At Gallaudet College, my job is to develop bilingual materials to teach deaf students English through ASL. The strategy I use is to demonstrate to deaf students the relationship between language expressions in ASL and language expressions in English, and thus facilitate their learning English through ASL. In 1977, I was doing informal research on how deaf people use ASL signs and how hearing people use English words. Through this research, I began to classify deaf students in terms of bilingualism. These groups are:

1. ASL-Dominant Bilinguals—they are comfortable expressing themselves in ASL better than English (in either printed or signed form);

2. English-Dominant Bilinguals—they are comfortable expressing themselves in English and are able to understand English (in printed and signed form) better than ASL;

3. Balanced Bilinguals—they are comfortable expressing themselves in both ASL and English and are able to understand ASL and English about equally well.

I would like to propose these classifications for the deaf students I have worked with at Gallaudet. It is possible that outside of Gallaudet College, there are more classifications in addition to the three given above; for example, there may be ASL monolinguals and English monolinguals. These classifications might also apply to deaf children and deaf adults.

Ideally, a deaf child should live in the best of two worlds and should be able to freely move from the Deaf community to the hearing community and vice versa. He or she should be able to communicate with deaf people in ASL or PSE, and to participate in their activities, should be able to use PSE to communicate with hearing people who know signs, and should be able to read and write English fluently. Speech, lipreading, and auditory skills of English should be considered for those who can speak or who have residual hearing. Our goal should be to have as many balanced bilinguals as possible in the deaf community.

What is actually happening now is that most of the schools for deaf children which turn to the philosophy of total communication employ varieties of languages between PSE and Manual English to teach deaf children. They try to achieve the three following goals simultaneously:

- to teach deaf children to talk and lipread English;
- to teach deaf children English as if it is their first language;
- to teach deaf children a subject matter using English as a medium of instruction.

It is too much for deaf children to try to learn how to talk, learn English as a first language, and learn subject matter in English all at the same time. In other words, why teach English through English?

We need to develop a bilingual and bicultural approach to education in order to prepare deaf children for both communities—deaf and hearing. In other words, we need to look at the deaf child as a whole child. At present, each communication method or each sign system used in educational systems in the United States develops only a small part of the child—that is, linguistic competence in English. But a bilingual and bicultural approach would foster the deaf child's positive self-image by developing linguistic and communicative competence in both ASL and English.

Sadly, there is a missing link between the researchers of ASL, the educators of deaf children, and members of the Deaf community. ASL research still has had relatively little impact on the educational systems that are supposed to serve the needs of deaf children. There is also substantial information about bilingualism in hearing children which could be usefully applied toward understanding the needs and abilities of deaf children. The Deaf community is beginning to change its own attitudes as a result of linguistic research on ASL; it is time for education to do the same. I hope to see in the future that researchers of ASL work together to promote a bilingual and bicultural education for deaf children.

References

Fant, Lou. *Ameslan: An Introduction to ASL.* Silver Spring, MD.: National Association of the Deaf, 1972.

Garvin, Paul and Mathiot, M. "Functions of a Standard Language." In R. Fasold (Ed.), *Topics in Sociolinguistics: Sociolinguistics of Society.* Unpublished collection of classroom readings.

Hornby, Paul A. *Bilingualism: Psychological, Social and Educational Implications.* New York: Academic Press, Inc. 1977.

Kannapell, Barbara, Hamilton, L. and Bornstein, H. *Signs for Instructional Purposes.* Washington, D.C.: Gallaudet College Press, 1969.

Kannapell, Barbara. Bilingualism: New Directions for the Education of the Deaf. *The Deaf American,* 1974, 26, 9–15.

_____. A Preliminary Report on Developing Bilingual Materials to Teach Deaf Students. A paper presented at the International Symposium on Sign Language Research. Stockholm, Sweden, June, 1979.

Lambert, Wallace E., Havelka, J. and Gardner, R. C. Linguistic Manifestations of Bilingualism. *American Journal of Psychology,* 1959, 72, 77–82.

Madsen, Willard J. *Conversational Sign Language II: An Intermediate-Advanced Manual.* Washington, D.C.: Gallaudet College, 1972.

Markowicz, Harry. Some Sociolinguistic Considerations of ASL. *Sign Language Studies,* 1972, 1, 15–41.

Stokoe, W., Casterline, D. and Croneberg, C. *Dictionary of American Sign Language.* Washington, D.C.: Gallaudet College Press, 1965. Second publication, Silver Spring, MD: Linstok Press, 1976.

Weinreich, U. *Language in Contact.* New York: Linguistic Circle of New York, 1953.

Sociolinguistic Research on American Sign Language: An Historical Perspective

by James Woodward

I will start this history with my own beginning in this field: how I met Bill Stokoe. The time was August, 1969. I had just returned from my senior year abroad in Taiwan. I was planning on going to graduate school on a scholarship, but my draft lottery number quickly produced a 1A classification and a notice for a physical exam, so I decided I would look around for a teaching position, which at that time offered the possibility of a deferment. By chance, I talked with my advisor, who suggested that I try Gallaudet College. I had never heard of Gallaudet College, but I called anyway and talked with the Chair of the English Department, William Stokoe. I explained my background and asked about teaching positions. Stokoe said that someone in his department was asking for a leave of ab-

James Woodward is Associate Professor and Chair of the Linguistics Department at Gallaudet College. He received his Ph.D. with distinction from Georgetown University in Sociolinguistics in 1973. His dissertation described grammatical variation in American Sign Language. He has done field research on the Toda-Sejeq dialect of Atayal and on Mandarin Chinese in Taiwan (1968–69), and more recently has studied Sign Language variation in Deaf communities in the United States, France, Colombia, and India. He came to Gallaudet College in 1969 as an Instructor in Linguistics and English. His publications have dealt primarily with regional, social, ethnic, and historical variation in French Sign Language and American Sign Language, and he is the author of two books: Signs of Sexual Behavior *(1979) and* Signs of Drug Use *(1980).*

sence and asked if I would be interested in coming over in a couple of weeks, since he was going on vacation the next day. Since I had my army physical in two days, I told him that I might not be around Washington, D.C. in two weeks. He suggested I come over that day for an interview. So I rode the bus to Gallaudet, interviewed, and got the job. Sometimes, when I look back on that day, I wonder what Stokoe had in his mind when he hired me off the street.

You, the reader, may be thinking, "What luck!" Actually 'timing' and 'chance' are better words, and they clearly describe the development of sociolinguistic research into ASL.

Many people assume that scientific research is the result of someone's carefully planned thought in an 'ivory tower' or that there is always some well-designed plan for research that is being steadily carried toward completion. Sometimes this is true, but in the field of sociolinguistics it is very difficult to do this, since no one can bring a society of language users into a laboratory.

In addition, many people think that professional contacts and relationships occur because of plodding, dilligent effort by researchers to make contact. In the case of sociolinguistic research on ASL in the U.S., this has rarely happened. Chance meetings and contacts are the norm. In this paper, I will try to describe the "interactive" history of sociolinguistic research on ASL by focusing on the personal as well as professional interactions between researchers and consultants that have influenced this research.

Before we start this interactive history, we need to first take a brief look at sociolinguistics.

What is Sociolinguistics?

Sociolinguistics is the study of the form and functions of language in society. What types of language or languages can be used in courts or educational systems? Is the same language used in both formal and everyday conversations, or are there different languages? What are the attitudes of majority and minority cultures towards language variation? What types of language variation actually occur? Often differences in the language used in a society are related to regional, social, ethnic, age, and even sex differences.

These questions and others are important for understanding how people actually use a language in real life situations. This information is important for understanding prejudice and discrimination in society, since very often people are stereotyped by the type of language they use. In addition, whenever language skills have to be taught in a classroom, there must be some decisions about which form of the language to teach, and this requires knowing how different forms of a language are used in a society. Interpreters also need to know more than just the appropriate vocabulary and grammar of a language, but also the appropriate situations in which this vocabulary and grammar can be used. For example, it is perfectly acceptable to me and many other people who were raised in the South to say, "He might could go." In fact, if you don't say "might could" people will often look on you as a snob or a Northerner. But all of us who use that form know that "might could" is inappropriate for written English; there we would use "might be able."

Like all other languages, ASL has variation: people from different places often sign differently (Woodward, Erting & Oliver 1976). Sometimes White signers sign differently from Black signers (Woodward 1976) and sometimes males sign differently from females (De Santis 1977). An understanding of this variation is crucial for planning educational and interpreting programs. One of the most important types of variation that occurs in the U.S. Deaf community is *diglossia*.

What is Diglossia?

In 1969, the Linguistics Research Lab at Gallaudet was in existence in the same offices as the English Department. At that time, Stokoe was Chair of the English Department and Director of the Linguistics Research Lab. He was also completing his classic article on "Sign Language Diglossia."

The term *diglossia* was first coined by Charles Ferguson (1959), who used it to explain the spoken language situation in Arabic countries, Greece, Switzerland, and Haiti. In the classic diglossic situation described by Ferguson, one variety of a language, generally a standard literary variety, has a special relationship to another colloquial variety of the same language. The literary variety is used in more formal situations with more formal topics and participants, while the colloquial variety is used in less formal situations. Native users generally consider the literary variety superior to the colloquial variety, and some people will even claim that the colloquial variety does not exist. The colloquial variety is generally learned at home, whereas the literary variety is learned at school. The literary variety is generally studied in the schools; the colloquial is not.

Many people study the grammar of the literary variety, but "descriptive and normative studies of the . . . colloquial variety are either non-existent or relatively recent and slight in quantity" (Ferguson, 1959, p. 432). Diglossic situations are typically very stable and may continue for several centuries.

Fishman further refined the definition of diglossia to include bilingual communities—communities in which more than one language is used. He pointed out that is is possible to have diglossia with bilingualism, diglossia without bilingualism, bilingualism without diglossia, and neither bilingualism nor diglossia. However, "only very small, isolated and undifferentiated speech communities may be said to reveal neither diglossia nor bilingualism" (Fishman, 1967, p. 37). Thus, the attitudes and patterns of language use that characterize diglossia are fairly common; it is also common to find more than one language used in a community.

What is Diglossia Like in the U.S. Deaf Community?

Since diglossic and bilingual situations are quite normal, it is not surprising to find them in the U.S. Deaf community. Stokoe (1969–1970) first pointed out the bilingual-diglossic situation between ASL and English. Stokoe identified the literary variety as English and the colloquial variety as ASL and showed that these languages shared the characteristics of other languages in diglossic situations. As in other diglossic situations, the literary variety (English) is used in formal conversations in church, in classrooms, for lectures, etc. The colloquial variety (ASL) is used in smaller, less formal, more intimate conversations. English is considered superior to ASL, and ASL is often regarded as ungrammatical or non-existent (Johnston 1977). Signers generally feel that "grammatical" English signing should be used instead of ASL for teaching. Much formal grammatical description has been done on English (in its spoken or written form) but only relatively recently has any research on ASL been done. Some signers feel that standardization is necessary, but Sign Language diglossia appears as stable as other diglossic situations.

There appears to be only one possible point of conflict between bilingual diglossia in the U.S. Deaf community and bilingual diglossia in Hearing communities—how the languages are acquired. In Hearing diglossic situations, the colloquial language is learned first at home and the literary at school. But only 5 to 7 percent of the Deaf population have two Deaf parents (Karchmer & Trybus 1977), so this can't be true for the Deaf community. However, if we remember that the home is the initial place for learning Hearing culture for Hearing children and that residential schools have served as the initial place for learning Deaf culture for many Deaf children of Hearing parents, this apparent contradiction is overcome. For we can now say that ASL is generally learned early in the initial place for enculturation: the home for Deaf children of Deaf parents and the residential school for Deaf children of Hearing parents. This acquisition of ASL takes place in informal situations. English (signed, spoken, or written) is usually learned in more formal classroom situations.

Why Does Diglossia Exist?

The negative attitudes of Hearing people and the discrimination of Hearing people against Deaf people are probably two of the reasons for the existence of diglossia in the Deaf community. With the seemingly hostile world facing most minority groups in the U.S., there is a feeling among members of the minority group that "outsiders" must be identified and not trusted until they have proved that they do not fit the minority group's stereotype of the majority. There is also a need to identify other members of the minority group so that a feeling of group solidarity can be achieved.

In principle, diglossia ensures that most Hearing people will be easily recognized and sterotyped as Hearing—and thus, excluded from intimate interactions with Deaf people. That is, since the majority of Hearing people do not know or use ASL, their more English-like signing shows that they are Hearing. When a Hearing person enters a conversation where Deaf people are using ASL, the Deaf people will automatically switch from ASL to a more English-like form of signing (Markowicz & Woodward 1975). This "code-switching" prevents the Hearing person from seeing and learning to use ASL and thus, from being able to participate in intimate interactions with Deaf people.

Many Hearing people, including some Hearing linguists, misunderstand the nature and importance of diglossia in the Deaf community. Sometimes Hearing people who are just beginning to learn to sign tell me, "Oh, now I have a class in ASL. It's fascinating." A few months later, they realize that what they are learning is Pidgin Sign English or some form of manually coded English. Then they start complaining that no Deaf person will teach them ASL no matter how much they beg. The Deaf people keep switching to English. I then suggest that they start taking the time to begin interacting with Deaf people in informal casual situations, and try to imitate the signing that Deaf people use with each other. The Hearing people reply that they don't have time and still ask, "Why can't someone teach an ASL class?" One reason it is so difficult for Deaf people to teach ASL is that it is presently not generally socially acceptable in the Deaf community to use ASL in classroom situations, especially when the class is full of Hearing people.

The point of this whole discussion is that diglossia acts as a "buffer" between Hearing and Deaf communities (Markowicz & Woodward 1975). It allows Hearing people to be identified as outsiders and to be treated carefully before allowing any interaction that could negatively affect the Deaf community. Hearing outsiders are stereotyped negatively until they prove themselves to the community. Any Hearing person who does not have the time to associate with Deaf people will be viewed as only another "hearie." At the same time, diglossia serves important functions in the Deaf community by maintaining the social identity and group solidarity of Deaf people, and thus is a very positive force in the Deaf community (Markowicz & Woodward 1975). The diglossic situation between ASL and English is complex. What is even more complex is the relationship between ASL and English signing in the Deaf community. To understand this relationship, we have to jump ahead in time to 1973 to the first Ph.D. dissertation that attempted to describe ASL in sociolinguistic terms (Woodward 1973a). The dissertation, supported by National Science Foundation and National Institute of Mental Health grants that Stokoe had obtained, was a discussion of the variation from ASL to English signing based on Stokoe's diglossic work, and sociolinguistic theory for analyzing variation along language continuums.

What is the relationship between ASL and English?

Because of the great variety of language backgrounds of Deaf students, the overt pressures of the Hearing community for Deaf students to learn English, the diglossic situation in the Deaf community, and perhaps other factors, we find a large amount of variation in signing. (Again it is important to note that variation is normal and, depending on sociological conditions, may vary in intensity from society to society.) This variation is *not* random but systematic and can be described in terms of modern sociolinguistic theory.

Let's take a look at one example of variation between ASL and English signing

One Example of the Continuum Between ASL and Manual English

(right hand)	FINISH ME	ASL
(left hand)	EAT	:
	EAT FINISH ME	:
	I FINISH EAT	Pidgin Sign English
	I END EAT	:
	I HAVE EAT	:
	I HAVE(V) EAT	:
	I HAVE(V) EAT FINISH	Manual English

In this example, meaning "I have eaten," "purer" ASL can sign EAT and FINISH simultaneously by using both hands, while no English variety does. Also notice that ASL does not have the same word order as English. English uses a different perfective (completed action) marker than ASL. ASL has one form for the first person singular pronoun, English has two. Certain types of English signing use an initialized handshape on HAVE (V). All of this may appear complex: it is. All of this may also appear random. IT IS NOT RANDOM, BUT SYSTEMATIC. If one uses the initialized sign for the English pronoun "I", they will use English word order. If one uses an initialized perfective marker, they will also use the sign for "I" and English word order. Depending on the social background of the signer and the appropriate language variety to choose, a person will use more ASL-like signing or more English-like signing. Of course, the use of any particular type of signing is dependent upon the signer's knowledge. People can't use a language variety they do not know.

The type of variation that we observe along the continuum between ASL and English is discussed theoretically below. PSE is not a discrete language from ASL or English. Please do not fall into the trap of trying to label each kind of signing you see with a specific name. A continuum by its very nature does not have discrete internal boundaries.

In my dissertation (1973a) and other papers (1973b, c, d, 1976) I have formally described the variation along this continuum and have shown that the variation is non-discrete, but regular, rule-governed, and describable in terms of sociolinguistic theory. This variation also correlates with social variables of whether a person is Deaf or Hearing, has Deaf or Hearing parents, learned signs before or after the age of six, and attended some or no college (Woodward 1973a).

Unfortunately, along with this recognition of variation has come a proliferation of names—American Sign Language, ASL (Stokoe 1960), Ameslan (Fant 1972), Ameslish (Bragg 1973), Signed English (O'Rourke 1970), Siglish (Fant 1972), (Pidgin) Sign English (Woodward 1972, 1973d), Manual English (Stokoe 1970).

What is wrong with having so many names?

This proliferation is unfortunate for two reasons: 1) it confuses people, and 2) it obscures the idea of a continuum and gives the impression that there are many discrete languages.

It should be remembered that there are only two discrete languages on the continuum: ASL and (a manual representation of) English. Intermediate varieties contain various overlaps and are not discrete, but are describable in terms of current variation theory in linguistics (Woodward 1973a, b, c, 1974). As stated earlier, these intermediate varieties along the American Sign Language-to-English diglossic continuum have certain sociological and linguistic characteristics of pidginized language varieties (Woodward 1973d; Woodward and Markowicz 1975).

Pidgin Sign English retains certain grammatical characteristics of both American Sign Language and English and some of the phonological characteristics of American Sign Language. Deaf signers retain more of the characteristics of American Sign Language in their Pidgin Sign English than do Hearing signers who retain more of the characteristics of English. However, because English and signs use different channels, it is impossible to keep as much English as ASL in Pidgin Sign English. Thus, Hearing people's Pidgin Sign English is much more reduced than Deaf people's Pidgin Sign English. Hearing signers are often said to sign without expression or to "mumble" because their use of the signing space is greatly reduced. However, Deaf PSE signers tend to use more of the signing space because this is a feature which can be carried over from ASL.

Some people are now saying that PSE is a separate language from ASL and English. While it is true that PSE is different from pure ASL and from pure English, it is not a separate language. There is no way in the world to define where PSE begins and ends. PSE was used specifically to label the situation that exists between ASL and English: there is no clearcut definable division between ASL and English. The term 'Pidgin Sign English' is merely used to describe the fact there is no clearcut division and allows one to talk about "English-y ASL" and "ASL-like English" for deaf people, and "ASL-like English" for a few hearing people and "English-y English" for most hearing people.

Although there is no clearcut division between ASL and English, there are research-based ways to describe the continuum. I have handled the description of this variation by using sociolinguistic variation theory (1973a, b, 1974, 1975). Through these techniques, it is possible to demonstrate statistically that Deaf signers tend to use more ASL-like signing than Hearing people (Woodward 1975), that Deaf people with Deaf parents use more ASL-like signing than Deaf people with Hearing parents (Woodward 1973a), that people who learned signs before the age of six will use more ASL-like signing than people who learned signs after the age of six (Woodward 1975), and that college experience is also an important variable (Woodward 1975). Lloyd Anderson has helped me realize that the original conclusion of the independent variable of college education was misleading. If signers are subdivided into those having Deaf parents and those having Hearing parents and then the variable of college is introduced, Deaf people of Deaf parents who attend college use less ASL than Deaf people of Hearing parents who attend college. The college experience then can be seen as reducing ASL use for Deaf students with Deaf parents and increasing it for Deaf students with Hearing parents.

This brings us to a crucial point. Most of the linguistic studies of ASL generally do not describe the Deaf people who participated as consultants in the research (usually only one or two), nor describe any empirical ways that they attempted to verify that what they were getting was close to "pure" ASL signing. But this kind of information is very important for understanding the results of their research. For example, such contradictory claims as "previous SOV (subject-object-verb sign order) and present predominant SVO sign order in ASL" (Fischer 1975) versus "free sign order in ASL" (Friedman 1975) versus "preferred SVO with variant sign orders depending on facial adverbials" (Liddell 1978) could be more easily resolved with a large scale study utilizing variation theory. I should point out that there are less than five consultants in each of these studies, that none of the linguistic consultants (informants) in each of these studies are from the Southeast, but all are White, middle class (in the Deaf community), and in at least two of the studies, college-educated. (This same trend for selection of consultants can be found in almost alll studies of ASL.) If one performed the same studies on a larger group of people, especially in the South, and more especially among Black signers, it is very likely that one would find a greater use of the historically older verb-final sign order among Southeastern consultants and within Southeastern consultants. Black signers might very well use more of the historically older verb-final orders than White signers of the same age. This is a reasonable hypothesis, since Southeasterners tend to retain older forms of signs more often than Northerners (Woodward 1976b, Woodward & De Santis 1977b). Also in the South, Black signers use historically older forms more often than White signers of the same age (Woodward & Erting 1975, Woodward 1976b, Woodward & De Santis 1977b).

What can we do to avoid these problems in variation?

The solution to this problem is to test out these studies that have the above problems on a fairly large sample of consultants from varying regional, social, ethnic, and age backgrounds. All of these variables significantly and independently influence ASL use. To give a brief illustration here of how complex the situation can be: regional, social, ethnic, and age and historical variations are often related. For example, Susan De Santis and I (1977b) have shown that French signers used more of the older two-handed signs on the face than American signers. In the same study, it was pointed out that in the U.S., Southerners use the older two-handed signs more often than Northerners. In the South, older White signers use the older two-handed signs more often than younger White signers. Also in the South, younger Black signers paralleled older White signers: that is, they use older two-handed signs on the face more often than younger White signers.

Having seen systematic variation along the diglossic continuum between ASL and English, we can now go back a little in time to

1970 to look at the historical development of sociolinguistic research related to region, sex, etc., within ASL.

Research on Variation in ASL

The year 1970 was primarily a year of development for the Linguistics Research Lab. By 1971, the Linguistics Research Lab was quite active and a number of events helped promote sociolinguistic research in ASL. First, the Linguistics Research Lab became an autonomous unit at Gallaudet College, and received funding from outside grants. This autonomy was necessary for expansion of staff and research. Second, I became involved in the newly established Sociolinguistics Program at Georgetown University, the first of its kind in the U.S. This led me to quite different emphases in my own research. Third, T. J. O'Rourke, then the Director of the Communication Skills Program at the National Association of the Deaf, with assistance from Stokoe, received a grant from the Bureau of Education for the Handicapped to establish a workshop at Western Maryland College, entitled "Psycholinguistics and Total Communication: The State of the Art." Stokoe was asked to teach at this institute, but since he had prior commitments, Stokoe asked me if I wanted to teach in his place. The institute at Western Maryland provided me with important contacts which led to specific field research at later dates.

Kay Meadow's paper at the institute, "Sociolinguistics, Sign Language, and the Deaf Sub-Culture" provided a summary of Stokoe's work on diglossia and brought out several other interesting areas for research (Meadow, 1972). Meadow herself refers briefly to Croneberg's work, especially his statement on ethnic variation in ASL (Croneberg 1965). My experience at the institute helped solidify my own thinking about where sociolinguistic research in ASL ought to move. At the December meeting of the Linguistic Society of America (LSA) in 1971 in St. Louis, I outlined our needs for future sociolinguistic research on ASL. This was the first paper on American Sign Language presented at a Linguistic Society of America meeting, and it helped other linguists to begin to recognize ASL as a language—a crucial step toward expanding the linguistic study of ASL.

In 1972, a second institute on Psycholinguistics and Total Communication was held at Lewis and Clark College in Portland, Oregon. In the Linguistic Research and Theory course in the institute, I began to switch the focus towards sociolinguistics. At the institute, I also made contact with Carol Erting and Harry Markowicz. We later worked together on various aspects of the sociolinguistics of American Sign Language.

During the Fall of 1972, Stokoe, Gil Eastman, Will Madsen, and I developed a course, "The Study of Sign Language," offered by the Audiology and Speech Department at Gallaudet. In the process of developing this course, I suggested that the course include ASL "dialects" and the other three people told me I should teach that part of the course. Since I didn't know anything about Sign Language varieties other than what was reported in Croneberg (1965), I decided that I would have to go and find out for myself. I contacted Carol Erting in Atlanta, since that was an area that might have significant variation. She set up an appointment for me at an Adult Basic Education class in Atlanta, and I went, with the trip partially paid by Stokoe from our meager budget.

That was the coldest winter Atlanta had had in years. I was in a motel that obviously had forgotten the insulation. I had turned the heat on as high as possible, pulled all the covers off both beds, and was sleeping in my clothes and still freezing. But the people I met were fantastic—signers from Alabama, Tennessee, Florida, and Georgia. Most of them used "Gallaudet" signs among each other, but when Erting and I started filming, they switched to their own regional signs. There were times when everyone was laughing so hard from the differences in signs that we had to stop the videorecorder.

What kinds of regional variation occur in ASL?

Regional variation occurs in American Sign Language phonology (formation), grammar, and vocabulary. One example of regional variation that has been researched is face-to-hand variation (Woodward, Erting & Oliver 1976). Certain signs that are made on the face in the Washington, D.C. area are instead made on the hands in some regions of the South. Some of these signs (that can be made on the face or on the hands) are MOVIE, RABBIT, LEMON, COLOR, SILLY, PEACH, PEANUT. Using 45 Southern consultants, we found that New Orleans signers made these signs on the face more often than Atlanta signers who made these signs more often on the hands.

Another example of regional variation concerns verbs that put the negative ('not') inside the verb sign by an outward-twisting movement of the moving hand(s) from the place where the sign is made. Verbs that do this "Negative Incorporation" include GOOD, KNOW,

WANT, LIKE, and HAVE. With 144 consultants, Susan De Santis and I (1978) found that Northwestern signers (in Montana and Washington state) used significantly more of this Negative Incorporation than Northeastern signers (Washington, D.C., New York, and Maryland).

There are also numerous variations in ASL vocabulary according to region. Very common signs such as BIRTHDAY, SHOES, GOAT, HALLOWEEN have a number of very distinct regional variants that are not formationally related.

Erting and I were both excited at the prospects for research in the future. I went back to D.C. and continued work on my dissertation. After the dissertation, I decided to go back to look at ethnic variation among Black Southern signers. Croneberg (1965) had said that variation existed between Black and White signers in the South. I wanted a larger scale study to find out: (1) if there was variation, (2) if so, what types of variation occurred, and (3) if this variation was purely conditioned by ASL or if there was some influence from Black English.

What kinds of ethnic variation occur in ASL?

With further support from the grants Stokoe had obtained, Harry Markowicz and I left for Atlanta in 1973. There Carol Erting, Harry, and I visited the Georgia School for the Deaf campus that had the largest percentage of Black students. We tried getting data at the school but the teacher who was assigned to help us interview students kept encouraging them to switch to White signs. Ultimately we got about 5 minutes of usable data out of a day and a half of work. But we had obtained the name of the leader of the Black Deaf community in Atlanta. Unfortunately we didn't have his address and he had no phone. We thought we perhaps could do something on the next trip. To salvage something from the trip, we decided to go to the Atlanta Club for the Deaf. We arrived but had little luck in getting data. It was the day before a holiday and everyone was more interested in partying than working. By 12:30 in the morning, we had decided to call it quits. Just as we were packing up the equipment, in walked about four Black people—all of the people in the club had been White. We watched the interaction and it seemed like one of the Black men was well known. Thinking maybe this person could use Black signs in addition to the White signs he was using, I decided to go up and introduce myself. He was the man we had been hoping to find. He said he hadn't been to the club in over three months, but had just decided to come because it was a holiday. We filmed from 1:00 A.M. to 3:00 A.M. and went home exhausted but excited. We had made contact with the Georgia Black Deaf community and we were welcome to come back.

The data we had obtained in Atlanta was used in a paper, entitled "Synchronic Variation and Historical Change in ASL" that Carol Erting and I presented in the summer of 1974 at the Linguistic Society of America meeting. In this paper, we hypothesized that Southerners tend to use historically older forms of signs than non-Southerners, and that in the South, Black signers tend to use historically older forms than White signers.

It was at this same LSA meeting where I became acquainted with Susan De Santis, who had interpreted some of the papers at the conference. Soon afterwards, she came to work at the Linguistics Research Lab where we frequently did research together. By this time Carol Erting was working at the Linguistics Research Lab and we planned another trip, this time to Atlanta and New Orleans under a grant from the National Science Foundation. Stokoe was the Principal Investigator and I was the Co-Principal Investigator. We obtained excellent data on this trip and found that of sign variants that could be made on the face or hands (such as LEMON), Black signers tend to use more hand variants as compared with White signers.

The years of 1974 and early 1975 were basically summary years, spent in putting some individual studies into more theoretical frameworks.

What kinds of general studies occurred?

In November, 1974, a number of researchers went to the American Anthropology Association meeting in Mexico City to present papers at a session organized by Bill Stokoe and Carol Erting. At the same conference Carol and I presented a summary of sociolinguistic research to date. A later version of this paper was published in *Discourse Processes* (Erting and Woodward 1979).

In 1975, there was also a good deal of research into the sociolinguistics of ASL. This research included papers on Pidgin Sign English and on language and the maintenance of ethnic boundaries in the Deaf community. All of this research was supported by grants with Bill Stokoe as Principal Investigator. Because of the overlap of regional, ethnic, and historical variation in ASL, I had become interested in finding out if the same historical processes were occurring in ASL and French Sign Language (FSL). I wrote a small grant to the National Endowment for the Humanities, using Stokoe's earlier grant proposals as a model and obtained a grant to study the "Historical Bases of American Sign Language."

What kinds of historical information resulted?

This grant brought Harry Markowicz, Sue De Santis, who was now majoring in Anthropological Linguistics, and me to France. Harry did historical research in the Library at the St. Jacques School for the Deaf, while Sue and I went to Paris, Toulouse, Albi, and Marseilles. This research resulted in several papers relating FSL and ASL. Three of the most important papers showed the first statistical relationship in ASL for sex and Sign Language variation (De Santis, 1977); showed the historical continuum between FSL and ASL and also demonstrated that FSL tends to preserve older signs more often than ASL (Woodward and De Santis, 1977); and showed a relationship of region and sex with linguistic variation in FSL (Woodward and De Santis, 1978).

Later in 1975, Sue De Santis and I again went to Atlanta to collect data and wrote a paper (1977b) which described the overlap of studies of regional, ethnic, age, and historical variation. We found that French signers tend to use older two-handed signs on the face more than American signers. In America, Southerners use these same forms more than non-Southerners. In the South, older signers used two-handed signs more than younger signers and Black signers tend to use these same older two-handed signs on the face more often than White signers of the same age. Having such information, we can more easily see that much of the variation in ASL has historical roots. In addition, such information makes it easier for us to speculate and hypothesize about older forms of signs that were not recorded earlier. We now can study those places and groups that still use those "older" signs. Thus, we can better reconstruct and understand the history of ASL.

The life of a language is intimately tied to the community that uses it. Sociolinguistics, since it focuses on language use in society, provides a very useful tool for understanding the Deaf community and its language varieties.

William Stokoe has played a major role in sociolinguistic research into ASL. His seminal work in Sign Language diglossia, his support of sociolinguistic research under grants that he directed, his dissemination of sociolinguistic research into ASL through the journal *Sign Language Studies*, and his writings on the practical applications of sociolinguistic research, all attest to his interest and support for the sociolinguistic analysis of ASL and the U.S. Deaf community.

References

Bragg, B. Ameslish: Our national heritage. *American Annals of the Deaf*, 1973, *118*, 672–674.

Croneberg, C. The linguistic community. In Stokoe, W., Casterline, D., & Croneberg, C. *A dictionary of American Sign Language.* Washington, D.C.: Gallaudet College Press, 1965.

De Santis, S. Elbow to hand shift in French and American Sign Languages. A paper presented at the annual NWAVE conference, Georgetown University, Washington, D.C., October, 1977.

De Santis, S. The deaf community in the United States. A paper presented at the American Anthropological Association meeting, Cincinnati, November, 1979.

Erting, C. and J. Woodward. Sign language and the deaf community: A sociolinguistic profile. *Discourse Processes*, 1979, *2*, 283–300.

Fant, L. *Ameslan.* Silver Spring, Md.: National Association of the Deaf, 1972.

Ferguson, C. Diglossia. *Word*, 1959, *15*, 325–340. (Reprinted in Hymes, D. *Language in culture and society.* New York: Harper & Row, 1964).

Fischer, S. Influences on word order change in American Sign Language. In Li, C. *Word order and word order change.* Austin, Texas; University of Texas Press, 1975.

Fishman, J. Bilingualism with and without diglossia: Diglossia with and without bilingualism. *Journal of Social Issues*, 1967, *23*, 2.

Friedman, L. The manifestation of subject and object in American Sign Language. A paper presented at the Annual Meeting of the Linguistic Society of America, San Francisco, December, 1975.

Hymes, D. *Pidginization and creolization of languages.* Cambridge: Cambridge University Press, 1971.

Johnston, G. George's Scope: The confusing terminology: Crisis for 1977, 1978, 1979, etc. *The Deaf Spectrum*, 1977, 20–25.

Karchmer, M. & Trybus, R. Who are the deaf children in 'mainstream' programs? Washington, D.C.: Gallaudet College, Office of Demographic Studies, 1977.

Liddell, S. Direct and oblique objects in American Sign Language. A paper presented at the Summer meeting of the Linguistic Society of America, Urbana-Champaign, 1978.

Markowicz, H. & Woodward, J. Language and the maintenance of ethnic boundaries in the deaf community. A paper presented at the Conference on Culture and Communication, Temple University, Philadelphia, March, 1975. To appear in *Communication and Cognition*.

Meadow, K. Sociolinguistics, sign language, and the deaf subculture. In O'Rourke, T. *Psycholinguistics and total communication: The state of the art*. Silver Spring, Md.: American Annals of the Deaf, 1972.

O'Rourke, T. Quotation in Stokoe, W. *The Study of sign language*. Arlington, Va.: Center for Applied Linguistics, 1970.

Padden, C. & Markowicz, H. Crossing cultural group boundaries into the deaf community. A paper presented at the Conference on Culture and Communication, Temple University, Philadelphia, March, 1975.

Samarin, W. Salient and Substantive pidginization. In Hymes, D. *Pidginization and Creolization of languages*. Cambridge: Cambridge University Press, 1971, 117–140.

Stokoe, W. Sign language structure: *An outline of the visual communication system of the American Deaf*. University of Buffalo, Occasional Paper 8, 1960.

Stokoe, W. Sign language diglossia. *Studies in Linguistics*, 1969–1970, *21*, 27–41.

Woodward, J. Implications for sociolinguistic research among the deaf. *Sign Language Studies*, 1972, *1*, 1–7.

Woodward, J. Implicational lects on the deaf diglossic continuum. Unpublished Ph.D. dissertation, Georgetown University, 1973a.

Woodward, J. Some observations on sociolinguistic variation and American Sign Language. *Kansas Journal of Sociology*, 1973b, 9 2, 191–200.

Woodward, J. Interrule implication in American Sign Language. *Sign Language Studies*, 1973c, *3*, 47–56.

Woodward, J. Some characteristics of Pidgin Sign English. *Sign Language Studies*, 1973d, *3*, 39–46.

Woodward, J. A report on Montana-Washington implicational research. *Sign Language Studies*, 1974, *4*, 77–101.

Woodward, J. Variation in American Sign Language Syntax: Agent-Beneficiary Directionality. In R. Shuy & R. Fasold, (Eds.), Analyzing

Variation in Language, Washington, D.C.: Georgetown University Press, 303–311.

Woodward, J. Black southern signing. *Language in Society,* 1976, *5,* 2, 211–218.

Woodward, J. & De Santis, S. Negative incorporation in French and American Sign Languages. *Language in Society,* 1977a, 6, 3, 379–388.

Woodward, J. & De Santis, S. Two to one it happens: Dynamic phonology in two sign languages. *Sign Language Studies,* 1977b, *17,* 329–346.

Woodward, J. & Erting, C. Synchronic variation and historical change in American Sign Language. *Language Sciences,* 1975, 37, 9–12.

Woodward, J., Erting, C. & Oliver, S. Facing and hand(l)ing variation in American Sign Language. *Sign Language Studies,* 1976, *10,* 43–52.

Woodward, J. & Markowicz, H. Some handy new ideas on pidgins and creoles: Pidgin sign languages. A paper presented at the 1975 International Conference on Pidgin and Creole Languages, Honolulu, January, 1975. Forthcoming in selected papers of the conference.

IV
USES OF SIGN LANGUAGE IN SOCIETY

Sign Language:
Teaching, Interpreting, and
Educational Policy

by Dennis Cokely

"The most powerful factors in the world are clear ideas in the minds of energetic men of good will."

J. Arthur Thomas

The other papers in this volume demonstrate that Bill Stokoe's contributions to linguistic research and the analysis of American Sign Language have had far-reaching implications. His work has also influenced, either directly or indirectly, the fields of education, Sign language teaching, and interpreting. Very often Bill has advocated methodological or attitudinal shifts in these fields when there was little visible support for his ideas. I hope this paper will show that

---

Dennis Cokely is currently a Research Associate in the Linguistics Research Lab at Gallaudet College. Before assuming this position, he was coordinator of Pre-College Manual Communication Programs at Gallaudet and a classroom teacher at Kendall Demonstration Elementary School. He is currently a doctoral student in the Sociolinguistics program at Georgetown University. His M.A. is in Applied Linguistics from American University with a dual minor: Teaching English as a Second Language, and Sign Language and Sociolinguistics in the Education of the Deaf. Dennis has served on the evaluation and certification team for the Sign Instructors' Guidance Network (S.I.G.N.) and holds a Comprehensive Teaching certificate from S.I.G.N. In addition, he has served on the national Board of Directors of the Registry of Interpreters for the Deaf (R.I.D.) and holds the R.I.D. Comprehensive Skills Certificate.

His present research interests include: interpreting, teaching American Sign Language, simultaneous communication and the development and implementation of communication policy in educational settings.

positive changes are taking place, albeit more slowly than one would prefer, and that many of these changes can be attributed in some way to the efforts of Bill Stokoe.

It may seem harsh to say that the fields of deaf education, Sign Language teaching, and Sign Language interpreting have suffered from linguistic myopia. However, the attitudes and actions of many people in these fields over the last twenty years clearly demonstrate a resistance to incorporate and act upon available research findings in the area of Sign Language. Of course, in any field there is a gap between research findings and application of those findings. In these fields, however, this gap has only recently begun to close.

Sign Language Policy in Deaf Education

In the late 60's and early 70's, educational programs for Deaf students began to embrace "Total Communication" in their efforts to improve student success. "Total Communication" was initially recognized as "the right of a deaf child to use all forms of communication available to develop language competence" (Denton, 1972). There are, however, two potential sources of difficulty with this view of "Total Communication." First, while the rights of the Deaf child are finally recognized, the responsibilities of teachers to improve their own communication abilities are largely overlooked. The second source of difficulty with this view of "Total Communication" is the fact that development of "language competence" is interpreted by most educators to mean the development of competence in the English language. In many cases, this view of "Total Communication" was used to justify or rationalize what teachers had already been doing in their classrooms. In a few cases, "Total Communication" provided the impetus to urge teachers to acquire some level of skill in the use of manual communication. In actuality, the communicative behavior of teachers and adults in educational settings can best be described as the use of simultaneous communication: spoken English accompanied by some manual coding of English.

In short, this initial view of "Total Communication," although it fostered the spread of manual/simultaneous communication, perpetuated the monolingual and naive views of language within the field. Despite statements to the contrary (Caccamise and Drury, 1976), what should have been a major tenet in a *philosophy* of education for Deaf students was instead viewed and discussed as a *method* of education. In fact, many educators have never viewed "Total

Communication" as a philosophy—a set of attitudes and beliefs which encourages teachers to be more flexible in how they communicate with their students, which encourages teachers to accept the communicative efforts of their students, and which acknowledges and accepts American Sign Language as a vital and valued fact in the education of Deaf students. Stokoe recognized this fact when he stated, "If Total Communication is to be what it claims to be, then it must include in its total more than just American English and all the many ways of coding it in visual symbols. Total Communication as a force in the education of the Deaf must include the knowledge and use of Sign (ASL)" (Stokoe, 1972b).

Going one step further, Stokoe has argued that failure to recognize and use ASL In educational programs and the failure to give a stronger voice to the Deaf community in educational programs amounts to cultural colonialism. Historically, conquering nations or dominant cultures have attempted to suppress or replace the language and values of "inferior" cultures. One motivating force behind such attempted suppression is that conquering nations or dominant cultures need to create a feeling of inferiority in others in order to maintain their self-imposed position of dominance and self-perceived superiority. Throughout history, dominant cultures have managed to create this feeling of inferiority in other cultures by denying access to any significant control or power in economic, educational or social matters to members of an "inferior" culture. The result is that members of the "inferior" culture must depend upon members of the dominant culture ("benefactors") to bring about significant, positive changes in the situation. In recognizing this situation, Stokoe states quite clearly, "Our counselors and rehabilitators and teachers and interpreters and psychologists and audiologists and so on do not keep slaves in the antique sense, but every one of them depends on more or fewer Deaf clients or pupils or patients to make them feel important, successful, and superior" (Stokoe, 1975). The harsh reality of this situation is even clearer when one considers that in the field of education alone there are approximately 10,000 individuals working in schools and programs for Deaf students in the U.S.—but the number of Deaf persons working in these schools and programs is only about 10% (Craig and Craig, 1979).

The rapid spread of "Total" Communication in the late 60's and 70's took place during a time when there was a sudden and seemingly uncontrollable increase in the development of artificial codes for representing English. In general, these codes not only require users to sign and speak at the same time (i.e. Simultaneous Communication) but also to use specific signs which are supposed to represent certain syntactic features of English (e.g. articles, affixes). For example, the sentence 'My friend writes clearly' would require six signs according to these codes: MY FRIEND WRITE +S CLEAR + LY. Thus for this four-word English sentence, six "signs" would be required to manually represent it according to the artificial codes for representing English. Given the difficulty which most hearing people encounter in trying to use Simultaneous Communication, it is not surprising that research has shown that there is a great deal of deletion and miscommunication which occurs among users of these artificial codes (Marmor and Petitto, 1979; Baker, 1978).

While there are some differences among these codes, basically they all share several features—first, signs no longer represent their actual referents but instead represent English words. Thus, the actual meaning of signs must fit the range of meanings of English words—no matter what the signs really mean and no matter how they are actually used by ASL signers. Second, the decision regarding which sign will be used to represent a given English word is based on arbitrary, invented criteria. Third, signs are invented or existing signs are modified in such a way that they do not consider the production constraints of naturally developed sign languages— thus some of these signs look like nonsense to many signers and are sometimes difficult for both children and adults to learn. Fourth, signs are invented to represent English affixes with little or no consideration of the relative importance or frequency of the affixes— thus there is no distinction made between affixes which are more commonly used in English (e.g. -ing, -ed) and those which are rare and infrequently used (e.g. -dom, -th). This also adds to the learners' difficulty since, in the case of hearing, native speakers of English, they do not think in terms of 'word + affix' and since there are no aids to learning these affixes (e.g. categorization according to importance or frequency) the learner must simply memorize all of these signs for affixes.

The use of manual codes for English have become quite widespread if one uses preferred or stated choice or reference texts in schools as an indicator (Jordan, Rosen and Gustason, 1979). Partly because of this, educators have equated the use of these codes with "Total" Communication. Historically, one of the primary reasons for encouraging the use of signs in educational programs is to facilitate successful and less frustrating communication between student and teacher. However, signing with these codes does not guarantee successful, less frustrating communication. Stokoe recognized this fact when he stated:

> The teacher who learns signs and puts them into English phrases and sentences to teach Deaf pupils will fail to communicate, unless pupils already have mastered the sentence-forming and the word-forming systems of English—a most unlikely chance. Just seeing signs that someone thinks stand for English words is by no means the same as learning the word-systems of English (Stokoe, 1978).

Stokoe has not been alone in addressing the linguistic and communicative naivete of the authors and users of manual codes for representing English. A variety of articles have been published which warn educators to be extremely cautious about how they use and advocate these codes or systems (Charrow, 1974; Cokely and Gawlik, 1973; Markowicz, 1974; Woodward, 1973; Woodward and Gustason, 1973; Cokely, 1979). The reader will find a more detailed discussion in these sources.

Recently, there have been formal attempts to examine more fully and carefully what is meant by "Total" Communication as a philosophy, not as a method. These attempts begin with a basic assumption—successful communication does not depend upon a person's competence in English (Cokely, 1979; Cokely and Kirchner, 1977). In short, English (in any of its forms—spoken, written, manually coded, etc.) is simply one vehicle through which successful communication can occur, not the only vehicle. Thus, it is viewed as a means to an end, but is not necessarily viewed as an end in and of itself. Total Communication as a philosophy focuses upon the type of attitudes which teachers need to have in order to successfully communicate with Deaf children. Methodological and instructional questions are, of course, important but are not as important or as crucial to a child's success as the question of teacher attitude.

The primary attitude required from teachers for a true "Total" Communication program is based upon two major premises: first, no single mode of communication is equally effective with all students in all situations; second, successful communication demands a certain "give and take" on the part of each participant. The practical implications of these two main premises are quite clear: educators must acquire reasonable levels of competence in a range of communication modes, and the deaf child has as much right and influence as the teacher in determining the choice of communication mode. Among the communication modes in which the teacher should be competent is the naturally developed, signed language of the U.S. Deaf community—ASL.

Competence in ASL, or at the very least a positive attitude toward ASL, and the recognition of ASL as a language open a new instructional possibility for the teacher—the use of ASL signing to teach English. Stokoe has argued for such an approach (Stokoe, 1972a; 1975) and, in fact, conducted a classroom experiment designed to explore this possibility (Stokoe, 1972). This experiment with a class of college students was designed to compare and contrast ASL and written English and is but one of the possibilities available when teachers approach ASL and English as separate languages, each worthy of recognition and respect.

At this point it seems appropriate to digress momentarily, to discuss my own association with Bill Stokoe. In the spring of 1972, after I had been teaching nine- and ten-year-old deaf students at Kendall Demonstration Elementary School for about one year, I made an appointment to visit the Linguistics Research Lab. I wanted to show Dr. Stokoe and his staff some videotapes that I had made of the students in my classes. I made the tapes because I had observed that these students, and most of the other students in the school, did not sign like the Deaf adults I knew. During the initial meeting I became excited because of Bill's obvious excitement with these tapes. His positive attitude and encouragement led me to analyze more than 70 hours of tapes, write an article with Rudy Gawlik on the results of this analysis, and prepare sets of special instructional materials for those students. My association with Bill has remained constant over the years and he has given me much encouragement, support and criticism. In fact, many of the projects on which I have worked were "fleshed out" in discussions with Bill.

Now to return to the discussion of "Total" Communication. Very few programs for Deaf students actively study how their students actually communicate with sign language. This type of investigation demands an open, positive attitude toward describing how students are actually signing, not superimposing a predetermined set of "rules" which students either follow or deviate from. In short, this means not judging students' signing only in terms of its adherence to or deviance from English. Moreover, recent Federal legislation has drawn attention to the need of schools and programs to find out how students actually communicate. In the rules and regulations accompanying Public Law 94–142, this need is quite clearly stated:

(1) In all direct contact with a child (including evaluation of the child), communication would be in the language normally used by the child and not that of the parents, if there is a difference between the two. (*Federal Register*, August 23, 1977)

Apart from actively focusing on students' actual communicative behavior, there are also very few schools or programs which have well-developed, well-thought-out policies on communication in the classroom and in the total educational environment. However, a growing number of administrators and educators believe that policies or guidelines are badly needed. These administrators and educators realize that selecting a schoolwide reference text and developing a policy are quite different matters; a reference text should be chosen because it best relates to a school's policy, instead of selecting a reference text and letting that text determine "policy." Some administrators and educators further realize that policies in this area must be based upon the best available linguistic research in Sign Language and signed communication. This search leads directly to Stokoe's work over the past twenty years, since so many research efforts in this field are based, to a greater or lesser extent, on the efforts or ideas of Bill Stokoe.

Currently, both Kendall Demonstration Elementary School and the Model Secondary School for the Deaf (Pre-College Programs at Gallaudet College) have an official policy that endorses ASL as an appropriate means of communication with deaf students (Cokely, 1979). Thus, in this educational setting the use of ASL is officially placed on a par with other forms of communication. However, real changes in practice, attitudes, and the educational potential of ASL cannot be dictated by official bulletins or pronouncements. Rather, a somewhat lengthy process of educating the educators must occur. This means that educators must have ample opportunities to examine their attitudes toward ASL (which traditionally have been negative) and must be informed anew about what sign languages really are (rather than operate on inadequate or erroneous information). This may be the only way to gain acceptance of the validity of using ASL within an educational setting.

There can be little doubt that ASL must be recognized and incorporated into any program advocating and espousing "Total" Communication—the supportive evidence is too convincing to be denied or swept aside. However, there is a vast difference between *recognizing* the role of ASL in a "Total" Communication program and *actually using* it in an educational setting. Recognition and acceptance of ASL on paper must be supported by in-service training and skill development of personnel. This is certainly consistent with the spirit and intent of recent public legislation (PL 94–142) and court decisions in a somewhat analogous educational situation (Martin Luther King Junior Elementary School Children *et al.* vs. Ann Arbor School District Board, 1979). PL 94–142 mandates that the child's language (i.e. what the child actually uses, not what some people think the child is using or should be using) must be considered in assessing and placing students in educational programs. The "Ann Arbor" case suggests that administrators have a responsibility to provide teachers with knowledge of students' language systems and to suggest ways and means of using that knowledge in educational programming.

The future success of "Total" Communication programs depends upon the ability and willingness of such programs to create and foster a positive, satisfying linguistic and communicative environment for students. Since the credibility of both individuals and institutions is judged by their access to facts and their willingness to act upon such facts, it is imperative that individuals and institutions in the field of education recognize and deal with the linguistic facts regarding Sign Language, the Deaf community, and Deaf students.

If the benefits and potential of "Total" Communication as a philosophical force in the education of Deaf students are to be realized, it is imperative that schools and programs begin serious efforts to incorporate and utilize the best available linguistic research in their policy development. Teacher training programs must also begin to provide information and training which will impart to their students positive, accepting attitudes toward ASL and the Deaf community. In this way, educational programs for deaf students will be better able to avoid the monolingual naivete which has existed for years and which, undoubtedly, has contributed to the rather limited success of the field in general.

Sign Language Teaching as a Profession

Another field which has been considerably influenced by linguistic research on Sign Language is the field of Sign Language teaching. Stokoe's own influence on the field of Sign language learning and teaching has ranged from materials preparation to program development to teacher training. Commenting upon Sign Language instruction, Stokoe (1978b) contends that often "[Sign Language] teachers say or imply that nothing is needed to communicate with deaf people except a knowledge of the signs: vocabulary drill, vocabulary drill and more vocabulary drill." In short, Sign Language teachers have, in many cases, assumed that ASL consists of signs used as if they were English words in English sentences.

If Sign Language teachers knew more about how languages work in general and, more specifically, how ASL is structured, then Sign Language instruction would be quite different. As Stokoe has said, "It would do no harm to reduce the number of courses in vocabulary and a lot of good to find introductory material that will show learners what they themselves must learn in order to have a real working knowledge of a real language that real people use." (1978b) Stokoe has constantly reminded Sign Language teachers that they, too, may be portraying an elitist attitude toward ASL.

However, in recent years, as more information from linguistic research on ASL has become available to teachers, we have seen that more positive, healthy attitudes are beginning to emerge in the field of Sign Language instruction. Such changes, appearing in the areas of materials preparation, program development and teacher training, have led to the emergence of Sign Language instruction as a "profession" practiced by "professionals."

Materials Preparation. In 1856, James S. Brown published the first known "dictionary" of signs used by deaf people in America. This fifty-page book was printed in Baton Rouge, Louisiana at the *Morning Comet* newspaper office and was entitled *A Vocabulary of Mute Signs.* However, from 1856 until 1960, only two other "dictionaries" of signs were published which were widely used—*The Sign Language: A Manual of Signs* by J. Schuyler Long (1910) and *How to Talk To the Deaf* by Daniel D. Higgins (1923). In large part these texts relied on verbal descriptions to show the reader how to produce the signs and also included photographs with superimposed arrows to indicate movement. From 1910–1960, other so-called "dictionaries" were published for use in sign classes but were not widely used. Most of these were written by educators and religious workers. All of these texts shared a number of common features and problems.

First, they were organized according to English glosses for signs. That is, the author selected an English word which might be an appropriate interpretation of the sign in *some,* but not all, contexts and then arranged the signs according to their glosses, "alphabetically"—either in groups (emotions, food, etc.) or in a single listing for the entire text. Thus the order in which a student would learn signs from these texts was determined by an English word list—not by the structure of the signs themselves, by the relationships among these signs, or by the frequency or importance of the signs.

Second, these texts provided very little, if any, information on how the listed signs are actually used by the Deaf community and any variations that may exist. Thus, these texts gave a number of possible wrong impressions—for example, that there is only a single sign for a single meaning, that signs are equivalent to English words, that signs are picture-like representations of English words, etc.

Third, these texts provided little, if any, information on the nature of ASL as a language. They did not help the student learn the syntax of ASL. Thus, the hearing student learned a list of signs and relied on the grammar of English to determine the appropriate sequencing of signs. It is probably safe to say that most students who used such texts learned a variety of Pidgin Sign English, not ASL.

In 1960 and 1965, two publications appeared which had a significant impact on the preparation of Sign language materials. The first was entitled *Sign Language Structure: An Outline of the Visual Communication Systems of the American Deaf* and was written by William Stokoe. This monograph marked the beginning of serious linguistic analysis of ASL as a language. Lou Fant made use of some of Stokoe's analysis in his book *Say It With Hands* (1964). Fant's book was organized so that the signs in each lesson used only one handshape. He felt that by teaching signs with the same handshape, but different movements and locations, that the students would learn more quickly and remember the signs more easily. Thus, for the first time in a popularly used book, English glosses were not used as the organizing principle. Instead, an aspect of the signs themselves— handshape—was used to determine the grouping and arrangement of signs.

Despite the publication of other texts from 1960–1965 (e.g. *Talking With The Deaf*, Springer, 1961; *Talk With Your Hands*, Watson, 1964; and *Talk To the Deaf*, Riekehof, 1963), Fant's book was the only major text which used some aspect of sign formation (not English glosses) to organize lessons within the text. However, none of those texts were, in fact, "dictionaries." That is, none of those texts did more than list English glosses with photographs or illustrations that showed a sign for each gloss.

The first text which could legitimately be called a "dictionary" of ASL signs was published in 1965 and was written by William Stokoe, Dorothy Casterline, and Carl Croneberg. This book was the first and, to date, the only attempt to prepare a dictionary of signs based on linguistic principles. This dictionary presents a range of appropriate English glosses for signs and is organized according to features of the signs themselves. It also provides some information about variations in signs.

Although this text represents a milestone in materials development for Sign Language learning and teaching, it has only been widely used by researchers, not by Sign Language teachers. There are perhaps two reasons for this: first, the dictionary contains few pictures or illustrations and the pictures which are in the text are of handshapes used in the production of signs. Second, a system of writing signs is used ("Stokoe notation system") which involves a symbol for the location (tab), handshape (dez), and movement (sig) of each sign. Entries in the text are arranged by handshape. In order to use the dictionary quickly and easily, a person needs to be familiar with this system of notation (for example, the symbols $O_T O_L{}^X$ represent the sign KISS). Because the notation system seemed "like Greek" to non-researchers, the text never gained much popularity with Sign Language teachers. However, it did have an impact on many of the materials which followed since it approached ASL as a language in itself, and not as a symbolic system dependent upon English.

Although a number of texts were published between 1965 and 1970 (e.g. *The Language of Signs: A Handbook of Manual Communication with the Deaf,* Davis, 1966), they were still lists of signs with English glosses. Even the most popular text—the National Association of the Deaf's *ABC* book (*A Basic Course in Manual Communication,* 1970)—provided no materials or lessons which focused on the grammar of ASL as a language. It was not until 1972 that texts were available which attempted to provide such information. In that year two texts were published which would be widely used by teachers and programs interested in teaching the language of the Deaf community. Lou Fant's book *Ameslan: An Introduction to American Sign Language* (1972) provided the first beginning level text for students interested in studying and learning American Sign Language, not just a list of signs. Willard Madsen's text *Conversational Sign Language II: An Intermediate-Advanced Manual* (1972) also provided material for those who had learned a basic vocabulary of signs and wanted to begin focusing on ASL. For the next four years, these were the only materials available for teaching ASL as a language.

In 1976, the NAD published a book by Harry Hoemann *(The American Sign Language: lexical and grammatical notes with translation exercises)* which not only provided ASL teachers with useful material for teaching ASL but also advocated a new teaching approach. In 1977, a second book by Lou Fant was published *(Sign Language)* which provided Sign Language instructors and students with another useful text for ASL courses. Finally in 1980 a series of five texts by Charlotte Baker and Dennis Cokely were published, two of which serve as a resource for teachers on curriculum, methods, evaluation, and the grammar and culture of ASL and the Deaf community *(American Sign Language: a teacher's resource text on grammar and culture* and *American Sign Language: a teacher's resource text on curriculum, methods, and evaluation)* and three which are for student use *(American Sign Language: Student Texts).*

The number of texts currently available for ASL courses is still rather small (approximately ten) and quite clearly needs to be expanded to provide the Sign Language teacher with a range of materials to choose from. However, fifteen years ago there was a complete lack of appropriate material to use in teaching ASL and Sign Language teachers were forced to determine program and course content based upon their own intuitions and knowledge. Obviously there was a need for some central resource to assist in the development of Sign Language programs.

Program Development. In 1967, the National Association of the Deaf (NAD) received the first of a series of grants from the Vocational Rehabilitation Administration (now the Rehabilitation Services Administration) to establish the Communicative Skills Program (CSP). One of the stated goals of the CSP was to become a national reference and information center for individuals and institutions who wanted guidance on the problem of Sign Language instruction (Covington, 1976). The first director of the CSP was Terrence J. O'Rourke who, before accepting the position, was a member of the English department at Gallaudet College. (Bill Stokoe was chairperson of the English department at that time and wrote a letter of recommendation for O'Rourke to the NAD.)

One of the initial projects undertaken by the CSP was the selection of sites for pilot Sign Language programs—one in each Rehabilitation Services Administration region. Classes were begun in September, 1963 with a total of 146 students in beginning classes. By 1972, intermediate and advanced-level classes were also being offered. The average total enrollment in these pilot programs was approximately 875 students per year for the first five years. The first text used for these classes was *Say It With Hands* by Lou Fant. At that time, a number of individuals served as consultants to the CSP director, including Bill Stokoe.

As CSP sponsorship and funding for these pilot programs was gradually phased out, each program assumed responsibility for seeking its own funding, and several programs began to develop their own materials. An example is the pilot Sign Language program sponsored by the District of Columbia Association of the Deaf at Gallaudet College. In 1971, Gallaudet College assumed responsibility for this program. The first director of Gallaudet's Sign Language Programs was Willard Madsen, who was also a member of the English department while Bill Stokoe was chairperson. The program has now expanded to the point where it presently offers classes all year round and has itself become a resource for other programs.

Recognizing the need for Sign Language teachers to share their ideas, methods, and materials, the CSP began a national organization of Sign Language teachers in 1975—the Sign Instructors Guidance Network (S.I.G.N.). This organization seeks to upgrade the skills of Sign Language teachers by providing workshops and short-term training, evaluating and certifying Sign Language teachers, and encouraging a closer relationship between teachers of Sign Language and the Deaf community. The first evaluation and certification of Sign Language teachers took place at the NAD convention in Houston in July 1976. Currently, S.I.G.N. has more than 200 members, 84 of whom hold some level of certification from that organization.

Apart from its involvement in Sign Language teaching during its early years, the CSP also became concerned with the uses of manual communication in the education of deaf children. The CSP was awarded two grants in 1971 and 1972 from the Bureau of Education for the Handicapped to sponsor special study institutes on psycholinguistics and Total Communication. The original grant was written with the assistance of Bill Stokoe, who was also a faculty member of the first institute, held at Western Maryland College, June 28-July 23, 1971.

Teacher Training. The need to train Sign Language teachers has always been a concern of the CSP. In the first ten years of its existence the CSP did much to improve and upgrade the skills of teachers by providing workshops, seminars, etc. However, two significant events have occurred within the last three years which may have more impact on Sign Language teachers than any previous CSP projects. The first event took place in May, 1977—the first National Symposium on Sign Language Research and Teaching (NSSLRT). This now-annual Symposium provided the first opportunitiy for researchers and teachers to meet, share information, and to influence each other's work. The faculty members included Bill Stokoe, Ursula Bellugi, Lou Fant and many other key people in both research and Sign Language teaching. These opportunities to share ideas on methodology, materials, and evaluation as well as to learn about current linguistic research on ASL, have had a very positive effect on the overall quality of Sign Language instruction.

Realizing that Sign Language teaching was becoming a profession in the fullest sense of the word, the CSP recognized the need for more formal training and preparation of Sign Language teachers. Consequently, in 1978 the CSP obtained a grant to establish a National Consortium of Programs for the Training of Sign Language Instructors (NCPTSLI). This consortium of programs located at ten different sites will provide the means for offering top-quality training for Sign Language instructors across the country. Undoubtedly, at least some of the ten sites (e.g. Gallaudet College, Northeastern University, California State University at Northridge) will be in a position to offer accredited courses which will lead to a Master's degree in Teaching Sign Language. The teacher training curriculum proposed by the CSP for the NCPTSLI sites includes such courses as: Structure of ASL I and II, Introduction to American Deaf Culture, Second Language Learning and Teaching, Sign Language Teaching, Sign Language Evaluation, etc. In other words, the NCPTSLI will provide the kind of basic training of Sign Language instructors which is necessary to truly consider Sign Language teaching a "profession."

In retrospect, quite a lot has happened in the field of Sign Language teaching in a relatively short period of time. From the CSP's beginnings thirteen years ago with pilot classes for 146 students to the present time when there are probably more than 400 colleges and universities that offer Sign Language classes; from Sign Language instructors who were willing, but untrained, to possible M.A. programs in teaching Sign Language; from Sign Language materials that were basically picture lists to texts that focus on ASL as a language; from relying upon hearsay or assumption in preparing Sign

Language classes to relying upon linguistic research as a base of preparation. Admittedly, there is still much to be done, but the day is approaching when Sign Language instructors can truly be considered the colleagues of other foreign language teachers.

Interpreting as a Profession

Another field which has been influenced by the work being done in the area of Sign Language linguistics is interpreting. It is probably accurate to say that for as long as there have been Deaf people, there has been at least one group of individuals who have facilitated communication between the Deaf community and the majority culture. Historically, this group of individuals is made up largely of hearing children of Deaf parents. These children often grow up with Sign Language as their first language and acquire English either in school or through association with English-speaking relatives or playmates. Since these children possess competence in both Sign Language and English, they are prime candidates to function as communication brokers.

Lacking training and an effective support system, it is not surprising that during childhood and early adolescence these brokers often develop feelings of embarrassment, anxiety, impatience and resentment which often are resolved by the time they reach adulthood (Bunde, 1979). Although perhaps generally successful in functioning as communication facilitators, even the most well-intentioned actions of untrained, unchallenged children and adolescents lacks the professionalism and quality control needed to reduce the confusion and misunderstandings which have often accompanied interaction between Deaf and hearing people. As a response to this need for professionalism and quality control, a national organization of interpreters was established in 1964 as a result of a workshop on interpreting for deaf people. The name of this organization (National Registry of Professional Interpreters and Translators for the Deaf) was changed in 1965 to the Registry of Interpreters for the Deaf (RID). It is noteworthy that a large number of participants at the initial workshop were hearing children of Deaf parents.

To most people, an interpreter (of spoken or signed languages) is seen as someone who knows at least two languages and is able to transmit messages from one of those languages to another. Of course, this is an oversimplification of an extremely complex process. It is precisely at this point where the work being done in Sign Language linguistics has had the greatest impact—helping interpreters understand exactly what it is that they do and must do to be effective. Such research has been valuable in beginning to sort out and explain the complex linguistic situation which Sign Language interpreters encounter. Obviously, an accurate understanding of this situation is vital in training and evaluating interpreters.

The linguistic complexities faced by Sign Language interpreters in the U.S. are quite unlike those faced by spoken language interpreters. First, for spoken language interpreters it is quite obvious that there are two distinct languages involved in their interpreting and, hence, it is relatively easy to distinguish the two. In spoken language interpreting, the distinctions and differences between two languages appear at all structural levels—sound, grammar and meaning. For the Sign Language interpreter in the U.S., the situation is much more complex and, oftentimes, much more ambiguous. These are, of course, two separate and distinct languages—ASL and English. When a Sign Language interpreter is transmitting messages from either of these languages to the other, he or she is functioning in a manner similar to the way spoken language interpreters function.

But unlike spoken language interpreters, Sign Language interpreters most often function in a situation where there are not two languages involved but rather two forms of the same language. That is, most often Sign Language interpreters find themselves in situations where they are transmitting messages from spoken English to some manual representation of spoken English (often including some features of ASL). This process (which is called *transliterating)* is unique to Sign Language interpretation. It would be equivalent, for example, to a spoken language interpreter hearing an English sentence and simply substituting German words for the English words but retaining English grammatical patterns. Thus, only the vocabulary would be German; the grammar would be English. Likewise, if a Sign Language interpreter uses signs which are part of the vocabulary of ASL but they are used in the grammatical patterns of English, he or she is transliterating, *not* interpreting. It is only when both the vocabulary *and* the grammar of ASL are used and are clearly distinguished from the vocabulary and grammar of English that the term *interpreting* can be properly used.

In the early years of the Registry of Interpreters for the Deaf (RID), there was an overt attitude of linguistic superiority and language chauvinism. I think this attitude did not result from a conscious attempt to suppress the language of the Deaf community, but rather from a lack of knowledge about the complex linguistic situation within the Deaf community and the unique task facing Sign Language interpreters. This attitude is most clearly seen in statements taken from the first book published about Sign Language interpreting—*Interpreting for Deaf People* (1965). This book is actually a report of a workshop on interpreting held at the Governor Baxter State School for the Deaf in Portland, Maine (July 7–27, 1965). The quotes which follow not only demonstrate a lack of awareness about the linguistic situation in the Deaf community, but also very clearly illustrate a sense of linguistic paternalism which was very evident in the early years of the RID:

> Interpreting requires adjustment of the presentation to the intellectual level of the audience and their ability to understand English. (p. 1)
>
> For many deaf people, it is necessary to paraphrase, define and explain a speaker's words in terms and concepts which they can understand. This is interpreting. (p. 1)
>
> A thought should be reduced to the simplest possible English expression—using words only in their commonest meaning to communicate with "Low Verbal" deaf people. (p. 39)
>
> In reverse interpreting, the interpreter must lower his own verbal level in order to grasp the message given him by a low-verbal deaf person before converting it into understandable English, with due regard to grammar and syntax. (p. 39)

These quotes are but a few indications of the underlying attitude toward Deaf people and their language which dominated the formational stages of the RID. They present the notion that Deaf persons who cannot or choose not to sign a manual representation of English are "low-verbal" or function at a lower cognitive level. Additionally, they suggest that any form of signing which does not represent English has no structure or syntax. This early focus on deviance and deficiency, which was primarily due to a lack of information, was also undoubtedly fostered by the fact that the majority of the original RID board members and participants in the 1965 workshop were educators. Thus, many of the false myths about ASL and about Deaf people which prevailed and which, in some cases, continue to prevail in the field of education were transferred to the field of interpreting.

Fortunately, these views are no longer officially expressed or endorsed by the RID and are no longer held by most professional interpreters. The increased activity in Sign Language research and the dissemination and utilization of this research have been the direct cause of this change in attitude. For example, in 1979 the RID redefined the term "interpreting" so that superior status is no longer attributed to English and has also done away with the term "reverse interpreting" (which referred to Sign-to-English interpreting). These changes, along with other changes in terminology, evaluation procedures, and attitudes, demonstrate a positive recognition of the value of Sign Language research. Needless to say, Bill Stokoe's role in spearheading such reasearch has been responsible for much of this change in attitude and perception.

Among the changes in terminology and attitude is the term "low-verbal." This term is currently undergoing a re-examination which reveals that the term has been used to obscure several kinds of language and communication profiles which are important to the interpreter. These communication profiles include:

- a Deaf person who is fluent in ASL but does not possess a comfortable, functional level of competence in English;
- a Deaf person who lacks competence in both English and ASL but uses another comfortable means of communication;
- a Deaf person who lacks competence in both English and ASL and also has no other comfortable means of communication.

Because the term "low-verbal" obscures these distinctions as well as conveys a negative value judgement, more appropriate terminology has begun to be used by interpreters and interpreter trainers:

- "minimal language skills"—refers to a person who lacks competence in ASL, English or any other language.
- "minimal Sign skills"—refers to a person who lacks competence in ASL or any ability to communicate comfortably using signed communication.
- "minimal English skills"—refers to a person who lacks competence in English—either spoken, written or manually represented.
- "minimal communication skills"—refers to a person who lacks competence in any language (spoken or signed) and who also lacks competence via any other means.

These terms attempt to accurately describe the various linguistic and communicative situations which an interpreter might confront without making value judgements and without claiming one language is better than another.

The shift in attitude and terminology indicates more openmindedness and acceptance which, in effect, is a positive response to

Stokoe's repeated demands for a less judgemental view of the Deaf community and its language:

> . . . no person's competence should be judged solely on performance in a second language to which he can have little or no direct exposure, and the competence in Sign Language is completely ignored or is unsuspected by those who apply, and by many who hear or read, the label "low-verbal deaf" and who can go on to infer deficits in language competence, cognitive skills, and intellect.

(Stokoe, 1976)

Perhaps the greatest visible effect of these more positive attitudes is that interpreter training programs now incorporate ASL research findings in an attempt to upgrade the signing skills of interpreters. We can also trace this focus on upgrading ASL skills to Stokoe:

> . . . the interpreter who puts signs in English order as if they were English words—which they are not—will usually confuse more than help one who cannot hear. To do this is not interpreting at all; it is more like what a stenographer does . . .

(Stokoe, 1978)

In summary, Stokoe has advocated linguistic and cultural equality for the Deaf community for many years. Unfortunately, advocates are frequently active ahead of their time; they are seldom recognized or properly acknowledged. A nation may neglect its prophets; the same is true when speaking of communities or disciplines and their advocates. While it is true that Stokoe's work has been responsible for fostering much of the research on the linguistic structure of American Sign Language, perhaps his most noteworthy and lasting effects will be seen in the education of deaf people and in the training of interpreters. For these areas hold the key to the future and the potential of Deaf individuals. Stokoe has forced people to focus on what Deaf individuals *do* instead of what they *don't do*. He has forced people to examine how Deaf people communicate, rather than letting people dwell on alleged communication inadequacies. In the context of the Deaf community, the following quotation applies to Bill Stokoe and his work:

> Each time a man stands up for an ideal, or acts to improve the lot of others, or strikes out against injustice, he sends forth a tiny ripple of hope . . . and crossing each other from a million different centers of en-

ergy and daring, those ripples build a current that can sweep down the
mightiest walls of oppression and resistance.

Robert F. Kennedy

References

Baker, C. How does Sim-Com fit into a Bilingual Approach to Education? To appear in proceedings of the Second National Symposium
on Sign Language Research and Teaching, San Diego, California,
1978.

Baker, C. and Cokely, D. *American Sign Language: a teacher's resource text on grammar and culture*. Silver Spring, Md.: T. J. Publishers, Inc. 1980.

Bunde, L. *Deaf Parents-Hearing Children*, R.I.D., Inc. 1979.

Caccamise, F. and Drury, A. A review of current terminology in
education of the deaf. *The Deaf American*, 1976, 29, 7–10.

Charrow, V. R. *A linguist's view of manual English*. Unpublished
manuscript, Gallaudet College, 1974.

Cokely, D. *Pre-College Programs Guidelines for Manual Communication*, 1979, Gallaudet College, Washington, D.C.

Cokely, D. and Baker, C. *American Sign Language: a teacher's resource text on curriculum, methods, and evaluation*. Silver Spring,
Md.: T. J. Publishers, Inc. 1980.

Cokely, D., and Gawlik, R. Options: A position paper on the relationship between manual English and Sign. *The Deaf American*, May
1973, 7–11.

Cokely, D. and Kirchner, C. *Pre-College Perspectives*, Pre-College
Programs, 1977, 10, Gallaudet College, Washington, D.C.

Covington, V. Problems for a Sign Language planning agency. In J.
Rubin (Ed.) *Language Planning in the United States. The Hague:
Mouton, 1976, 85–105.

Craig, W. and Craig, H. (Eds.) *American Annals of the Deaf*, 1979,
124, 113–219.

Davis, A. *The Language of Signs: A Handbook of Manual Communication with the Deaf*. Executive Council of the Episcopal Church,
1966.

Denton, D. A Rationale for Total communication. In T. O'Rourke
(Ed.), *Total Communication: The State of the art*. Washington,
D.C.: American Annals of the Deaf, 1972, 53–61.

Fant, L., Jr. *Say It With Hands*. Silver Spring, Md.: National Association of the Deaf, 1964.

_____. *Ameslan, An Introduction to American Sign Language*. Silver Spring, Md.: National Association of the Deaf, 1972.

_____. *Sign Language*. Northridge, Ca.: Joyce Media, Inc., 1977.

Federal Register, Department of Health, Education and Welfare, Office of Education, August 23, 1977.

Higgins, Daniel. *How to Talk to the Deaf*. Newark, N.J., 1959.

Hoemann, H. *The American Sign Language: Lexical and Grammatical Notes with Translation Exercises*. Silver Spring, Md.: National Association of the Deaf, 1975.

Jordan, I. K., Gustason, G. and Rosen, R. An Update on Communication Trends at Programs for the Deaf. *American Annals of the Deaf*, 1979, 124, 350–358.

Long, J. Schuyler. *The Sign Language: A Manual of Signs* (2nd ed.). Washington, D.C.: Gallaudet College Press, 1962. 1st ed. 1918.

Madsen, W. *Conversational Sign Language II: An Intermediate-Advanced Manual* (Rev. ed.). Washington, D.C.: Gallaudet College, 1972.

Markowicz, H. *Is Sign English English?* Paper presented at the meeting of the First Annual Conference on Sign Languages, Washington, D.C. (Gallaudet College), 1974.

Marmor, G. and Petitto, L. Simultaneous Communication in the Classroom: How Well is English Grammar represented? *Sign Language Studies*, 1979, 23, 99–136.

Quigley, S. (Ed.) *Interpreting for Deaf People*, U.S. Department of Health, Education and Welfare, Washington, D.C., 1965.

Riekehof, L. *Talk to the Deaf*. Springfield, Missouri: Gospel Publishing House, 1963.

Springer, C., C.S.S.R. *Talking With the Deaf*. Baton Rouge, Louisiana: Redemptorist Fathers, 1961.

Stokoe, W. *The Study of Sign Language*. Silver Spring, Md.: National Association of the Deaf, 1972.

_____. A Classroom Experiment in two languages. In T. O'Rourke (Ed.) *Total Communication and Psycholinguistics: the State of the Art*. Washington, D.C.: American Annals of the Deaf, 1972a, 85–92.

_____. It Takes Two to Total. Address delivered at the Maryland School for the Deaf, Frederick, Md. November, 1972b.

_____ . An Untried Experiment—Bicultural Bilingual Education of the Deaf: Crammatte and Crammatte (Eds.) *Proceedings of the Seventh World Congress of the World Federation of the Deaf*. Silver Spring, Md.: National Association of the Deaf, 1976.

_____ . Sign Language and the verbal/nonverbal distinction. In Sebeok (Ed). *Sight, Sound and Sense*. Bloomington, Indiana, Indiana University Press, 1978a, 157–172.

_____ . Signs and Systems: What the student of sign language should know. MS. Gallaudet College, 1978b.

Watson, D. *Talk With Your Hands*, Vol. I, II. Silver Spring, Md.: National Association of the Deaf, 1964.

Woodward, J. C., Jr. Some observations on Sociolinguistics Variation and American sign languages. *Kansas Journal of Sociology*, 1973, 9, 199–200.

_____ . Manual English: A problem in language planning and standardization. In G. Gustason and J. C. Woodward, Jr. (ed.) *Recent developments in manual English*. Papers presented at a special institute at Gallaudet College (Washington, D.C.), July 1973.

Sign Language and Communication Between Adults and Children

by Carol Erting

I first met Bill Stokoe during the summer of 1972 in Portland, Oregon. He was a guest speaker at a special study institute sponsored by the National Association of the Deaf entitled "Psycholinguistics and Total Communication," which I was attending. I had finished my M.A. in deaf education that spring and was preparing to begin my new job as parent-infant educator at a day school for deaf children. The institute marked a turning point in my professional life. The ideas I encountered and the people I met that summer combined to influence the direction of my work profoundly. And no single person influenced the direction of my professional growth more than Dr. William Stokoe.

In the fall of 1972, I eagerly began my new job as parent-infant educator. My experience at the summer institute had taught me that

Carol Erting is currently a member of the Research Faculty at Kendall Demonstration Elementary School at Gallaudet College. She has long had a professional interest in the education of deaf children and communication issues in the classroom. After receiving her B.S. (1970) and her M.A. (1972) in Education of the Deaf from Northwestern University in Illinois, she spent two years directing and teaching in a program for parents and infants at the Atlanta Area School for the Deaf. In 1974, she began her doctoral studies in social and cultural anthropology at the American University in Washington, D.C. Since then, she has directed or participated in a number of sociolinguistic studies of Sign Language and the communication of mothers with their young deaf children.

the best way to learn Sign Language and to learn what I needed to know to help deaf children was to associate with deaf people and their families. During the next year, I did that. As I became involved with the deaf families whose children attended the school and participated with them in activities in their homes, at the deaf club, at the school, and at their church, I came to see the complex social and linguistic forces at work in their lives. I also realized that the school program did not reflect much awareness of these forces. The result was often a curriculum which did not meet the needs of the deaf children, to say the least.

The problem I wanted to investigate was how the school program could be designed so that it helped to prepare deaf children for their future lives as competent, happy deaf adults. Many deaf children were growing up to be just that, but it was usually in spite of the educational establishment. A key to some of the answers seemed to lie with the deaf people I knew and their language, American Sign Language.

Signing had only recently re-entered the school as an acceptable means of communication with the "total communication" movement. However, this signing was actually manual coding of English rather than ASL, the native language of deaf people. Formal classroom signing used by the hearing teachers was strikingly different from the Sign Language conversations of deaf people—both adults and children. This situation raised several questions in my mind which needed to be studied—questions concerning the adequacy and efficiency of the invented sign systems, the roles of American Sign Language and English in the lives of deaf people and the hearing people they interact with, the ways deaf children are socialized, and many, many more.

I could find very little research directed at these basic questions; school programs and curricula were being designed without the answers, usually relying on someone's opinion rather than substantiated research findings. I decided to return to school and prepare myself to do some of that research and consulted Dr. Stokoe and his colleagues at the Linguistics Research Laboratory (LRL) for some advice. Bill recommended that I study anthropology, since he felt that the social sciences would give me the best base to approach the questions of interest to me. I knew very little about anthropology, but decided to become more familiar with the discipline. I liked what I learned and decided to take his advice.

During the several months before school began, I worked as a research associate at the LRL. It was a stimulating and exciting experience for me and Bill gave me much needed encouragement as I launched my research career. He often talked about the bilingual abilities of some of the deaf people he knew, and I was especially impressed with his account of Todd Williams, a preschool deaf child who used ASL at home but Sign English at school (Williams, 1976). I was fascinated. How had Todd developed these language skills? Was he an extraordinary child, or did other deaf children learn to function in this same way if they had the opportunity?

I began to focus my research interests. We needed to have more information about the way in which deaf children interact in natural situations with a variety of people. We needed to know what deaf children know about communicating and how they learn it. Adults and children, children and other children influencing each other as they interact—this phenomenon was what I wanted to study and I knew where I wanted to begin to study it. At the school for the deaf where I had been working, there was a classroom that seemed to be ideal for research. This class had eight preschool deaf children, one hearing teacher and one deaf assistant. Four of the children came from deaf families and were learning ASL as their native language. Dr. Stokoe was enthusiastic and provided me with the time to collect the data. Later, as I attempted to make sense out of my observations, he encouraged me to develop my ideas. That was the beginning of an analysis which is still going on; the questions generated by that data are still the major questions I am pursuing in my work.

Before discussing some of the results of that classroom research, it might be helpful to review the few studies of adult-child interaction which have been done. I am only concerned with those studies in which Sign Language was used. An important reason for the limited number of studies is the negative attitude of the schools and society in general toward signing until very recently. Also, most of these studies focus on only one of the participants rather than focussing on the interactions of the participants.

One of the earliest studies of mother-child interaction which included hearing mothers who signed was reported by Hilde Schlesinger and Kathryn Meadow in their 1972 book *Sound and Sign*. These researchers studied forty deaf children and their hearing mothers and compared them with a group of twenty hearing children and their mothers. They found that mothers of hearing children rated higher than mothers of deaf children on nine out of ten dimensions of behavior. Mothers with hearing children were:

- more permissive—Mother allowed the child freedom to do things her or his way. She did not try to control the child's behavior more than necessary.
- non-intrusive—Mother played with the child in an informal way, often letting the child lead the way. Sometimes she let the child play alone when he or she wanted to do so.
- non-didactic—Mother did not see herself as a teacher. She shared discoveries with the child through play activities.
- flexible—Mother set up rules which could be changed depending on the situation, the child's mood, etc. She tried to explain the reasons for the rules.

Mothers with hearing children also showed more approval of the child.

Assuming that it was the communication difficulty which differentiated these two groups, the researchers divided the deaf children into two groups, high (good) communicators and low (poor) communicators. They found that on four of the five dimensions mentioned above (flexibility, nondidactic behavior, nonintrusiveness, and the approval of the child) the mothers with deaf children who were high communicators ranked second while the mothers with deaf children who were low communicators ranked last. That is, the mothers with deaf children who could communicate better were more like the mothers of hearing children. Differences were also seen among the children. Those in the low communication group appeared to be less happy, to enjoy interacting with their mothers less, to be less compliant, less creative and to show less pride in his or her own accomplishments than the deaf children with more communication skills or the hearing children.

I should point out that only four of the forty mothers of deaf children had decided to use signs with their children at the time of that study. The other thirty-six were all attempting to communicate orally. These numbers reflect the situation in deaf education at the time of that study. Most deaf children were still being taught orally, although the move toward "simultaneous communication" (speaking and signing at the same time) had begun. Six years later, Greenberg was interested in the interaction of hearing mothers and their deaf children and compared two groups, one using oral means of communication and the other using some form of simultaneous communication with signs and speech. By the mid-1970's the majority of deaf children were being taught some form of simultaneous communication, making such a study possible.

Greenberg (1978) wanted to examine the communication and social behavior of profoundly deaf children with their hearing mothers. He studied twenty-eight mother-deaf child pairs, fourteen who used oral communication only and fourteen who used simultaneous communication. Like Schlesinger and Meadow, Greenberg videotaped interaction and conversation. However, while the former study utilized rating scales, Greenberg counted the frequency of various specific behaviors, as well as functional communications. When Greenberg began to analyze his data, he found that he needed to use the concept of communicative competence in the same way that the previous study had used it, since the communication skills represented in each of the groups were so varied. There were equal numbers of high communicators and low communicators from the oral-only and simultaneous communication groups.

One of Greenberg's hypotheses was that the communicative competence of the simultaneous communication pairs would be significantly higher than that of the oral-only communicators. The study did not confirm this hypotheses, and Greenberg suggested two possible reasons for this result. One was that about half of the simultaneous communication pairs had a lack of skill in using simultaneous communication. The researchers had tried to select only mothers and children who could be labeled "optimal" simultaneous comminicators, but he could not find enough pairs who qualified. The second reason he suggested was success of the oral programs, which have become smaller and more selective as a result of the expansion of "total communication" programs. I would like to suggest another possibility. Rather than emphasizing the lack of signing skill on the part of the simultaneous mothers, perhaps we should be questioning the feasibility of the type of manual communication they were attempting to use. Questions that need to be addressed are:

- Can people physically perform what is required by manually-encoded English systems?
- Can speech be added to these systems without negatively affecting the user's speech or signing?
- If simultaneous communication is workable, how effective is it for communicating, or for teaching English?

Recent research findings suggest that simultaneous communication is a very difficult system to use (Crandall, 1974; Baker, 1978; Cokely,

1979). Also, there has not yet been any research which indicates that this system is effective for communication or for teaching English.

Even though there were no significant differences between the oral and the simultaneous pairs in communication, there were significant differences in the area of interaction. The simultaneous mothers and children showed more complex and sociable interactions than the oral pairs. Simultaneous children did not look away from their mothers as much as oral children and they touched their mothers more often. The simultaneous mothers laughed more frequently than the oral mothers. Furthermore, the simultaneous communicators spent more total time interacting together in play, they sustained each interaction longer, and they had more interactions in which both the mother and the child elaborated on the topic. Greenberg also concluded that the simultaneous children used communication in a more active and responsive way than the oral children since they had higher rates of spontaneously initiated communication and they complied with their mothers' demands and requests more often. Greenberg suggested that this indicates an increased desire of both simultaneous mothers and children for sustained joint interaction. It is particularly striking that for all measures of interaction, except total interaction time, the *low* communicators in the simultaneous group showed higher mean scores than even the *high* communicators in the oral group. Thus it appears the the communication mode itself strongly affects the flow of interaction between mothers and their deaf children.

These studies point out that normal mother-child interaction is threatened when the child is deaf and the mother is hearing, due to the communication problem. As Hilde Schlesinger (1972) suggests, both meaning and enjoyment suffer and the interaction is strained. Early use of manual communication seems to promote understanding and pleasure so that as communication improves, interaction improves, too.

But what happens when both mother and child are deaf? A recently published article (Galenson *et al.*, 1979) claims that deaf mothers are unskilled mothers who have disturbed interaction with their deaf children. The article does not fully explain how the researchers conducted their research nor how they came to their conclusions. However, we are told that the data were collected by hearing staff who did not use Sign Language, placing these parents "in their usual predicament vis-a-vis the hearing world" (132). This condition alone should cause us to question the validity of this research.

In an important area like this which affects all deaf people, research such as this must be adequately reported and well-designed to be useful.

Currently, Dr. Kathryn Meadow and I are working on a research project involving seven deaf mothers and their preschool deaf children. We are using Greenberg's coding procedures so that our group of deaf mothers can be compared with his three groups of hearing mothers: hearing mothers with deaf children using oral communication, hearing mothers with deaf children using simultaneous communication, and hearing mothers with hearing children. Our preliminary observations of our videotapes indicate that the interaction of deaf mothers and their deaf children is more similar to the interaction of hearing mothers and their hearing children than it is to interaction of either of the other two groups. It seems that when communication is comfortable and natural for both mother and child, there will not be any negative effects on their interaction.

Now I would like to return to the classroom research I began when I was working with Dr. Stokoe. Instead of mother-child interaction, we will look at the interaction of a hearing teacher and a deaf adult with eight deaf children. To collect the data, I spent three weeks videotaping the preschoolers and their teachers in a variety of everyday situations at school (a day school for deaf children): structured classroom activities, informal classroom activities, and lunch time interaction. When I reviewed the tapes, I noticed that the signing of both the children and the teachers looked different depending on the situation and depending on the people involved in the conversation. For example, the deaf assistant and the children used a specific variety of Sign Language during refreshment time. The assistant's language changed from a more ASL-like signing and became more like English. Similarly, the children's requests changed from their usual style to questions which followed English word order. Another example is the use of voice. The hearing teacher often stopped using her voice when she began signing to the assistant or when she joined a conversation in which the deaf assistant was involved. One of the children who has deaf parents seemed to use his voice repeatedly in structured situations with the hearing teacher, where he was producing one-word responses. Occasionally, he even used his voice alone, dropping the signs. However, he never communicated with the deaf assistant in this style.

I also noticed that the deaf assistant seemed to have a special role in the classroom. She was a language teacher, interpreter and a positive adult model. When questions came up about a particular sign, the teacher and the children asked the assistant first; she was the Sign Language authority. If there was no ASL sign, one of the new signs that the school developed for instructional purposes was used. When the hearing teacher could not understand one of the children, she asked the deaf assistant to interpret. The deaf woman was also a source of information for the children. Since she communicated with them fluently and since she knew the children of deaf parents as members of the deaf community, she and the children shared experiences and a familiar communication system which encouraged true communicative interchange in the classroom. Examples appeared on tape where the children asked for explanations of people and events and specific information, such as the fingerspelling of names. This kind of communication seemed to occur most often between the children and the deaf adult. It seems that the hearing teacher gave the children information about classroom activities through the structured lesson and the deaf assistant gave them enjoyable interpersonal experiences through informal conversations.

After these initial observations, I decided to analyze a portion of the interaction in some detail. I chose a five-minute section of tape in which the class and the deaf assistant were seated around a table while the hearing teacher presented a structured lesson. To begin, I simply counted the number of times a child began to communicate with one of the adults, and vice-versa. I did not pay attention to how the children communicated with each other. Then I counted the responses of each participant during each communication exchange. I wanted to know who initiated communication to whom and how long those communicative exchanges were, i.e., the number of turns in each exchange. Figure 1 is a diagram of that analysis. It shows that the children who are involved in most of the conversations are children of deaf parents. But it also includes "L" who has hearing parents; she spent a year at a residential school before coming to the day school, and she appears to have some competence in ASL. These conversations involve the deaf assistant more often than the hearing teacher. A closer look at the exchange between participants reveals that there is a difference in the kinds of exchanges which take place between the children and the deaf adult on the one hand, and the children and the hearing teacher on the other. For the assistant, 55% of the conversations in which she participated had three or more turns. For the hearing adult, this was true only 31% of the time. Another way to describe the difference is to say that the conversa-

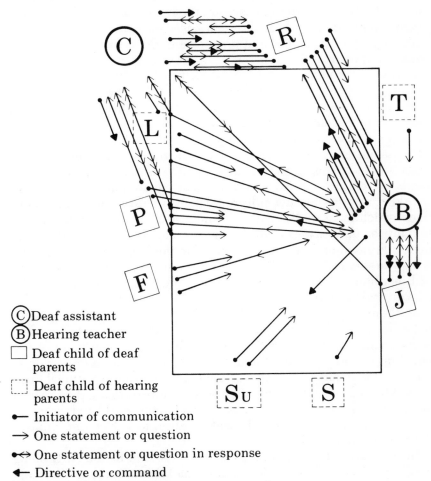

Figure 1. Classroom interaction: a 5-minute sample

tions with the deaf adult had three turns (3.0) while the average number of turns for the hearing teacher and a child was less than two turns (1.6). In this particular sample, the children were able to have longer conversations with the deaf assistant. This provided them with language experience and practice and the possibility of a satisfying interpersonal relationship.

Recently, a colleague and I went back to the data from this study (Johnson & Erting, 1979). We were interested in the socialization of deaf children—in other words, how deaf children learn what it means to be a deaf person. Since Sign Language is so important in the lives of deaf people, we decided to focus on how children learn Sign Language. The classroom seemed to be a particularly good place to study this question for several reasons. First, the school wants the children to learn and use English so that they will fit in with the majority hearing culture. Schools are the American institutions which have traditionally assumed that English fluency is important for minority groups. In educational programs for deaf students, this assumption is usually stated in the language policy (as the school in this case did). Simultaneous communication was the official medium of instruction and interaction; the primary goal of the educational program was acceptable English communication. Therefore, there was pressure for the teachers to use English. Another pressure to use English came from the relationship between deaf and hearing employees at the school. Hearing people were in the positions of authority, and the deaf people played little or no role in the decisionmaking. English was the language used for official business. Third, most deaf adults themselves believe that a deaf person must have good English skills to get ahead in the world and therefore they want to use English with deaf children to help them improve their knowledge of English.

In this particular classroom, we also expected to see ASL being used. The deaf children of deaf parents had learned ASL as their first language. It was natural for them to communicate in ASL. Likewise, the deaf adult in the classroom, who was a member of the same deaf social group as those children, tended to communicate in ASL with the children in the same way their family or friends would.

With these things in mind, we began to look at the interactions between the adults and children as well as the interactions of the children among themselves. We assumed that both the deaf adult and the deaf children of deaf parents would informally and formally teach the deaf children of hearing parents. We began by looking at the children's interactions with each other. The children seemed to divide into two groups. In group A, consisting of children whose first initials are R, P, L, F, the children were fluent users of ASL; three had deaf parents and one had hearing parents but had been at a residential school for the deaf for a year before coming to the day school. Group B, the other four children, whose initials are J, T, Su, S, were not skilled in the use of ASL. Three of them had hearing parents who did not sign with them at home. The other child in group B had deaf parents but the deaf assistant, as well as the child's parents, described his signing as "funny" or "strange." There are several examples on the tape of this child making incorrect or nonstandard signs.

But these were just impressions. In order to verify our impressions, we decided to analyze the interactions of the children. We wanted to know which children chose to sit with each other and which children chose to communicate with each other. Our analysis showed that there were two groups and the differences in their behavior were based on differences in language use: Group A children were skilled in ASL, whereas Group B children were not. Furthermore, the adults interacted differently with these groups. We found that during structured classroom situations, the teacher and the assistant both gave Group A considerably more linguistic and interactional experiences. For example, children in group A had more chances to initiate communication, received more initiations from the adults, received more responses from the adults and had more total turns in a communication exchange.

Our next question was whether or not the teacher and the assistant communicated differently to the two groups of children. We had already determined that Group A children used more ASL signing than Group B and the B children tended to copy signs from A children's conversations. Next, we were interested in how the two adults communicated with the two groups of children. We looked at one section of videotape where the deaf assistant was signing the same sentence to children from the two groups. She was serving food at the lunch table and wanted to know if each child wanted more. She used different types of English-like signing with Group A and B children. Her signing with A children was more fluid and conversational, but with B children her signing was segmented and more school-like, that is, more like manually-coded English (MCE). This seems surprising, since we usually think of eating as an informal kind of activity. However, the lunch situation is one which seems to influence the teachers and children to use English, perhaps because the curriculum in a school for deaf children often uses the distribution of food as a means of teaching English. Therefore, it is not so surprising that English-like signing is used in this situation. Another time, also at the lunch table, the deaf assistant was having a conversation with one of the Group A children when the child asked for the last piece of bread. The assistant turned to one of the Group B children who had not yet had her piece of bread and asked her if she wanted it. Her signing was more conversational in style than formal. The informality of the situation influenced the assistant's signing so that it was more conversational and less like MCE than it usually was with the children from Group B.

Another aspect of adult-child interaction which we investigated was intentional language teaching. We found examples of the deaf assistant correcting one child's baby sign for WATER (four fingers extended and touching the chin) to the standard adult sign (three fingers extended). She also changed the children's local signs and incorrect signs into standard signs. The hearing teacher, on the other hand, translated the ASL of a group A child into MCE for a group B child.

Both the teacher and the assistant attempted to teach the children English. However, they used different methods. It seemed that the hearing teacher assumed that the intentional coding of speech into signs, MCE, would provide a good English model for the children and that the children would learn English through exposure to this model. Table 1 is a typical example of the simultaneous speech and manually-coded English the hearing teacher used. It clearly shows that the signs and speech do not match. In fact, sometimes the meaning of her signs contradicts the meaning of her speech. Other researchers have found similar problems with the simultaneous communication used by teachers (Marmor & Pettito, 1979). However, the deaf assistant used a different strategy. She used contrastive examples in Sign English to teach specific English structures. For example, when signing to a group A child, she signed (J) NOT WANT EAT CHOCOLATE PUDDING. She followed that with DON'T-WANT CHOCOLATE PUDDING DON'T-WANT. These two sentences showed the children two different ways of signing the same thing. The first seems more like English; the second is more like ASL, since it uses the form of the verb WANT that incorporates negation. Another example involves a group B child: (J) NOT WANT TO EAT H H̲IS HIS CHOCOLATE PUDDING. She started to fingerspell

Table 1   Simultaneous Communication of Hearing Teacher Using Speech and Manually Coded English (MCE)*

Speech: Tell . . .
Signs: TELL

 tell the Easter Bunny   . . .
 SAY   HORSE RABBIT

 He said: "no", he's all   out.
           NO   ALL OUTSIDE

 You can take a different   color.
                 DIFFERENT COLOR HIM (INDEX)

 You forgot to   say you've . . .
      FORGET   TELL

 say thank you
     THANK-YOU

 Ah, well go   back and   make him say   thank you . . .
     COME BEFORE   MAKE   TELL THANK-YOU
     (PAST)

---

*These utterances by the teacher occurred sequentially. The children's utterances which occurred during this segment are not shown in this table.

H-I-S, changed to initialized MCE sign HIS, and finally gave the ASL sign HIS.

Finally, we looked at the interaction between the children in each group and the two adults in the lunchroom. We had already seen one pattern of interaction in the classroom; the group A children initiated more conversations than the B children with both the teacher and the assistant, and they had a greater number of total turns within those communication exchanges. We wondered if there would be a similar pattern during lunch time, which is more informal and unstructured. We chose three different lunchroom situations to study. During the first one, the deaf assistant was serving food to the children (see Table 2). Group A children did not initiate any interactions with group B children. They did not initiate any with the deaf assistant either. Instead, they chose to initiate communication to other group

A children. Group B children initiated their communication equally with the deaf assistant and other group B children, but most of their time was spent communicating with the deaf adult. They had a total of 59 turns with the deaf assistant, but only 13 turns with other members of group B. Group A members, on the other hand, communicated with other members of group A even more than they communicated with the deaf adult. They had 45 turns with the deaf assistant and 61 turns with other members of group A. The deaf assistant initiated communication the same number of times with children from each group but had more total turns with group B (59) than with group A (45).

During the second lunchroom situation the deaf assistant was seated at the table with the children. We found a different pattern of interaction (see Table 3). The group A children initiated most of their communication with the deaf adult rather than with other children and had more than three times as many total turns with the deaf assistant (45) as with other children (14). Group B children also initiated more to the deaf adult (8) than to the other children (4) and had twice as many total turns with her (30) as with the other children (14). The deaf adult initiated more communication with group B (8) than with group A (2), but had more total turns with group A members (45) than with group B members (30). It appeared that when the deaf adult was seated and eating lunch with the children, group A members communicated with her as if she were part of their group. However, when she was in her more formal role as teacher's aide, distributing food and communicating in a more formal, classroom-type English signing, she was not part of their group and they communicated more among themselves.

The third situation in the lunchroom involved the hearing teacher. She was seated at the table having lunch with the children. We found that the interactions here were more similar to the first situation with the deaf adult than the second (see Table 4). Group A children initiated more communication to other members of group A (9) than they did to group B children (2) or to the hearing teacher (4). They also had more total number of turns (19) with other children than they had with the teacher (17). Group B children initiated more to the hearing teacher (9) than to the other children and also had many more total number of turns with the hearing adult (26) than with the other children (5). The teacher initiated communication equally with each group of children but had more total turns with group B children (26) than with group A (17). When the observed number of turns

Table 2. Lunchroom Interaction: Total number of turns at 3 different times

Time		*	N
Time #1:			
Deaf Assistant	Group A with Group A	34%	61
serving food	Group A with Group B	—	0
	Group A with Deaf Assistant	25%	45
	Group B with Group B	7%	13
	Group B with Deaf Assistant	33%	59
	Total	100%	178
	$X^2 = 125.0$ p $\leqslant .001$		

Time		%	N
Time #2:			
Deaf Assistant	Group A with Group A	8%	8
seated at the	Group A with Group B	6%	6
table	Group A with Deaf Assistant	46%	45
	Group B with Group B	8%	8
	Group B with Deaf Assistant	31%	30
	Total	99%*	97
	$X^2 = 69.952$ p $\leqslant .001$		

Time		%	N
Time #3:			
Hearing teacher	Group A with Group A	26%	17
seated at the	Group A with Group B	3%	2
table	Group A with Hearing teacher	26%	17
	Group B with Group B	5%	3
	Group B with Hearing teacher	40%	26
	Total	100%	65
	$X^2 = 42.2$ p $\leqslant .001$		

Group A consists of four deaf children who are fluent in sign language.
Group B consists of four deaf children who are not fluent in sign language.
*Total does not equal 100% due to rounding.

for each group was compared with the number of turns which might have been expected if all participants were communicating equally with each other, the chi square values for each situation were significant at the .001 level. This means that the numbers shown in Table 2 for Time 1, Time 2, and Time 3 would have occurred by chance only one time in 1000.

When the deaf adult is serving food (situation #1) and when the hearing teacher is seated with the children (situation #3), the patterns of interaction are similar. Those patterns are significantly different from the situation where the deaf assistant is seated with the children. What do situations #1 and #3 have in common? Perhaps the similarity is the kind of signing the adults are using. When the deaf assistant is distributing food at lunch she seems to use the activity to teach English. This situation is similar to refreshment time in the classroom where the teachers ask questions in English and the children are expected to respond in English sentences. At lunch, the deaf woman signs, for example, D-O YOU WANT BREAD? D-O YOU WANT APPLE SAUCE? Her signing is more formal and deliberately English-like throughout this situation than it is when she is seated with the children. The hearing teacher, on the other hand, attempts to make her signing code her spoken English in every situation where she interacts with children, including the time during lunch when she is seated with the children. It may be that the formality of the situation, i.e., how "school-like" it is, is communicated to the children by the type of signing which the adults use. (In formal, "school-like" situations in most classrooms the teacher does most of the talking. She initiates with the children by asking them questions. They respond by giving the answers.) This may be especially true for the deaf adult when she communicates with group A children since she used both formal and informal kinds of signing with them. When she switches from more ASL-like, informal signing to English signing, she signals that the situation is more formal than casual and the children respond accordingly. In the more formal situations, we see the children in group A initiating communication more among themselves than with the adults, interacting with the adults primarily when it is the teacher who initiates. When the deaf adult joins them as a member of the group, signalled by her more informal style of communication, the pattern changes. The children include her as a member of their communication group and initiate many conversations with her. Here the signing is more ASL-like than it is English-like.

Summary and Implications

What does this research tell us? One thing we see is that children initiate interaction more often and have longer interactions when they can communicate in a way that is natural and comfortable for them. This is supported by Greenberg's research as well as the classroom research by Johnson and Erting:

- Greenberg's research suggests that mothers and children who include signing in their communication enjoy communicating and playing together more than mothers and children who communicate orally.
- In the classroom study, the children who knew ASL chose to communicate a lot with the deaf adult and the other children who knew ASL, but very little with the hearing teacher and those children who were not skilled in ASL.

As teachers and parents, we want deaf children to interact and communicate with us. Through enjoyable interaction they will learn about themselves and others, and they will improve their communication skills. It is our job to make positive interaction possible for them:

- We need to communicate with them using a language they will understand.
- We should not try to communicate with them only through oral language when they want and need Sign Language.
- We should have deaf adults in every classroom, especially when there are children in the class whose first language is ASL.

Only if we take these steps will it be possible to help deaf children to learn the important things they need to know about themselves and the world they live in, including new ways of communicating.

Acknowledgements

I would like to thank Dr. Robert Johnson and Dr. Kathryn Meadow for their comments on earlier drafts of this chapter.

References

Baker, Charlotte. "How does 'Sim-Com' Fit into a Bilingual Approach to Education?" Paper presented at the Second National Symposium on Sign Language Research and Teaching, San Diego, October, 1978.

Cokely, Dennis. *Pre-College Programs Guidelines for Manual Communication*. Washington, D.C.: Gallaudet College Press, 1979.

Crandall, Kathleen. A Study of the Production of Chers and Related Sign Language Aspects by Deaf Children Between the Ages of Three and Seven Years. Unpublished Ph.D. dissertation, Northwestern University. 1974.

Galenson, Eleanor, Miller, Robert, Kaplan, Eugene, and Rothstein, Arnold. Assessment of Development in the Deaf Child. *Journal of the American Academy of Psychiatry*, 1979, 18 (1), 128-142.

Greenberg, Mark. Attachment Behavior, Communicative Competence and Parental Attitudes in Preschool Deaf children. Unpublished doctoral dissertation. University of Virginia, 1978.

Johnson, Robert and Erting, Carol. Sign, Solidarity and Socialization. Paper presented at the annual meeting of the American Anthropological Association. Cincinnati, Ohio: November, 1979.

Marmor, Gloria Strauss and Petitto, Laura. Simultaneous Communication in the Classroom: How Well is English Grammar Represented? *Sign Language Studies*, 1979, 23, 99–136.

Schlesinger, Hilde. Meaning and Enjoyment: Language Acquisition of Deaf Children. In O'Rourke, T. J. (Ed.) *Psycholinguistics and Total Communication: The State of the Art*. Washington, D.C.: American Annals of the Deaf, 1972, 92–102.

Schlesinger, Hilde and Meadow, Kathryn P. *Sound and Sign: Childhood Deafness and Mental Health*. Berkeley: University of California Press, 1972.

Williams, Judith. Bilingual Experiences of a Deaf Child. *Sign Language Studies*, 1976, 10, 37–41.

Education in Schools for Deaf Children

by Raymond Stevens

Introduction

My first impressions of Bill Stokoe were negative. During the summer of 1966, when I was a graduate student at Gallaudet College, Bill was the leader of a bagpipe-blowing, kilt-wearing Scottish music group. Bill and his group practiced on the campus of Gallaudet College. Obviously, very few of the students at Gallaudet College were bothered by this strange music. It bothered me, however, because I am a hearing person. Early every Sunday morning, Bill and his group came on campus and, with their music, awakened us few hearing people. Since then, people have told me that Bill is a fairly good piper, but early on a Sunday morning, I was not an appreciative audience! I also remember the professional gossip that was circulating about Bill. It seemed that he was maintaining that Sign Language

Raymond Stevens is presently Principal at the Austine School for the Deaf in Vermont. Before assuming this position, he was a social studies teacher in schools and programs for deaf children for four years. He has a B.A. in History from Augustana College (1964), an M.A.T. in teaching social studies to deaf students from Gallaudet College (1967), and a Ph.D. in Instructional Technology from Syracuse University (1977).

Formerly a strong proponent of the oral method of educating deaf students, Ray is now a firm advocate of Sign Language and is concerned with how deaf children learn language and culture and with how research findings can be used to guide the development of educational programs for deaf children.

177

was really a language in and of itself, it wasn't simply "poor English." I didn't appreciate the argument or the singular stand that he had taken.

Since that summer of loud music, 13 years have passed and much has changed in regard to the professional view of Sign Language and the status of Bill Stokoe. Bill's role as English professor at Gallaudet has been realized much more in his study of American Sign Language than in the nouns and verbs he taught his students. His unwillingness to accept commonly held views of Sign Language served as inspiration to both students and teachers alike. As a graduate student, I had little opportunity to talk to him and had very little knowledge to share with him. But as a doctoral student at Syracuse University, I interned at the Linguistics Research Lab in the summer of 1975. During that summer, I spent several hours talking with him, listening to his fellow workers in the lab, and developing a very positive image of him. On one occasion, Bill asked me to lead one of the regular Friday discussion groups. Because I did not see how I would be able to offer anything to six practicing linguists, I told Bill that I would like to decline the invitation. Bill's response was simple and direct: "No, because every time I talk to you, I get a good idea." I can well imagine Bill saying that to hundreds of individuals throughout his career. His willingness to listen, to learn, and to exchange ideas and information with colleages, with his deaf and hearing students, and with visitors is the foundation of his reputation as a scholar. In my eyes, he is one of the best role models in the field of education: good students make good teachers. Bill Stokoe is a good student. Living as a student of American Sign Language, he has become a teacher of many researchers. In fact, in a few short years, some of his students may be better known than himself. Most of the current research in American Sign Language can be traced back to Bill. Most of the people presently conducting research in American Sign Language trace their interest to Bill's original works. Those who do not relate their work to his, empirically, are supported, at least in attitude, by his work. Where once Stokoe stood alone and received the criticism of the majority of leaders in our professional community, many now stand unafraid and supported in their work. What was once a quirk of a young professor at Gallaudet, is now a field of research that demands the respect of professionals around the world. I believe that Bill's leadership in the field of Sign Language research has crucial implications for the education of deaf children. Unfortunately, documentation of cause-effect relationships in education, as in most social sciences, is difficult to obtain. Thus, the remainder of this essay will be a personal opinion rather than a summary of research studies in the field of education.

The Problem

The education of deaf children is a failure. It is especially a failure in the light of the criteria used to measure success. By and large, the criteria of success has been the acquisition of speech and reading skills. However, the deaf child cannot acquire English, speech and reading skills without the prerequisite of communication skills and an understanding of the meaning of things. Knowledge of English, speech, grammar and reading and the acquisition of facts are surface skills. They are measurable, but are not fundamental. They are what most teachers are trained to teach, but they are not all that the deaf child must learn. Communication, semantics, and culture are the prerequisites to a so-called normal education.

Unfortunately, the deaf child has not acquired these prerequisites because, in the attempt to "normalize" deaf minority students, the hearing majority has oppressed them. This cultural and linguistic oppression is the result of regarding deaf people as "without a language." For years, the manual communication system used by deaf people has been described as "bad English" or as a negative off-shoot of communication systems used by hearing people. Thus, in the attempt to "give" the deaf minority a language, the hearing majority has sought to forbid, or at least restrict, the use of their manual communication.

Language has often been described as the most essential human characteristic and ability. Extensions of this position might be: (1) If you do not accept the person's language, you do not accept the person, and (2) If you do not believe the person has a language, you do not believe the person is a complete, whole person. Such has been the case with deaf people. Hearing people have attempted to "give" the deaf community English in order that the members of the community will be whole people. In order to assure that the deaf community acquires English, the manual communication of the deaf community has been suppressed.

Too many professionals have viewed signing as a symptom of deficiency to be avoided whenever possible, rather than simply as a natural and comfortable way to communicate. Some examples of suppression are worth citing . . .

At the 1st National Tripod Meeting in 1971, Dr. Hilde Schlesinger and Dr. Kay Meadow reported that many deaf parents would not admit to them that they used signs with their children. When a deaf adult did the same survey, many of the same deaf parents disclosed that they did sign to their deaf children. Evidently, the deaf parents were afraid of rejection by two hearing people with such high status in the educational community.

Deaf teachers have been traditionally used in the older and/or "slow-learner" classrooms. Hearing teachers have traditionally been used in the preschool and with the "normal" deaf students. Obviously, one reason for putting deaf teachers in with less capable students is that deaf teachers could communicate with the less able deaf students, whereas the hearing teachers could not. A second reason for such selective placement of deaf teachers was to "protect" the normal deaf children from the "poor English" and "deafisms" of the deaf teachers. Constant communication in less than "perfect" English was viewed as harmful to the deaf students.

An expert was invited to speak on the need to develop a statewide program for deaf students. After the formal meeting had closed, this so-called expert on deafness was challenged by a deaf adult on some of her opinions. While communicating his disagreements, the deaf adult used Sign Language. But the "expert" simply took hold of his hands and said, "You do not have to sign. You can talk, put your hands down."

This suppression and oppression have deprived deaf children of a language, and have, in turn, deprived them of a culture. Language and culture cannot be separated. It is not possible to learn a language without knowledge of the culture. Conversely, it is not possible to acquire the culture without knowledge of the language because language is the major vehicle by which culture is transmitted from one individual to another and from one generation to another. When deaf children were not allowed to learn Sign Language, many of these children were deprived of the only communication system which could effectively transmit the culture to them. Consequently, the natural bonds between these children and their hearing parents, the community, and, ultimately, the general culture were not established. These children then entered school in a cultural "limbo," without language, and unable to ever again have the preschool experiences so crucial to success in school and adulthood. Fairy tales, cops and robbers, ring around the rosey, church and table talk left no marks on the great majority of deaf children. Thus, these children entered school without a knowledge of their culture because of linguistic suppression and remained in this cultural limbo because of the educational system itself.

In recent years, however, "total communication" has swept the country in a wave. Schools have invented sign systems willy-nilly. Different forms of signing are being taught all over the United States. It may even be true that more hearing people than deaf people can use some form of signing simply because so many hearing people have taken sign courses and because there are relatively so few deaf people. Again, much of the acceptance of total communication is the result of giving Sign Language an elevated status in the world of language.

Unfortunately, the acceptance of manual communication in the classroom has not been accompanied by a change in the content or form of instruction. Manual communication has simply been added to the repertoire of teaching skills. It is viewed as a *method* of teaching rather than as a *language*.

Re-Educating the Teacher

In order to improve the educational system for deaf children, we must first re-educate the teachers and reduce the prejudice that leads to oppression.

In the past several years, Sign Language research has demonstrated quite clearly that American Sign Language is a language in and of itself. Many deaf people who were formerly called "low verbal," only because they had low English skills, are now more correctly described as monolingual people. "Slang signs" and "idioms" are now more correctly described as American Sign Language signs that do not happen to correspond to English words; no value judgment is implied. American Sign Language has been accepted in several universities on the graduate level, as both a subject of linguistics and as a language requirement for graduate work. In short, the linguistic community has accepted American Sign Language as a language. Unfortunately, the professional community in the education of deaf children still does not.

Research in psycholinguistics indicates that deaf children of deaf parents acquire American Sign Language skills similarly to the way hearing children acquire spoken language skills. The rate of learning, specific semantic and syntactic constructions, and specific vocabulary items of American Sign Language learned by deaf children, all parallel spoken language learning by hearing children. This demonstrates that American Sign Language is a language and that deaf children have normal language learning capacities. Thus, not only should we view the deaf community as whole and complete, but we should also view deaf children of deaf or hearing parents as strong, capable human beings.

Until professionals have faith that deaf students can be competent language learners, the education of deaf students will not improve. Somehow, teachers must acquire more faith in the power of humans. While very few people would choose to become deaf, many deaf people would choose to remain deaf. Teachers must learn that deafness itself does not alter a human sufficiently to make him or her incomplete as a functioning member of society. Failure to acquire speech is unfortunate but it does not predict ultimate failure in life. Likewise, failure to acquire competence in English does not predict ultimate failure. Tremendous frustrations and failure are predictable, however, when the deaf child has no language or when his or her only language (e.g. American Sign Language) is unacceptable to the hearing majority.

Therefore, in order to improve the education of deaf students, it is necessary to change the attitudes of teachers towards deaf students and eliminate oppression based on cultural and linguistic prejudice. Teachers must be helped to see that the richness of language, whether it be American Sign Language or English, reflects the richness of the person who knows that language.

Educating the Deaf Child

Teachers of deaf children are right, in one way, when they identify language as the focal point in the education of deaf children. Deaf children do not succeed in the academic subjects because they do not know English. Presently, academic instruction depends on textbooks produced for public school students. Without the ability to read, deaf students cannot acquire the knowledge and information necessary to succeed in the traditional classroom.

However, the manner in which the profession attempts to prepare the young deaf child for formal, academic instruction should be seriously questioned. At present, there seem to be some major problems in the way infant and elementary school programs are structured.

For example, infant programs have been started in which the clinician takes the role of the parent. For one or two hours a week, the clinician visits the home and tries to interact with the deaf infant in order to stimulate language development. Often the infant has no stimulation between the visits of the clinician. These programs do not focus enough on developing communication between the parents and the child. Consequently, parents do not become the child's major source of language learning as they are for hearing children.

Secondly, elementary school programs focus on "blackboard English" rather than allowing skills in American Sign Language or English to develop naturally through communication about specific concepts and ideas. Formal instruction in vocabulary, phrases, and grammar to children who are functioning linguistically as infants seems to be inappropriate. Child developmental stages, language learning processes, and the cultural consequences of deafness must be more carefully considered.

The following is an attempt to outline an educational program for deaf students. The most salient characteristic of the program is the creation of a *normal* learning environment.

Culture

Children are born into families. Families are members of communities. Communities make up societies. A society's way of life is a culture. The culture is, by and large, communicated through language. Thus, in order to communicate the culture of the society to the deaf child, he must be surrounded with language. Values, aspirations, expectations and attitudes of the family, and in many ways of the culture, are first communicated at home. By the time the hearing child is three, he has mastered the rudiments of his language. By the time the deaf child (with hearing parents) is three, he generally has very little or no knowledge of any language. By the time the hearing child is six, he has acquired a wealth of knowledge about his family, his environment and society's general expectations of him. He knows that work follows school, that marriage is for big people and that grandfather and grandmother are finished work. The great majority of knowledge, information and language that the hearing child knows has been learned incidentally through natural, normal communication in the family and around the community. Deaf children of deaf parents are able to do much of the same. Unfortunately, less than ten percent of all deaf children have deaf parents and, consequently, most do not live in a normal environment.

The mother of the hearing child may spend hours telling stories, reading stories and talking about the activities in a child's environment. The deaf child of hearing parents seldom learns fairy tale characters and community helpers and, consequently, does not play-act our culture. When grandfather dies, the hearing child may learn about death through a story that mother reads. Parents select the book that reflects their attitude towards death and the hearing child learns that attitude through the real experience of grandfather's death and through the symbolic experience of the story. When the deaf child's grandfather dies, little is said, and less is understood.

Father's absence from supper is explained to the hearing child. The child learns that father works hard to earn money, to save money so the child can have nice clothes, go on vacation and go to college. In short, one missed meal can trigger a statement describing the lives of a great majority of people.

The continued explanation of experiences day in and day out, year after year, helps the hearing child to develop a sense of culture. The absence of these explanations day in and day out, year after year, puts the deaf child in cultural limbo. The *normalization* of the deaf child's early experience is dependent on clear, unambiguous, signed communication. Parents and siblings alike must communicate to the deaf child in order that the deaf child can incidentally acquire the culture of his society.

The acquisition of cultural knowledge is a never-ending process. Continued communication and participation in society help the individual continue to grow and change as the culture grows and changes. Without such involvement, the individual cannot acquire knowledge about his culture, nor be a full member of it.

Understanding of one's culture is important for developing reading skills. Reading is not simply looking at and being able to recognize words on paper. Reading is a process of using one's knowledge of the environment to understand the printed word. Without knowledge of one's environment and culture, it is impossible to give meanings to individual words and sentences. Thus, deaf children who are in cultural limbo cannot read because they do not have the shared meanings of the culture represented by those words. While specific syntactic constructions (e.g. passive voice, relativization) are particularly difficult for deaf students, the way in which we use passive voice and relative pronouns are culturally determined. They are not simply grammatical constructions in the abstract. Thus, the most pervasive, yet unmeasurable, consideration in the education of the deaf child is culture.

Bilingual-Bicultural Education

The most prevalent educational goal in schools and classes for deaf children is the acquisition of English. However, this goal is too narrow and the methods used to reach it are too limited for the goal itself to be obtained. Much of the time and energy devoted toward reaching the goal are wasted because the cultural aspects of education are ignored, and because the teachers, by and large, do not foster growth in general areas of language and thought development. A much expanded educational curriculum must be developed in order for the deaf child to acquire competence in English.

I have seen that deaf children learn American Sign Language with ease. It does not take long for the deaf child to become more skilled in manual communication than his hearing teachers. Their American Sign Language competence grows with the same rapidity that a hearing child's competence grows in a spoken language. Unfortunately, this wealth of language and knowledge of language is an untapped resource of both English language learning and general concept development.

It seems clear that a bilingual, bicultural educational program should be developed. Such a program would not de-emphasize English language learning, but rather, help the child acquire bilingual and bicultural skills. Bicultural education implies the development of a curriculum in which not only the culture of the majority is studied through the social sciences and literature, but the minority culture of the deaf community is also studied. Bicultural studies attempt to provide the learner with a knowledge of, and an appreciation for, both the differences and the similarities of the two cultures. Likewise, the two languages which represent the two cultures are studied. Each is given its due respect, and the function and use of each is examined. Thus, deaf students will study both languages and, ultimately, become consciously bilingual.

Within the framework of bilingual, bicultural education, there are special considerations that might be made because of deafness, and because the parents of the majority of deaf children are not deaf.

1. *Deaf professionals:* More deaf teachers and deaf house-parents should be hired in educational programs for deaf students. The psycho-social identity necessary for any person can be developed only through association with adults who share characteristics which are significant to the subgroup. While hearing adults are good role models as teachers, workers, and credit card carriers, they cannot

serve as adult deaf role models. Even though communication between deaf students and hearing teachers is very useful, deaf children also need deaf role models; it is crucial for them to see that
success in school and learning is not limited to hearing people. In
addition, hearing teachers need deaf teachers as their peers and as-
sociates. Deaf teachers are examples of "successful" deaf people and
consequently lead hearing teachers to have higher expectations of
their students. Prior to the newly elevated status of American Sign
Language, deaf people continuously relied on hearing people to inform them about English. Now the relationship should be two-way.
Deaf people now have the opportunity and the "right" to inform
hearing people on how to sign. Having more deaf teachers in educational programs will facilitate this two-way learning. Certainly the
deaf child will need to continuously see and use both American Sign
Language and English in order to acquire competence in both languages and the cultures of these languages.

2. *Child Language Development:* The onset of formal instruction
in both American Sign Language and English must depend on the
level of language and thought development of the child. Hearing
children are fairly competent in their language before entering
school. Deaf children need the same "normal" experience if they are
to become competent adults. Language acquisition is a natural process: it cannot be hurried through coercion or bribery. Research
clearly indicates that deaf children have normal language learning
capacities and, thus, formal instruction should not, cannot, be introduced prematurely. "Instruction" should not be confused with "exposure." Deaf children need to be exposed to the fairy tales, games
of imaginary play, and to the mythical characters of a culture(s).
Storytelling precedes reading, just like knowledge of animals, trees
and people precedes biology. The preschool curriculum for the deaf
child needs to be broader than the preschool curriculum for the
hearing child, simply because the deaf child of hearing parents is
often culturally deprived. Exposure to the cognitive world of the
young child does not include calendar work, rote counting, and
memorizing sight word lists. The cognitive world of the child is full
of sights and sounds, sensory-motor play, and the give and take of
unstructured, yet meaningful communication. In short, the language
of the young child should be learned or, perhaps, played, but never
taught.

3. *Curriculum:* A much broader preschool and elementary school
curriculum for students must be developed. The curriculum should

not depend on the printed word in the early years of school. Typically, there has been too much concentration on language acquisition and not enough on concept acquisition. Specific concepts in the traditional academic disciplines of math, language, social studies, and science must also be taught.

Fortunately, the educational system can be changed. Deaf children have normal language learning abilities, and thus, by inference, have normal thinking and learning skills. Similar to hearing children, deaf children can learn a great variety of concepts and information from face-to-face interaction before they are able to read and write. In fact, hearing children learn to read because they have knowledge of the concepts reflected in books. Deaf children must also be exposed to the concepts which naturally interest young children. Regardless of their later success in learning to read, deaf children and adolescents need to have a base of knowledge about their world in order to become knowledgeable adults. Whether or not they learn English and, finally, learn to read, is a separate issue. The simple fact is that deaf children are ignorant not because they are intellectually deficient, but because the educational system has focused too narrowly on the acquisition of English.

Sign language research demonstrates that American Sign Language is a full language and, therefore, can function as a vehicle for communicating concepts and information to deaf students. The meanings and principles expressed through the spoken and printed word can also be communicated through manual communication. Thus, the deprivation of knowledge is not a result of any inadequacies of manual communication, but rather in the attitude of the professionals working with deaf children.

This attitude is expressed in either "they won't be able to understand that . . . " or "English and reading must come first." I contend that young, deaf children are willing and interested to learn about fire engines, polar bears and Indians of America. One time a 6th grader explained how he had been bored for the last five years in school. When asked what happened five years ago, he said he had learned about "Indians of America." He then sat for five years waiting for the next social studies course.

Ironically and happily, there can be many different curricula. Every school could have a very different curriculum with different emphases yet still convey important concepts, facts and learning skills to their students. Deaf students cannot acquire knowledge, however, unless professionals make a conscious effort both to devise specific academic curricula and to focus on knowledge as well as on language.

4. *Language Adapted Materials:* The most elementary and essential thing in present day educational programs is the book. Books have made mass education possible. Without books, very few people could become well-educated. Possession of books has almost become synonymous with an education itself. Yet the great majority of deaf children are not given books that they can read and understand. It is not uncommon to see deaf students carrying books that everyone knows they cannot read. They will avoid easy books because they are "kid stuff" and use books that are unintelligible to them because they have seldom had the experience of being able to read a book.

In order to help deaf students learn and have equal access to the ideas of the world, a great volume of books and other printed materials must be produced specifically for them. Sign Language research and research on the written skills of deaf adolescents now provide sufficient information and guidelines to write these materials in such a way that the great majority of students at each age and/or reading level will be able to use them productively.

Professionals have often argued that language adapted materials will make deaf students lazy and dependent on "easy books." Such dependency will, in turn, hinder deaf students from using "public school texts." Yet, no explanation is given to why the great majority of deaf students who "use" public school textbooks fail to learn how to read them, and do not acquire broad competency in English, or at least acquire the knowledge contained in the books.

In the final analysis, language adapted materials is another way to normalize deaf children's educational experience. Adults, especially hearing adults, do not "read" books they cannot understand because of language or content. They simply exchange the book for a more suitable one. However, deaf students are expected to "read" books which they cannot understand. They do not have the same freedom of choice, and yet professionals are disappointed when deaf adolescents and adults do not "see the need" for reading. Until books are produced for deaf students, they will continue to be dependent on their teachers for the ideas, information and concepts that other students generally obtain from books. Dependency in learning fosters dependency in other areas of life. While specially prepared books will not make the deaf child a free adult, without them, many deaf students will be denied access to information that they need in order to become well-informed, competent adults.

5. *Formal Language Instruction:* The teaching of English is the most discussed subject in the profession. Generally, the approach is to start early, start simple, and start structured. Research on child language acquisition, cognitive development, and second language learning have been largely ignored, and little thought has been given to the usefulness of Sign Language in teaching English. Over the years, several systems have been tried and discarded, only to have another system take the place of the last one.

In a bicultural, bilingual education program, formal language instruction helps the child use his first language to help him acquire proficiency in his second language. In order to assure that justifiable instructional methods are used, the child's cognitive and linguistic development are carefully examined. Formal instruction in either language does not begin until the child is cognitively mature enough to perceive the system in the language itself. Such maturation occurs around the time of puberty.

Once the child is cognitively mature, he can be instructed in the grammar of the second language, and how that grammar differs from his own everyday language. The intent of such instruction is not to judge or to criticize, but rather to help the student see differences and when to employ those differences.

Bilingual instruction is based on the supposition that the content of the two languages are basically the same; both languages can communicate the same meanings. However, the form (i.e. the grammar) of the languages are different. Instruction should proceed from the grammar of the first language to the grammar of the second language. The vocabulary of the first language should be used to develop the vocabulary of the second language. (Generally, the deaf child's signed vocabulary is larger than his sight-word vocabulary and yet teachers often do not first teach the printed form of the child's signs before moving on to new words.)

6. *Songs and Signs:* The final special area of consideration for a bicultural, bilingual education program is music.

Songs are a special form of language use and an expression of cultural values and attitudes. Wars of love and hate, work habits and folk heroes are all described in songs. Thus, songs provide a unique opportunity to understand the culture of a people in condensed time. Songs help individuals maintain contact with their culture and also help them deal with the frustrations of their daily life. Teenagers are noted for using songs to help them understand conflicts with their parents, their first love, and their roles in society.

Deaf students also need well accepted expressions of their culture(s). They face trials and conflicts, joys and successes as they grow up. Unfortunately, they cannot turn to music and song to help them understand themselves and their expected roles.

Therefore, in order to further the cultural development of deaf students, songs (and music) should be incorporated into their curriculum. In addition to the specific meanings of a song and its implications for the individual, the deaf child will obtain a much more real and up-to-date view of the broader culture. Secondly, in the process of translating the song into American Sign Language, the student will experience not only bilingual, but very clear bicultural differences and similarities. The experience of learning songs, interpreting them, and then recreating them in another language would help the deaf child understand the changes in himself created by the normal maturation process and the conflicts that may be present due to conflicts across cultures.

Song is an art form. Deaf children need to experience and to express art. Art speaks to the emotional, to the affective part of our existence. Song is such an art form, but it is also a very practical and general unambiguous way by which members of different cultures are assisted in communication. Through such communication, the deaf child should be more able to develop into a productive member of both cultures. To settle for less is both unfair and unnecessary.

Conclusion

The arguments presented in this paper are both incomplete and sometimes unsubstantiated. They are, however, attempts to confront our present educational practices. These practices must be called into question because they are not successful.

Fundamental to the educational profession is the need to grow and learn. Without change and growth, the profession cannot hope to remain a viable institution, for the essence of education is learning. In other words, while the practice of education is teaching, the heart of it is learning by the teachers themselves.

Therein lies the beauty of Bill Stokoe. His willingness to learn, even under severe criticism, must serve as an example to us all. Our profession of teaching deaf children has had too many narrow-minded arguments. The oral/manual controversy has divided our field for the past 150 years. We have depended too much on our training and not enough on our thinking. We have depended too much on our private experience and not enough on research. Bill Stokoe has used research and thinking with great skill. He has shown that American Sign Language is a true language. But his research has not solved all the problems in our field. We must be careful that we do not develop new disagreements and arguments that will hurt deaf students. American Sign Language has become popular and widely used. Other forms of manual communication are also being widely used. Is another war going to begin between the supporters of American Sign Language and the supporters of Signed English? As a practicing professional and as a supporter of research, I strongly advocate that we do not exclude either American Sign Language or Signed English. I believe we must do research on the effectiveness of both of them. I also believe we must be careful that the use of American Sign Language does not alienate hearing parents of deaf children. We must also be careful that the use of Signed English does not alienate deaf people. In the end, we must commit ourselves to learning. We must commit ourselves to improving the education of deaf students through research and thinking. We must not again take sides and argue against each other. I believe that is Bill Stokoe's message. We have applauded him for his research on Sign Language. But we must also applaud him for helping us all to become better students of our profession.

Drama and Poetry in Sign Language: A Personal Reminiscence

by Louie Fant

Like most children of deaf parents, I grew up with no conscious awareness that ASL was a language. I thought of ASL as an ungrammatical parody of English. It was not until I reached my mid-thirties, about a dozen years ago, that I was relieved of this misconception. My enlightenment came from people who were not native users of ASL. They were people who had come into the field of deafness with no preconceived notions, and bound to no points of view regarding deaf people and their language. They looked at the signed language of deaf people with fresh eyes and described to people like me what the situation really was.

Lou Fant is presently a Lecturer in the Department of Special Education at the California State University at Northridge, where he teaches American Sign Language. He also gives public lectures and workshops about ASL and dramatic presentations in the language. Lou received his B.A. from Baylor University in 1953, and his M.A. in Special Education from Teachers College, Columbia University in 1955.

Lou's interest in deaf people and American Sign Language began with his parents, who are deaf. He became a teacher at the New York School for Deaf Children and later, an Associate Professor of Education at Gallaudet College. Lou was a founding member of the National Theater of the Deaf and has played a variety of roles on television and in films. In partnership with John Joyce, he has made a series of filmed stories in ASL from the Bible, and has made a variety of educational Sign Language productions. Lou has also written three texts: Say It With Hands (1964), Ameslan (1972), and Sign Language (1977).

Foremost among those people is William C. Stokoe of Gallaudet College. More than anyone else, he is responsible for awakening people like me from our fuzzy slumber, causing us to look again at how deaf people really communicate with one another. Bill shook us all by the shoulders and said, "Hey, look at what's really happening!" He launched the movement to accept ASL as a language and to subject ASL to rigorous linguistic analysis, a movement that now has scores of people involved in researching ASL in prestigious institutions from Boston to San Diego and in teaching ASL in numerous colleges and universities.

I was a member of the faculty at Gallaudet College when Bill Stokoe's first publication, *Sign Language Structure: An Outline of the Visual Communication Systems of the American Deaf*, came out in 1960. I think my reaction to it was typical of the majority of the people in the field. I felt that it was merely the attempt of another opportunist to make a name for himself. I saw little in his work to change my attitude toward ASL. For most of us, Sign Language was a tool to be used as a last resort to teach English, it was not anything to be dignified with scientific scrutiny. How would we ever get deaf children to learn English if we accorded Sign Language equal status with it? This anxiety, which is still widespread today, prevented me from realizing the significance of Bill's insights at that time.

When Bill's first work was published, there were few classes in Sign Language. Gallaudet had a class for those graduate students studying to become school teachers, the "teacher-in-training" as we called them. A few schools for deaf children had 'survival' classes for new teachers to help save them from being completely lost, and a few classes thrived in church basements. None of these classes taught ASL, but rather taught a system of manually coded English. Prior to the publication of Bill's work, no one gave serious thought to a career as a Sign Language instructor. One could not even imagine conducting sober research on Sign Language. Such activities could only be considered amusing hobbies.

Four years after Bill's work was published, I decided to write a Sign Language textbook. I concluded that Bill had come up with at least one valuable thing about signs, and that was that each sign had three parts to it: the handshape, the place where the sign occurred, and the type of movement. I organized my book so that the signs in each lesson all had the same handshape, and only the place and movement varied. I felt this organization would facilitate learning the signs. To my knowledge it was the first attempt to use a linguistic analysis of ASL to organize the teaching of signs.

In 1965, I felt there was a need for Gallaudet College to become more actively involved in the area of manual communication. I proposed the establishment of a Department of Manual Communication that would:

1. Train new faculty and staff members to use the simultaneous method of manual communication.
2. Train new students and graduate students to use the simultaneous method.
3. Provide the college with interpreters for all college activities.
4. Develop methods and materials for teaching manual communication and for training interpreters.
5. Establish a program of research that would (a) improve the learning of manual communication, and (b) explore the effects of manual communication on the intellectual and social development of deaf children.

The term "simultaneous method" meant speaking English at the same time one is signing manually coded English. I did not use the terms "ASL" or "American Sign Language" because it then had not yet become a part of our vocabulary. During the preceding five years I had gotten to know Bill much better and I considered him a friend. I listened with interest to his explanations of what he was discovering, but I still could not accept the idea that ASL was a language. By this time Bill had set up the Linguistics Research Laboratory, and I suggested that the proposed Department of Manual Communication could work closely with the Lab to develop teaching materials. However, no action was taken on the proposal, and it died quietly.

In 1967 I left Gallaudet to become one of the founding members of the National Theater of the Deaf (NTD). Nearly all of the productions of the NTD were rendered in manually coded English, because ASL was considered bastardized English and not proper for use on the stage. Occasionally we would throw in some colloquial expression from "real sign language." That was our term for the signed language used by most adult deaf people when communicating among themselves. I did a monologue called "On the Evils of Tobacco," in which I used "real sign language," and it caused some consternation among a couple of the members of the company. Somewhere in the recesses of my mind was a growing awareness that Bill was right, and that what we were calling "real sign language" was in fact ASL.

While I was with the NTD, I received a phone call from Dr. Ursula Bellugi of the Salk Institute for Biological Studies, inviting me to lunch. She wanted to ask me some questions about Sign Language. I had no idea who she was and I accepted the invitation with little enthusiasm. She, her husband Ed Klima, and I lunched in the faculty dining room of Rockefeller University in New York City. She was interested in studying how deaf children developed their Sign Language. As the conversation progressed, my attitude underwent a rapid transformation. In her warm, winning way, she made me realize how little I really knew about Sign Language, even though I had known it since childhood. Her questions shook the foundations of my beliefs about ASL. Her praise for Bill and his work made me wonder if I was missing something.

I left the NTD and moved to Los Angeles in 1970. Soon after arriving in California, I met Dr. Earl Walpole, who was teaching French and ASL at California State University, Hayward. I asked him what he thought of Bill's work. I half expected him to say that it was interesting but of little substance, so I was quite taken aback when Earl poured forth a torrent of praise for Bill and his work. I became a convert. I ceased to resist the idea that ASL was a language, and submerged myself in studying it so that I could teach it as a language. Unfortunately, I was poorly equipped with the necessary linguistic tools to do an adequate job.

My fascination with artistic signing, which had been fanned into flames during my experiences with the NTD, receded into the background as I became more involved with trying to understand how ASL worked and how to teach it to my students. I had some correspondence with Bill in which I eagerly shared my discoveries, and Bill tried like a fatherly priest to cool the over-heated zealot, and to steer me in better directions. I am sure Bill's counsel saved me from dashing down many avenues that would have been unproductive dead-ends.

By 1975 I convinced myself that I should leave the linguistic study of ASL to the linguists, and focus my energy on the area in which I could make a more meaningful contribution: ASL artistic signing, and dramatic interpreting from English into ASL. One of my concerns in this area was, and still is, that too much of what passes for artistic interpretation of English literature into ASL is not interpretation at all, but rather a rendering of spoken English into manually coded English.

In the November 1972 issue of the *Deaf American,* I tried to explain what I perceived to be the situation with regard to the misuse of the terms "interpret" and "translate." The Registry of Interpreters for the Deaf had defined "interpret" as moving from English to an edited paraphrase in signs, while "translate" meant moving from English to some form of manually coded English. I pointed out that interpreting and translating are two sides of the same coin. In either instance, one moves from one language into another. By definition, moving from spoken English to manually coded English could not be considered translating. In this process, one does not move from English to another language, but rather from one system of coding English to another system of coding it, much as one moves from spoken to written English. I said that this act should be called "transliterating," reserving the words "translating" and "interpreting" for the act of moving from English to ASL, and from ASL to English.

Bill's work had been in print for a couple of years before the Registry was formed, but we chose to ignore it, because most of us believed that there was no such thing as a real language of signs. A confusion of terminology followed because we failed to perceive what was really happening with interpreting situations. As late as 1980, we are still trying to unravel the confusion that resulted from our insulating ourselves against Bill's profound discovery.

I will illustrate the difference between "transliterating" and "translating" with the opening line of Hamlet's soliloquy, "To be or not to be: that is the question." A transliteration of the line might be: TO BE OR NOT TO BE THAT IS THE QUESTION, using signs from one of the systems of manually coded English, which has a sign for each of the English words. Another rendition might use fingerspelling: T-O B-E OR NOT T-O B-E THAT TRUE QUESTION. Other combinations are possible, but none of them require much thought or imagination, because transliterating is a fairly automatic process. Its advantage over translating is that transliterating may be done instantly with no preparation. In fact it is usually done simultaneously with the spoken word.

The translation of this line from Hamlet follows a completely different course. First one must have some idea of the meaning of this phrase "To be or not to be," and reading some of the commentaries on it surely helps. Since ASL does not have a sign that means "to be," the translator is faced with several choices. One might interpret the line "to live," or "to act," or "to go ahead," or several other alternatives. In my translation, I chose to use the sign DECIDE, since to me Hamlet is having difficulty deciding what to do.

Before deciding upon DECIDE, however, I had to give some thought to how I would negate it. One could, of course, sign DE-CIDE DON'T, but there is no artistry in that. The sign POST-PONE came to mind as I experimented with ways to negate DE-CIDE, because both signs have identical handshapes. To postpone is the antithesis of making an immediate decision, so it seemed an artful way of negating DECIDE. Because DECIDE may be trans-lated by such expressions as "to be resolute," "to come to a deci-sion," "to stand firm," and POSTPONE may be variously translated as "to put off," "to delay," "to procrastinate," the pair seemed to balance each other quite well. But it was artistically significant to me that I did not have to change the handshape to achieve these oppo-site meanings.

Something more was needed, however. Hamlet is obviously weighing which course of action to pursue, so I needed somehow to convey this, but I did not want to break the continuity of handshape in order to sign OR, and I also wanted to express it in a more subtle way. The solution was to face slightly left while signing DECIDE, then face slightly right while signing POSTPONE. This device is used in ASL to set up alternative choices. If the signer places a person, object, or event left of center, and another right of center, the observer knows that two different things are going to be compared or contrasted in some way.

Finally, I chose to use the sign WHICH rather than the sign OR (which really belongs to manually coded English) because the movement of WHICH resembled scales moving up and down as if weighing something, and thus it creates a stronger visual image. I altered the sign WHICH slightly so that the left hand is in the space where I signed DECIDE, and the right hand is in the space where POSTPONE was signed. So the sense of the signed line comes out, "To stand firm and to be resolved or to put off and procrastinate: which shall it be?"

My translation may not be the best, but it does illustrate the kinds of things one needs to consider when translating into artistic ASL. All along, the artistic translator must appeal to the eye. In our exam-ple there is symmetry in handshape and placement, and opposition in meaning. There is the weighing movement expressing doubt and question. The observer now knows that Hamlet is trying to make up his mind to do something, and the observer has been told this in a way that is different from everyday ASL conversational signing.

What about other forms of artistic signing? ASL poetry is very slowly developing. In November 1978, the first conference on ASL poetry was held at the University of Indiana at South Bend. It brought to light the efforts of some deaf and hearing poets to creat ASL poems. Many of the participants were inspired by this meeting to create more such poetry and perhaps soon we shall see the fruits of their work.

Deaf children are rarely encouraged to create ASL poetry. The emphasis in most schools is exclusively on the writing of English poetry. This places an unfortunate obstacle in the path of deaf children who have vivid imaginations but who have limited ability to express their thoughts in English.

The poetry of a spoken language is recognized as poetry because it deviates from the conventional style of everyday conversation in that language. In ASL poetry, the poet strives to use signs in ways that are different from the ways they are used in everyday conversation. The poet may attempt to create visual images by making signs fit into some sort of pattern, by distorting signs, and by creating new signs. The possibilities are as infinite as the imagination.

Here is an ASL poem I composed that illustrates a few ASL poetic devices. Throughout the poem, I use only one handshape, the "5" handshape, with all fingers spread; both hands are in motion all the time. I begin with CLOUD and then change it to depict "larger and stormier clouds," then to "light rain," then to "heavy downpour," using variations of the sign RAIN. Next the hand movements change into the sign WATER-FLOWING, first showing "small rivulets," then becoming a "raging torrent flowing over rapids," then changing into a "waterfall," and "whirling vortex," which then "flows out to sea," and becomes the sign OCEAN-WAVES. At first the waves suggested are small, then they become quite large. The hands next change to WIND, then EVAPORATE, and finally back to CLOUD, ending the poem. Although the hands remain in the 5 handshape, I do wiggle and bend the fingers from time to time. I think we might legitimately call this "poetic license."

This poem begins in the space above and to the right of the signer, moving downwards, then to the left, then to the space above and to the left of the signer, and finally back to where it all began. This added feature reinforces the signs, showing the rain and river images going downward, the flowing out to sea image moving to the left, the evaporation image moving upwards, and the cloud image floating from left to right. Furthermore, this adds a visual cycle to the whole presentation, which I call "The Wartercycle."

I have a naturally developed interest in artistic ASL, but my interest also stems from my desire to encourage deaf native ASL users to be proud of their language, and to enjoy it to its fullest. I know that many of them feel embarrassed by ASL because they have been conditioned to think of it as inferior to English, as an adulterated, watered-down version of English. I know this because I once felt the same way. If Bill Stokoe had not done what he did, I might still be feeling that way. I close this article with a quote from one of Bill's letters to me, which expresses my own feelings as well:

> I can hardly give up English now, but if I had to make a choice I would rather have the language and thought of a deaf man who is making it in the world than the language and thought of one of these teachers of the deaf who think that the only "straight" language is Miss Fitz's English.

Sign Language, Power, and Mental Health

by Raymond Trybus

What I present in this paper is really only a metaphor and symbol, a way to recall yet one more area in which Bill Stokoe has led the rest of us. For in this matter of Sign Language and mental health, Bill has opened the major highways and drawn the initial maps, as he has in so many other realms. We who come after him can pave and smooth, build secondary roads, and add the color coding to the maps, but the main features are already there.

Power and Significance in Mental Health

The major issue that I would like to discuss has been raised and studied by Bill Stokoe and his co-workers in a very broad and basic

Raymond J. Trybus, presently Dean of the Research Institute at Gallaudet College, received his Ph.D. in clinical psychology from St. Louis University in 1971. He has been involved in research, teaching, and clinical psychology services with deaf people since 1969, when he served as a psychologist for the Rehabilitation Program for the Deaf at the St. Louis Jewish Employment and Vocational Service. Since 1971, Ray has been at Gallaudet College, initially as a psychologist in the Counseling Center, later as a research psychologist and Director of the Office of Demographic Studies. His current interests include psychological and educational research related to deafness and deaf people, and activities in which these research interests are put into practice for the benefit of hearing and deaf people. Most people, with the occasional exception of his wife and children, believe his hearing to be normal.

way. Perhaps the best and simplest statement of this issue, however, can be found in Schlesinger (1978), who was building on earlier work by Coopersmith (1967): *power* and *significance* are major ingredients in self-esteem, and thus in mental health or well-being. Schlesinger takes the point of view that mental health is something more than the absence of mental illness. Instead, it is a condition of well-being which is related to a set of feelings about oneself, about the world, and about other people. A sense of one's power, that is, one's ability to influence and control others, is one of the major ingredients in Schlesinger's positive concept of mental health. Another major component is a sense of significance, which means the ability to obtain acceptance and affection from others simply because one exists.

Psychologists and psychiatrists, especially those who engage in clinical practice, look for the roots of well-being or of illness in an individual person's background and experiences in life. Certainly this is valuable and necessary, particularly for clinical purposes. However, I believe it is useful also to consider these same issues of power and significance on a collective or social basis. In other words, apart from any specific individual, what are the social conditions of deaf people's lives which provide them with the sense of power and significance needed for mental health and well-being? In this paper we shall look at social issues, at the position of deaf people as a group in contemporary society, and at ways in which the position of deaf people as a group affects the mental health and well-being of the individuals within the group. As we will see later in the paper, the language of a group, and the way in which that language is treated by the group itself and by others, is one of the most significant factors in the position of a group of people within society at large. Following the broad leads of Bill Stokoe, then, this paper will examine issues of the signed languages of Deaf communities, the communities' sense of power and significance, and consequently, the mental health and well-being of individuals within those communities.

The Meaning of Language in a Community

How much difference does a language really make to a community? Some historical examples show that it makes all the difference in the world. Kelman (1972) speaks of "individual and group needs for finding roots and a deep appreciation of the emotional, esthetic, and practical significance of a group's unique cultural products—

and particularly of its language—in confirming its sense of rooted-ness." Similarly, Fishman (1972) notes, "the view that a people's individuality resides in its language is very old . . . language has been regarded as a defining characteristic of a nationality, within the sphere of the Judeo-Christian tradition, since Biblical days." Fishman goes on to explain that a language has traditionally been considered one of the absolutely essential characteristics of a group which is trying to achieve recognition as a legitimate entity, as a nation. A language and a history, he says, are the two first needs of a people. In fact, he goes so far as to say that, "the essence of a nation-ality is its spirit, its individuality, its soul. This soul is not only re-flected and protected by the mother tongue but, in a sense, *the mother tongue is itself an aspect of the soul,* a part of the soul, if not the soul made manifest."

If a people's language is so central to its very being, then the loss of its language must be among the worst disasters that can befall it. This point of view has been held for a long time. Davies (1945, originally written in 1845) said:

> To impose another language on . . . a people is to send their history adrift . . . to tear their identity from all places . . . to lose your native tongue, and learn that of an alien, is the worst badge of conquest—it is the chain on the soul . . . a people without a language of its own is only half a nation. A nation should guard its language more than its territories—'tis a surer barrier, a more important frontier than fortress or river.

Many more examples could be presented. I think it is clear at this point, however, that communities of all sorts down through the ages have considered their language to be one of their major assets, and often their most precious possession.

Language Control as Power: External Forces

If a language is such an essential part of a community, then clearly the control of that language must be one of the major ways of control-ling the community and the individuals within it. To the degree that individuals define themselves as parts of such a community, control of the community constitutes control of the individuals who form that community. Control of a community through control of its language can occur from within a community or from outside of it. If control comes from outside, then the community and its members are sub-jected to external power, and will develop a corresponding sense of powerlessness themselves. On the other hand, to the degree that the control of a community through its language occurs within the community, the community and its members experience a feeling of self-direction, power, and significance in controlling their own destiny.

There has been considerable study of power and significance with respect to language, as these issues concern nations and the impact of nationalist movements throughout the world. O'Barr (1976) says, for example, "Those involved in the formulation and realization of language policies are quick to recognize the enormous power over people which stems from the ability to manipulate their language." It is not by accident that powerful or conquering groups down through the ages have sought, with varying degrees of success, to impose their own language on minority people. One of the prominent ways of enforcing such control of language is through the educational system, which forms and influences children during their most impressionable years. Leibowitz (1976) says directly:

> The thesis to be presented here is simple: language is primarily a means of control. I believe this proposition is generally true, as true as 'language is a means of communication' or 'language is a means of social intercourse' or the host of other definitions which come to the fore when language is discussed ... when politics and language relate most openly, we can see more clearly the use of language as a means of expressing power, as a way of controlling and manipulating people in society ... language designation was almost always coupled with restrictions on the use of other languages; it was also coupled with discriminatory legislation and practices in other fields ....

In reviewing the history of education in the United States, Leibowitz indicates that in the early years, official policy was mostly neutral on the issue of language of instruction in school, with large numbers of German language and other non-English language schools flourishing in the middle 1800's. He then shows that, beginning in the 1880's, there was a shift to a heavy emphasis on English in the schools and in official policy generally. This shift was part of a movement which was largely intended to exclude new immigrants from participation in schooling, voting, and a variety of other rights ot citizenship. As an example of this period, Leibowitz cites the establishment of boarding schools for American Indian children that were located off the reservations, and had instruction in English:

> The purpose of this school became clear in the succeeding decades: to separate the Indian child from his reservation and family, strip him of

his tribal lore and mores, emphasize industrial arts, and prepare him in such a way that he would never return to his people. Language became a critical element in this policy. English language instruction and abandonment of the native language became complementary means to the end.

Leibowitz concludes that this emphasis shifted again, beginning after World War II, to a new period of increasing tolerance of linguistic difference, and to some extent, even of encouragement of the use of languages other than English.

Language Control From Within: Language Planning

We have seen that a people's language is central and all-important, and that control of a people's language by outsiders is a disaster and a tragedy. And yet languages are living realities, not eternal, mystic entities. This fact leads to the need for what is called "language planning," which means the systematic development and expansion of a language to suit new times and circumstances, new challenges. When people are proud of their language, they try to ensure that it is used more and more widely. However, natural changes occur in all languages, as their users adapt to changing demands and to other languages used in the locale. Therefore, as a community takes charge of its language and attempts to promote its greater use, it is also setting forces in motion which will certainly change the language in a variety of ways.

But changes of this kind may be debasement of the original, "pure" strain of the revered language. One of the common problems when attempts are made to develop or rejuvenate a language, is that certain intellectually and culturally elite groups within the language community typically use an expanded and therefore "contaminated" version of the language. The language patterns used by such elite groups simultaneously define "high" culture and those who are its custodians. In the late 1700's, some of the leading scholars in Germany argued that their language had been debased because it included many foreign (especially French) expressions and constructions, when used by the educated people. They felt that to use such foreign expressions was to claim that the German language in its pure form was not capable of expressing learned and higher thoughts. Similar complaints have been made about many of the major languages as they incorporated words, expressions, and constructions borrowed from other languages.

Because languages are used by real people in real situations, new emphasis on the development and expanded use of a language is almost inevitably a part of a broader rearrangement of social roles and social structures. Therefore, the rejection of foreign borrowings in a language is also a rejection of the educated elite, who were the primary users and developers of such foreign borrowings. At a time of social upheaval, when the movement was to unseat the powerful and prestigious elite groups, and to place greater emphasis on the power of *all* the people, people frequently rejected the educated form of the language with its foreign borrowings, and called for a return to the purity of the language as it once was. In these situations, people frequently focused on studying the national language as it had been in the past, before foreign influences and models had begun to spoil the authentic linguistic heritage from past generations. More and more, then, the leaders of the community seeking to reestablish its authenticity would locate groups of users of the national language who have been least exposed to recent developments and foreign borrowings, and to define their usage of the language as the pure form, to which all members of the community should return. Many nationalist movements were therefore accompanied by extensive study of the national language as it had been used in the past, and as it is used in the present by those groups of people who have had the least contact with modernizing and therefore "corrupting" influences.

There is a significant contradiction here. On the one hand, those who are leading the community to a new self-definition and a new awareness of their own power emphasize the need to rediscover the "natural" and historic state of their language and attempt to return current linguistic practice to those roots. At the same time, as Fishman (1972) notes:

> The users of developing languages are particularly aware of their lexical shortcomings . . . the developing language is always relatively impoverished when it comes to the more abstract subtleties of imported or recently innovated higher learning and fashionable society. One sign of the development of the language is its growth in exactly these respects.

Within communities striving for self-definition and power, therefore, one can expect to see evidence of this contradiction. On the one hand, there is an emphasis on return to the pure sources of the community's language; on the other hand, there is a need to adapt and enrich the language to handle new social and intellectual needs which did not exist when the community's language originally developed.

Deaf Communities and Their Languages: Unique Communities

One of Stokoe's major contributions has been his convincing argument that deaf people can be usefully studied as linguistic and cultural communities, and not only as unfortunate victims with similar physical and sensory pathologies. This definition of deaf people as being those who belong to the Deaf community, the chief badge of which is the use of its own language, American Sign Language, is a view which is in substantial agreement with very ancient traditions. We saw, earlier in this paper, evidence of many historical parallels. It is clear, however, that the Deaf community is a different sort of entity than are most ethno-cultural communities. Although the Deaf community possesses its own language and other characteristics of such groups, it exists to a much greater extent as the result of "voluntary" affiliation rather than birthright. The most recent available information indicates that less than 3% of deaf children are descended from two deaf parents (Karchmer, Trybus, & Paquin, 1978). Only this tiny minority, whose parents are largely users of ASL, have ASL as a native language and are members of the Deaf ethno-cultural community as a matter of birthright. Extrapolating the figures obtained by Karchmer et al. to the national population, one would expect to find 2,200 to 2,500 deaf children in this situation. There is a larger, though still small, group of deaf children who have one hearing and one hearing impaired parent. This group constitutes 10% of the group studied by Karchmer, Trybus, and Paquin, and would suggest that there are about 7,500 such children nationally. However, the available data indicates that these families with one hearing and one hearing impaired parent are socially and culturally more similar to families with two hearing parents than they are to families with two deaf parents. The overwhelming majority of hearing impaired children, numbering approximately 65,000 nationwide, have two hearing parents. The vast majority of deaf people, therefore, have not had two deaf parents and could not therefore have ASL as a "native" language. Such persons have become members of the Deaf ethno-cultural community by a process of choices made over a lifetime. To say that this majority does not have ASL as a native language is not to imply that they do have English as a native language. The communication difficulties between deaf children and their parents are very well known, and it may well be that such individuals, or a large proportion of them at any rate, cannot be said to have any language as truly a native language. It is also true that a significant proportion of this majority may learn ASL fluently through peer interactions at school and elsewhere, and consider and use ASL as their "primary" language. The point is simply that the process of acquiring a primary language at age 4 or 6 or 8 from peers is not the same as the process of acquiring the language of one's parents from the day of birth.

What does it mean to call membership in the Deaf community "voluntary"? It does not mean that the choice to affiliate with the Deaf community is made easily or without significant influences and consequences. But it does suggest that the process of affiliating with the Deaf community is not identical with the process of becoming a member of the Black community, for example: that affiliation is given, not chosen, irrevocably from birth and even before. In the past, the choice to affiliate with the Deaf community was substantially influenced by attendance at special schools for deaf children. Even though many of these schools did not use Sign Language in instruction, they still provided a conducive social atmosphere in which the native ASL minority could, through peer influences, encourage the development of a "Deaf identity" and provide a ready replacement for the native language many deaf children never experienced. At present, however, the majority of deaf children do not attend such special schools, but receive their education in local public schools. At the same time, the large majority of those deaf children who have two deaf parents continue to attend the special schools for deaf children. Their peer influence of socializing deaf children into the Deaf community, therefore, is being limited to a smaller and smaller proportion of deaf children as time goes on. Although deafness imposes the need for a visual-gestural communication system and is not itself a matter of choice, as time goes on affiliation with the Deaf community will be more and more a matter of conscious choice during childhood, adolescence, or young adulthood.

Because deaf people do not belong to the Deaf community in the same automatic and irrevocable way that Black persons belong to the Black community, it is probably not surprising that the Deaf community has developed a sense of cohesiveness, power, and significance so slowly. This issue of "voluntary" affiliation, influenced by educational and childhood history, may also account largely for the multiplicity of schisms and internal disagreements over the very central feature of language. For example, consider the group which identifies itself as "oral deaf adults," and which makes rejection of the cultural language its defining characteristic. Consider also how a number of better educated deaf adults reacted to Stokoe's initial claim that ASL was an entire language of its own: "We do not use some foreign language, but use proper English in a form that is appropriate for our sensory capacities."

Deaf Communities and Their Languages: Parallels With History

Although deaf people form Deaf communities which are unique in many respects, let us see what the parallels are to the language situations in other national groups.

As Leibowitz indicated, the period since World War II has seen an increasing tolerance and even encouragement of linguistic differences in education and in society at large in the United States. Thus the current emergence of American Sign Language as an accepted and legitimate language of a cultural minority is one of many similar developments that fit into a background of increasing general tolerance of cultural and linguistic diversity in the United States. This is certainly a hopeful situation, since it indicates that the general social climate is likely to support, rather than hinder, the further emergence of the Deaf community and its American Sign Language as a legitimate and respected group.

It is clear that the current revitalization of interest in ASL is part and parcel of a broader "deaf power" movement, which is seeking expanded power, significance, and self-determination for members of the Deaf community. This closely accords with Fishman's finding that nationalist movements are usually accompanied by extensive periods of study and renewed interest in the language, literature, and culture of the emerging group. The work of Stokoe and the others who have followed thus parallels the work on French, German, Gaelic, Tagalog, and many other languages at comparably critical periods in the development of those national groups.

Considering Leibowitz's example of the boarding schools for American Indians, it is easy to see similarities in the schools for deaf children: separating the child from his family, eliminating identification with tribal customs, emphasizing industrial arts, and preparing them in such a way that they would never return to their people. In the schools for deaf children, as in the American Indian schools, language has been a critical element in this policy. However, because of the "voluntary" nature of affiliation with the Deaf community, this example cuts both ways, and has therefore generated significant emotion in two opposite directions. For those children who came from a native ASL background or who adopted this language early on, the school's emphasis on English and oral communication prevents or removes the child from identification with the Deaf community, its ways, and its language. At the same time, as these schools began to use Sign Language, or to the extent that signing flourished unofficially as a means of communication among the children, the vast majority of hearing parents could see the school as separating their deaf child from them, and enculturating him into a language and community which was not theirs.

And so, much of what we see occurring now with the Deaf community and its American Sign Language is the repetition, with relevant modifications, of processes that have occurred again and again at other times and in other places with other languages. This broader historical context does not belittle these processes, but gives us a perspective from which to view events as they pass before our lives.

What Will The Future Bring?

Looking back through this brief review of the place of language in political and nationalist movements, and making the appropriate "translations" from the struggles of nationalist groups to the struggle of Deaf communities within the United States and other countries, what can we expect to see in the years ahead as the recognition of Sign Language and the development of deaf awareness rapidly proceed? We will continue to see repeated expressions of the beauty, the grace, and the ingenuity of signed languages, as the unique expression of the particular "soul" of deaf individuals and Deaf communities. Because of the visual rather than auditory nature of signed languages, we will see expanded examinations of the ways in which knowledge about signed languages expands the human consciousness, understanding, and appreciation of the rich variety of human communication.

We can expect to see more emphasis on codifying and creating a history and folklore of deafness, as evidence that the Deaf community has a past, and that much of what is best in the past is conveyed and preserved in the signed languages used by Deaf communities. This has, in fact, already begun. At the 1975 meeting of the World

Federation of the Deaf in Washington, D.C., and subsequently at the 1977 Special Conference of the World Federation of the Deaf in Copenhagen which focused on families with deaf members, there was a call for the preservation through video-taping and filming of jokes and folktales of Deaf communities from around the world. More recently, Gallaudet College has requested and received a planning grant to consider developing an encyclopedia of deafness and deaf people. The parallels with nationalist movements in Europe and throughout the world are incredibly close.

We can expect to see continued studies of American Sign Language among those groups of users who have been the least influenced by contact with users of English. The study of these relatively isolated groups will be part of the process of documenting the language in its purest and least contaminated form. At the same time, the signed language of more educated communities where the contacts with the products of other cultures and in particular with the English language have been much more extensive and intense, will be described as a "pidgin" Sign Language (a term which often carries pejorative connotations), rather than as a blend or as a natural evolutionary step in the history of the language. We will see, and are seeing, an increasing emphasis on the use of the older, "more authentic" Sign Language, rather than signing as it has been modified by the natural process of interaction with hearing culture and spoken English. This can be expected to produce some confusing and potentially divisive issues, bearing in mind the "voluntary" nature of membership in the Deaf community, and the fact that the vast majority of deaf children cannot claim Sign Language as a native language. We can expect to see a particularly concerted effort to define American Sign Language in such a way as to exclude those borrowings from the English language which are seen as prostituting the soul of Sign, and as adopting the speech of the invader. At the same time, borrowings from other foreign signed languages will be welcomed as a more authentic means of enriching the language and shaping it into a vehicle for high culture, literary discourse, and international exchange.

As all of these developments occur in Sign Language itself, and as Deaf communities throughout the United States see themselves increasingly as communities worthy of respect and self-determination, we can expect to see deaf people increasingly viewing themselves as having power and significance in the world, both as individuals and as collective groups.

Sign Language, Power, and Mental Health

And what has all of this to do with mental health? As I indicated at the beginning of this paper, a major element in mental health or well-being is a sense of self-esteem, a sense that one has some control over one's life and destiny; and a sense of power and significance is a major component of the feeling of self-esteem. Although psychologists and other mental health practitioners have traditionally looked within the individual for the sources of health or illness, and have focused on the internal psychic transactions of an individual, it is becoming more and more clear that both biological and social determiners have a major impact on the psychic state of the individual. We shall pass over the question of biological determiners for the present; our interest here is in the social determiners.

Epidemiological studies in the past, and careful attention to the mental health needs of ethno-cultural minorities more recently, have emphasized again and again that the relative status, power, and prestige of a group of persons within society at large has a major impact on the mental health and well-being of individuals within the group. Therefore, mental disturbance, depression, and the like are more often found among economically disadvantaged groups and among others who have at least partially internalized societal evaluations of themselves as inferior in one or more ways to the societal norm or ideal. As a group breaks out of its disadvantaged status and achieves societal power and recognition, mental disturbances within individuals decrease correspondingly.

A case study may give one example of how this dynamic may be expected to operate among deaf persons. Among the patients with whom I worked clinically some years ago was a young deaf woman who complained of anxiety and nervousness about the future, and an inability to make personal vocational decisions or progress. As our initial sessions probed into this problem, the young woman began to explain that a major component of her difficulties was that, as a result of her deafness, she was unable to comprehend or follow instructions in the English language. This, she indicated, meant that she was unable to profit from reading instructional and self-development manuals in her vocational specialty of accounting, as well as in a variety of other areas. For example, she could not understand written materials on the basic workings of automobiles and thus could not diagnose and remedy minor difficulties with her own car. In the course of our discussions, she acknowledged frequently that she was very fluent and respected as a master of Sign Language, and was in constant demand as a teacher and tutor of signing. However, she dismissed this as "kid stuff," and indicated that all that really mattered in life was the ability to perform linguistically in English. What became more and more apparent as our sessions continued was that her English language abilities were in fact very adequate. By all the formal and informal measures I was able to devise, she was perfectly able to read, understand, write, and speak perfectly grammatical, idiomatic English. There was, in fact, not the slightest factual basis for her complaint of inadequacy in English. It finally became clear that the source of the difficulty was that she had internalized a message which she had heard frequently during her years growing up: deaf persons depended for success on their mastery of English, but that at the same time deaf persons were very unlikely to be able to master the English language. At the same time, she dismissed her competence in American Sign Language as of secondary importance at best, as a kind of "crutch" for those benighted souls like herself who were unable to achieve mastery in the *proper* language, that is, English. This young woman's difficulty, in other words, was at root a deficiency in her sense of power and significance as a deaf person, which expressed itself most pointedly in her complaints of linguistic inability. God alone knows how many other deaf persons, to one or another degree, have experienced comparable feelings of personal failure, frustration, and inadequacy, with little or no factual basis for their self-deprecations. This is one of the clearest examples I know of the potential mental health consequences of a lack of power and significance, as symbolized linguistically. It is a situation which I expect to diminish rapidly and then disappear as Deaf communities struggle for and begin to achieve self-determination and linguistic self-respect.

Such effects to not occur automatically, of course. Several actions which can be taken by special education programs for deaf children and by their families may reduce and eliminate the kind of psychic situation described in the example. For one, school programs and school personnel will need to keep in mind a clear distinction among interpersonal communication, Sign Language, and English language. As for the two languages, it is entirely possible for children to learn both Sign Language and English, just as children in many other bilingual situations learn two languages side by side. Implied in the very meaning of learning a language is that there are beginning and intermediate steps which occur prior to full mastery of the intricacies of the languages. Therefore, deaf children learning Sign Language, English, or both, will by the very nature of things acquire each language over a period of time, and will therefore use neither language in its full and perfectly grammatical form during the developmental period. It is even probable that the rate of linguistic development will not be equal in the two languages, and therefore parents and teachers need to be aware of the child's developmental level in each of the languages. Equally important is remembering that *human communication is not limited to any language.* The need of children at all ages to communicate with their parents, their peers, and their teachers must take precedence over their learning of any and all languages. None of the people in the deaf child's environment can afford to focus so exclusively on language development, whether Sign Language or English, as to require that communications with the child be in a grammatical form appropriate to either of the languages in its finished adult form. Human communication includes action, demonstration, gesture, facial expression, body language, and the like. While learning to speak and learning to sign are both of great importance, neither must be permitted to stand in the way of free and easy interpersonal communication, occurring by whatever means.

A second major consideration for parents and teachers is that deaf children have some sense that there are others who are "deaf like me." Whether or not the child tends to identify with a Deaf community, and regardless of whether the child's parents and teachers do or do not wish to see the child identify with a Deaf community, it should be made possible for the child to know that there are Deaf communities and deaf persons of all ages who identify with these communities. The point is that the child should know that there are many ways of being human, many ways of being a deaf human, and that the mastery of the English language desired by hearing parents and teachers is not the only route to success, self-determination, and self-esteem. Certainly deaf children should learn to master English and feel proud of their accomplishment in doing so. Just as certainly, they should not be led to feel that this is the only accomplishment worthy of them, or the only accomplishment which matters.

At the same time that we expect developments in Sign Language to improve some of the basic conditions for the mental health and well-being of deaf persons, we can expect the very same process to create increasing difficulties in the technical process of providing psychotherapeutic and psychodiagnostic services to deaf persons. As members of the Deaf community gain an increasing sense of power and significance, they are likely to become increasingly critical of mental health services provided by practitioners who know little or nothing of the culture and language of the Deaf community. Deaf clients are likely to increasingly demand that practitioners substantially improve their understanding of the culture of deafness and their Sign Language ability as an emblem of that understanding. This can be expected to be much like the rejection by Black Americans of services provided by white therapists. These therapists did not have, or did not seem to have, sufficient appreciation of the Black life experience, as revealed in the therapists' inability to understand or to "talk Black," This may result in hard times ahead, since studies such as those of Levine (1974) have indicated again and again that the large majority of mental health practitioners working with deaf clients are hearing persons who rate themselves as having very minimal competence in Sign Language. Presumably, the evaluation by deaf clients of such practitioners' competence will show an even more dismal picture. What we can expect to see ahead, then, is increasing criticism and rejection of mental health services offered to deaf clients by hearing practitioners so removed from the Deaf ethno-cultural community as to be considered simply foreigners. These practitioners, in turn, can be expected to respond with resentment, confusion, and some bitterness, when their attempts to be of service are rebuffed or criticized by their actual or potential clients. There are, of course, a few deaf clinicians now in practice, for whom the issue of familiarity and identification with the Deaf ethno-cultural community should not present the same problem faced by hearing practitioners. This is not to suggest that all deaf clinicians are therefore competent or successful, but simply to indicate that their membership in the Deaf community should reduce the significant issues to those of competence, without the additional difficulties of social identity and affiliation.

What can be done about this state of affairs? A number of very useful directions are suggested in the excellent paper by Stokoe and Battison (1975), in which they offer several specific examples of how communication between patient and therapist can be misinterpreted because of differences between the hearing culture and English language of therapists and the Deaf culture and Sign Language of the clients. The remedy to this situation is, in many ways, obvious. On the one hand, native signers and members of the Deaf community should have access to the training programs in which they can acquire professional credentials in psychology, psychiatry, and other mental health fields. On the other hand, hearing professionals in these fields who wish to serve deaf clients effectively will need training programs which focus heavily on understanding the cultural and linguistic patterns of the clients they propose to serve. Doing either of these in practice is, of course, not an easy matter.

The future, then, of Sign Language and the mental health of deaf persons is not entirely rosy or without difficulties. However, thanks to the "nationalist" feeling developing among deaf people in the United States and elsewhere, the future can be expected to be productive. To change from a past in which not all has been well to a more productive future means that a variety of circumstances and relationships must change. Such changes are by definition disruptive and very often difficult for the parties involved. Fishman (1972) offers us this plea for understanding: "This is happening again today. It will happen again in the future. It is part of the social drama of humanity. Would that we could help it happen with less wear and tear and with more mutual acceptance among all concerned."

References

Coopersmith, C. *The Antecedents of Self-Esteem.* San Francisco: W. H. Freeman & Co., 1967.

Davies, T. *Essays and Poems With a Centenary Memoir: 1845.* Dublin: Gill, 1945.

Fishman, J. *Language and Nationalism: Two Integrative Essays.* Rowley, Massachusetts: Newbury House Publishers, 1972.

Karchmer, M., Trybus, R., & Paquin, M. Early Manual Communication, Parental Hearing Status, and the Academic Achievement of Deaf Students. Paper presented to the American Educational Research Association, Toronto, Ontario, Canada, April 1978.

Kelman, M. Introduction. In Fishman, J. *Language and Nationalism: Two Integrative Essays.* Rowley, Massachusetts: Newbury House Publishers, 1972.

Leibowitz, A. Language and the Law: The Exercise of Political Power Through Official Designation of Language. In O'Barr, W., & O'Barr, J. (Eds.) *Language and Politics.* The Hague: Mouton & Co., 1976.

Levine, E. Psychological Tests and Practices With the Deaf: A Survey of the State of The Art. *Volta Review,* 1974, 76, 298–319.

O'Barr, W. The Study of Language and Politics. In O'Barr, W., & O'Barr, J. (Eds.) *Language and Politics.* The Hague: Mouton & Co., 1976.

Schlesinger, H. Mental Health and Deafness. *Gallaudet Today,* 1978, *9(1)*, 14–18.

Stokoe, W., & Battison, R. Sign Language, Mental Health, and Satisfactory Interaction. To appear in E. Mindel & L. Stein (Eds.) *Deafness and Mental Health.* New York: Grune & Stratton.

V
SIGN LANGUAGES IN OTHER COUNTRIES

The Social Movement
Surrounding French Sign
Language

by Bernard Mottez and Harry Markowicz

Bernard Mottez, Senior Researcher at the Centre National de la Recherche Scientifique (National Center for Scientific Research), is a sociologist associated with the Centre d'Etude des Mouvements Sociaux (Center for the Study of Social Movements) in Paris. Following his studies in philosophy, he received a doctorate in sociology in 1963. For many years, he studied labor movements and also spent 18 months in Chile as visiting professor at the Faculdad Latino Americana de Ciencias Sociales (The Latin American University of Social Sciences) and working with the Ministry of Labor. From 1968 to 1975 he studied problems relating to alcoholism and to handicaps in general. In 1975, after meeting Harry Markowicz in Paris, he visited Gallaudet College and attended the World Congress of the Deaf in Washington, D.C. Since then he has been doing research on the sociology of deafness.

Harry Markowicz is a sociolinguist, also at the Centre d'Etude des Mouvements Sociaux in Paris. He first became interested in signed languages in 1969 while teaching French and pursuing an M.A. in applied linguistics at Simon Fraser University in Vancouver, Canada. From 1973 to 1976, he worked in the Linguistics Research Laboratory at Gallaudet College. Harry is working toward his doctorate in sociolinguistics at Georgetown University and is studying the problems of Deaf people as an ethnic group. With Bernard Mottez, he co-edits a French language newsletter, Coup d'Oeil, *which publishes news about Sign Language research, publications, congresses, artistic productions, and related matters.*

This chapter is based on a research report titled "Integration ou droit à la difference: Les consequences d'un choix politique sur la structuration et le mode d'existence d'un groupe minoritaire, les sourds." ("Integration or the right to be different: The consequences of a political choice on the structure and way of life of a minority group, the deaf.") CORDES, 1979. The project was supported by CORDES grant no. 103/76.

221

Introduction

In this paper we discuss a social movement that is beginning to
gather force in France: a movement to recognize French Sign Language (FSL) as a language, and to change social policies and social
institutions to incorporate this point. Although the story begins in the
last century among educators of the deaf, the fate of French Sign
Language is not currently being decided in the schools; it is in the
hands of deaf people themselves.

A black marker in the collective memory of deaf people, the Congress of Milan (1880) is inevitably brought up, to the point of becoming tiresome, whenever the status of Sign Language is discussed.
The period preceeding the Congress is said to be the Golden Era
when Sign Language had a place of honor. After the Congress, presumably Sign Language became oppressed and stigmatized, and
thus started to degenerate. It is true, of course, that during the earlier
period, Sign Language and deaf culture reached some great mo-
ments. But since the language was not recorded, it is no longer ac-
cessible to us. Its treasures left their mark only in the memory of
those who participated in it. Several generations separate us from
that time.

While Sign Language was used in the schools during the period
before the Congress, it was never triumphant. Sign Language was
under constant attack. The Congress of Milan happened to be a more
decisive battle. That Congress put an end to a century of pedagogical
quarrels about the choice between what was called the pure oral
method (oralism) and the mixed method (total communication). It
ended with the shout "Viva la parola!" (Long live speech!). One
speaks of methods, but what triumphed in Milan is a clear statement
of the objectives of deaf education. Speech had previously been one
of several methods, but it became the only one. It was elevated from
a "means" to an "end", the ultimate goal where education was concerned and the necessary "passport" for access to the general culture. Deaf people of the time saw their famous institutions of learning transformed into "speech clinics."

The consequences were brutal in France. In the schools, the incoming deaf children were taught separately from the older generations. To prevent contamination, no contact of any kind was allowed
between them. When the last students who were educated with Sign
Language had graduated, the deaf teachers were dismissed from
their jobs. This was done to prevent them from perpetuating Sign

Language, a "shameful anomaly" that was expected to die out soon. The fanaticism did not end there; books on Sign Language were thrown out of the library of the National Institute for the Deaf in Paris. Disillusionment with these actions started a decade later. However, the objectives established earlier were not challenged. A simple criterion had been found for judging the quality of a school. A school was valued highly if little "gesturing" went on. Essentially, it is still the criterion used today!

The Movement

More recent events help us understand the current picture. The 6th Congress of the World Federation of the Deaf, held in Paris in 1971, caused many educators to question their position on Sign Language. Total communication had begun to spread in the U.S., and the participants were impressed by the American interpreters. Was it really posssible to say everything with the hands? Even abstract things?

However, after the 6th Congress in Paris, most people were preoccupied with a new law effecting the education of the handicapped, early detection of deafness, pre-school education, and the problem of integration (mainstreaming). Those who favored integration took an outright position against Sign Language. To ask that it be used in the schools seemed to them like a throw-back to the dark ages. After all, a way had finally been found to make *all* deaf people talk! The idea of using Sign Language in the schools was not even worth considering. The deaf people who spoke up in its favor were ignored, in the way one ignores old fashioned people or those who are too naive to know what they are talking about.

On the other hand, the 7th Congress in Washington in 1975 was a shock for all the French participants. It convinced those who had been swayed by the Paris Congress and it shook up those least ready to be convinced. Sign Language seemed to have its place under the sun in the United States and the consequences were clearly observable.

Only those few who had close contacts with linguists and progressive members of the deaf intellectual milieu realized that the situation in the United States was not quite as clear as it appeared. The real battles for the recognition of American Sign Language (ASL) were only beginning. At the time, artificial sign codes for English were triumphant in the schools and in Sign Language courses for parents. While they used some signs borrowed from ASL, most Americans were still a long way from recognizing ASL as a language.

The Congress in Washington hastened what the Congress in Paris only suggested: French Sign Language could have a status like that obtained by deaf people in other countries for their signed languages. Around the same period, articles favoring Sign Language began to appear in some publications. Until then, any mention of Sign Language had always been disparaging. But the recognition of a language cannot be based on lip service alone, and cannot consist merely of a more tolerant attitude towards it. It must be realized in facts and in institutional changes. In late 1975, things began to change. A national television network began a weekly news program for deaf and hard-of-hearing people. Thus, Sign Language made its appearance on the TV screens. A committee was set up by the Confederation Nationale des Sourds de France (the French National Association of the Deaf) to study the problems of communication, including the concept of "total communication."

These were important changes, surely. But when we started our research project in November 1976, it seemed to us that three criteria would have to be met before we could say that French Sign Language (FSL) is recognized as a language:

1. It must not be banished from the schools for the deaf, neither by law nor tradition.
2. There must be places where those who feel the need or simply the desire to learn it, can do so.
3. A professional corps of interpreters must be available.

At that time none of these three conditions existed in Franch and they appeared only as long term objectives.

These three conditions may be accompanied by other transformations. On the one hand, they reflect self-assertion and development of the deaf culture, and on the other hand, a greater participation by deaf people in the social and cultural life of the society at large. Contrary to what is sometimes assumed, these two developments are not mutually exclusive: they are the two faces of the same coin.

There are other consequences of recognizing a signed language as a language.

- The development of Sign Language linguistic research;
- The expansion of artistic creations (theatre, poetry, films, visual music, etc.) that are characteristics of the deaf culture, not only for internal consumption, but for the general community;

- the possibility of interaction between parents of deaf children and deaf adults, and consequently, between the young and adult deaf;
- Deaf people gaining control over the institutions which concern them (e.g., the schools);
- A higher level of education for deaf people;
- A greater access for deaf people to university studies, continuing education, and to information in general;
- Access to professions from which they were previously barred, in particular, teaching.

While Sign Language remains unrecognized, deaf people tend to have only utilitarian contacts with hearing people—their families, employers, colleagues at work, and professional workers in deafness. With the recognition of Sign Language comes an expansion of relations with various hearing individuals who are not motivated by a desire to "help" but simply by interest, curiosity and friendship.

Information and Planning

One indication of this latent interest in Sign Language was the large number of requests for scientific information we started receiving as soon as we undertook our research project. The same questions came up continuously. Is it a real language? What about abstractions? Is it possible to be precise? Does it have a grammar? Doesn't it vary from region to region? Shouldn't it be codified and enriched?

Answering these questions in person and by mail became monotonous and time-consuming. We decided to begin a publication and a public forum. In January 1977, *Coup d'Oeil*, a French-language newsletter that reported on Sign Language activities was born. The first issue announced a monthly seminar on "Sign Language and the Deaf Community." For the next two years, we ran this seminar at the Ecole des Hautes Etudes en Sciences Sociales (School of Advanced Studies in Social Sciences), with which our Laboratory is affiliated.

In this seminar series, we began to present the major American research on ASL, which had been totally ignored in France. This provided a perspective to view FSL, one which contrasted sharply with the prevailing attitudes in France at that time. Several outside speakers were invited to make presentations: William Stokoe, on sabbatical in Great Britain at the time; Carol Padden, formerly of the Linguistics Research Laboratory at Gallaudet; Tom Humphries, then professor of English at Gallaudet; Shelley Lawrence, an interpreter at California State University at Northridge; and René Préneau, French psychologist and expert in the history of the education of deaf people. The participation of deaf people was made possible by Bill Moody, an American interpreter residing in France, who served as an FSL interpreter. It was the first and still is the only seminar in a French university to be interpreted.

We had hoped that the participants in the seminar would begin to make waves around them. They did, because they represented the whole scale of involvement in deafness: from deaf people and parents of deaf children to professionals, including specialists working with deaf people (teachers, speech therapists, interpreters) and researchers (linguists, psychologists). Perhaps it was no coincidence that the seminar included some of the individuals who later became the vanguards in the battle for the recognition of FSL! The following innovations can be attributed to them: the first bilingual (FSL-French) kindergarden class; a bi-weekly TV program in which fairy tales are told in FSL for deaf and hearing children; planning an interpreters association; the establishment of the Academie de la Langue des Signes Française—and many others. The Academie de la Langue des Signes Française (Academy of French Sign Language) is one of several new associations which were created to propagate Sign Language. Others include the Socio-Cultural Center of the Deaf in the Chateau de Vincennes, the Association Ferdinand Berthier in Bordeaux, and the national association "Deux Langues pour une Education." These associations consist mostly of deaf people with a few hearing members. Their activities include teaching FSL, linguistic analysis of that language, preparing dictionaries of signs, and organizing social activities with parents of deaf children and others interested in meeting deaf adults.

The initial model for our newsletter, *Coup d'Oeil*, was William Stokoe's newsletter, *Signs for our Times*. Like him we chose a pun, or play on words, for our title. Curiously, people generally focus on the ear when they have to find a title, a label, or an insignia for deafness. We wanted our title to reflect what seemed obvious to us: the eyes, their expression and their observations characterize deaf people, not the ears. We settled on *Coup d'Oeil*, because it includes the French word for "eye" (oeil) and translates as a "quick look" or a "glance." This title suited our objectives: to give short news items, and at the same time cast an eye on everything related to Sign Language.

Coup d'Oeil announces and reports on Sign Language conferences and meetings, and gives accounts of relevant research projects, books, and articles. New Sign Language courses in France and in neighboring countries are announced, as well as TV programs and artistic productions which use Sign Language. The information focuses on France, but the U.S., Denmark, Sweden, and Great Britain also receive a lot of coverage, because of the many innovations in those countries. Correspondents provide information about Sign Language developments in about 20 different countries.

Like the seminar, the initial purpose of *Coup d'Oeil* was to economize: to provide information which was sought by numerous individuals in different parts of France. But demands for information increased and subsequently *Coup d'Oeil* took on a new role; it became a catalyst.

FSL was not considered a language when we started *Coup d'Oeil*. However, the newsletter soon began to have a surprising impact on the status of FSL in France simply by reporting that linguists in several countries studied signed languages, published books and articles based on their analyses, and held national and international academic meetings regularly where this research is presented and discussed by scholars.

We reported on all the projects and experiments related to Sign Language teaching, research, interpreting, education, and artistic endeavors. By becoming known through *Coup d'Oeil*, these activities gained legitimacy and encouraged others to pursue projects themselves. The chronicle of events in *Coup d'Oeil* gave the movement for the recognition of FSL a visibility, and many other people began to take it seriously. We ourselves initiated various public events: showing video-tapes made in Sign Language; workshops on non-verbal communication as a Sign Language base; lectures on the linguistics of Sign Language, deaf pride, interpreting, and continuing education. Many of the speakers were American specialists passing through Paris, including Joe Castronovo, Linda Donnels, Gil Eastman, Barbara Kannapell, Harlan Lane, and William Stokoe. Speaking engagements were planned in Belgium and in France for Dr. Hilde Schlesinger, a well-known authority in early education of deaf children and mental health. Carol Padden and Tom Humphries lectured their way through five French cities where the Sign Language movement had been the most active. Wherever they spoke, these deaf professionals had a tremendous impact, particularly on the deaf people in the audiences who discovered that their language could be taken seriously.

Last but not least, we organized one-month training sessions for French people in cooperation with Gallaudet College, through its School for Continuing Education and its International Center for Deafness. During the Summer of 1978 and again in 1979, a total of 69 deaf and hearing French people discovered at Gallaudet College the possibility of a different kind of relationship between deaf and hearing people, one based on mutual respect.

The program gave the participants an overview of the lastest developments concerning deafness, including all levels of education, continuing education, interpreting, psychiatric services, TV programs, etc. Considerable time was alloted to learn FSL, to work with Gil Eastman on nonverbal communication, and to learn about Sign Language linguistics. William Stokoe, his colleagues in the Linguistics Research Lab, and other visiting linguists provided this information. These summer sessions were planned for those who wanted to see for themselves and bring back whatever was relevant to French problems and issues. One indication of their success is that a group of deaf and hearing people who participated are now planning a similar session to be held in France for the first time.

Considering the changes in attitudes towards Sign Language over these past few years, where is the movement for the recognition of FSL today? How close are we in France to the three minimal conditions we established earlier: Sign Language teaching, interpreting, and Sign Language in the schools?

Sign Language Teaching

The first Sign Language course in France began in November 1976. Half official, half clandestine, it was held weekly at the Institut National of Paris, the school founded by l'Abbé de l'Epée's successor, l'Abbé Sicard. It was soon followed by others in Paris and in the provinces. Deaf adults were trained to teach by Bill Moody, and began teaching FSL in the Socio-Cultural Center of the Deaf at the Chateau de Vincennes. Graduates of his rigorous and imaginative program also teach at the Institut National and other places in the Paris area. Moody was also instrumental in setting up several classes in the provinces, and in neighboring Belgium. The number of French cities that offer Sign Language has grown to about twenty. While they are sometimes held in schools, they almost never have official approval.

A few Sign Language teachers are hearing people whose parents are deaf, but the majority are deaf themselves. The courses are not linked to any pedagogical project to use Sign Language in the schools. The classes are usually conducted without speaking a word. The objective is communication between deaf and hearing people, not the education of deaf people. The participants are primarily parents and speech therapists.

To find deaf people who are willing to teach Sign Language in their spare time has been difficult; the recruitment of new teachers has not kept up with the increasing demand for Sign Language classes. Their reticence may be due partly to their inexperience as teachers, the lack of teaching materials and methodology, as well as the unavailability of training, except at the Chateau de Vincennes. Some deaf people also seem to "exclude" the Sign Language teachers, as if it was wrong to reveal their language to ousiders. This feeling reflects the prevailing relations between deaf and hearing people.

With each new class comes the question of which signs to teach. Regional varieties of FSL were initially considered to be a problem, however, it later became the rule to teach the signs normally used by the teacher. The other major kind of variation, the continuum of sign varieties between FSL and signed French, was not perceived as a problem. William Stokoe has noted that when Sign Language is oppressed and deaf people begin to defend their language, they usually argue for a manual representation of the country's spoken language. They often consider only that version of signing worthy to teach. This seems to be the case in France; most classes teach a kind of signing that is close to the "signed French" end of the continuum. A few teachers, in particular those who have been exposed to linguistics or to Gil Eastman's workshop at Gallaudet, will teach varieties of signing closer to FSL.

We have observed two unexpected benefits of these Sign Language classes. First, hearing and deaf people are meeting outside of the usual paternalistic patterns—deaf people are teaching hearing people—second, because of new relationships developing with hearing people, deaf people often want to improve their knowledge of French and to find out what it is like on the "outside."

Interpreting

The interpreting situation in France today is roughly the same as in most countries around the world. Hearing children, usually the first-born, are weighed down with the responsibility of interpreting for their parents in their dealings with government services, businessmen, doctors, etc. Other deaf people depend on volunteer interpreters who are known in the community, usually hearing people who have deaf parents, or teachers or chaplains. They may also interpret at meetings and congresses where both deaf and hearing people participate.

For the professional interpreter who works according to the ethical code of his or her profession, the ways of the volunteer interpreters appear outrageous. They may not be familiar with interpreting techniques, or they may not even know Sign Language well. However, it is their attitudes toward deaf people in the interpreting situation which causes indignation. These interpreters often overstep their role of interpreter to adopt a paternalistic attitude. Instead of interpreting everything and providing a communication link, they decide themselves what is important, and give only a summary. Rather than simply interpreting, they explain, they comment, they intervene, and they act as lawyers, counselors, or even specialists in human relations.

This way of going beyond the role of interpreter cannot be attributed entirely to the fact that they are volunteers, or to the family ties between the interpreter and the deaf person. Both the deaf and hearing participants in the exchange often expect the interpreter to function this way. Sometimes the deaf person expects to be advised or counselled by the interpreter. Conversely, the hearing person may also depend on the interpreter for information or advice. Under these conditions, it is difficult to resist acting as an advisor.

Interpreting is beginning to be established in police stations and courts in France. In these situations, communication is considered important. The deaf person must be able to explain himself, to understand the explanations of others, and to understand the decision of the court when it concerns him. For all of France, only a handful of interpreters are recognized by the courts. They must fit their interpreting duties around their regular occupations of teachers, office employees, or technicians. In addition, judges tend to suspect defendants of faking deafness. This suspicion is sometimes reflected in a negative attitude of the courts toward the interpreter.

The interpreting situation may improve in the near future. A special issue of *Coup d'Oeil* (no. 10) focused on this problem to create more sensitivity to the needs of deaf people. While the status of FSL in these past few years has become an extremely controversial issue, especially where schools or television are concerned, everyone seems to agree that we must create a professional corps of interpreters. Interpreters have formed an association with the support of the Ministry of Health. They are still trying to define their roles and objectives. If their activities increase the number of qualified interpreters who are able to observe a rigorous code of ethics, they will make a positive change in the lives of deaf people in France.

Signing in the Schools

Our optimism about Sign Language teaching and interpreting cannot be applied to the attempt to use Sign Language in schools for deaf children. The problem first arose in the schools, and no doubt the schools will be the last place where it will be resolved. Some teachers claim to be in favor of Sign Language but blame the parents' expectations and the directives from the Ministry for their inaction. However, the parents' expectations may have been poorly interpreted, in particular because they do not know what a "bilingual education" would involve. This information is never given to them.

The majority of schools for deaf students are under the Ministry of Health. During these past few years, the Ministry has made some rather important decisions. The first, in December 1976, gave deaf people the right to become teachers in private schools. They had previously been excluded from teaching deaf children because of their own deafness. The second decision, in 1977, added an introduction to Sign Language to the training program of the future teachers of deaf children at the four National Institutes.

The first two hearing impaired individuals to be accepted in the teacher program are now taking part in an experiment with Sign Language involving a whole school. It is a school for multiply handicapped deaf students, most of whom are considered to be mentally retarded. The first official experiments are generally reserved for these special cases. In addition to several clandestine experiments, there are a few more semi-official experiments, but in all their number is quite limited.

The current big problem is a recent law that will make all the schools for deaf students depend on the Ministry of Education; more specifically, it will attempt to integrate all the deaf students among hearing students. Previous experiences in France and in other countries have shown the major problems associated with such a proposal to integrate. However, on the positive side, the presence of Sign

Language in these schools may, as it has done elsewhere, incite the hearing students to become interested in learning Sign Language.

Conclusion

It seems to us that the main characteristic of the situation in France is the contrast between the grass-roots efforts in favor of Sign Language, and the indifference and lack of initiatives of the schools. The most significant event in France is the development of unofficial Sign Language courses over the past three years. There are several curious consequences of this situation. For instance, almost all the Sign Language teachers are themselves deaf, and most are native signers who have limited education. As a result, unlike other countries where signing has been introduced in the schools, there have been no attempts yet to create artificial sign codes for the French language. While this reflects the current lack of interest in introducing signs in the educational system, it is a positive factor in the battle for the recognition of French Sign Language as a language.

While some courses tend to teach signs that accompany spoken French, in other courses deaf teachers attempt to teach FSL. Contact with American linguistics has made them aware that FSL is a real language. Lectures by Carol Padden and Barbara Kannapell, as well as other linguists from the Linguistics Research Laboratory at Gallaudet College, were successful in supporting that point. It is our hope that by the time signing is introduced in the schools, FSL will be so well established that it will be possible to consider true bilingual and bicultural education. This will require the active participation in the schools of those who pioneered the teaching of Sign Language—deaf people themselves.

The Renaissance of British Sign Language

by Mary Brennan and Allan B. Hayhurst

Introduction

Four hundred years ago, during the lifetime of William Shakespeare, a great debate was taking place on the worthiness and adequacy of the English language. Before that time, most of the important work in religion and philosophy, for example, had been written in Latin or Greek, and it was assumed that it was impossible to express abstract ideas and complex thought in English. Seen from the perspective of the twentieth century, this seems incredible.

Mary Brennan is currently a Lecturer in Linguistics at the Moray House College of Education in Edinburgh, Scotland, and Principal Investigator of a research project on British Sign Language. Her Bachelor and Master degrees are in English, Philosophy, and Linguistics. During the past seven years, she has taught courses on language development and linguistics for teachers of deaf students and more recently, for social workers who work with deaf people. Her research interests include syntax in British Sign Language and the linguistic abilities of deaf children in schools that use a Total Communication approach to education.

Allan B. Hayhurst is General Secretary of the British Deaf Association, based in Carlisle, England. After an early involvement in commerce and accountancy, his life has been concerned with community work with deaf people—for which he was honoured by the Queen in 1967. He became a principal officer of the BDA in 1951 and one of his main interests has been to promote the use of Sign Language among educators of deaf children in the United Kingdom. He developed the Communication Skills Programme of the BDA, helped to produce the book on Gestuno (published by the British Deaf Association in 1975), and will soon publish a long-awaited dictionary of British signs.

Today English is the first language of hundreds of millions of people all over the world. It is a language widely used in international affairs and in the circulation of scientific and technical information. Yet in the sixteenth century, many writers regarded English as inadequate and inelegant. In fact, the word that was frequently used was "barbarous" and writers used a number of equally derogatory words such as "vulgar," "rude," "without logic," and "cruel" to expound their views.

One of the greatest controversies concerned the translation of the Bible into English: many authors thought that to translate the Bible into such a "primitive, wild" language was nothing short of blasphemy. However, the comments of St. Thomas More on this matter seem to be true not just for the English of 400 years ago, but also for the Sign Language used by the British deaf today:

> That our language is called barbarous is but a fantasy, for so is, as every learned man knoweth, every strange language to any other. And though they would call it barren of words, there is no doubt that it is plenteous enough to express our minds in anything whereof one man hath used to speak with another.

St. Thomas More's words are echoed today by linguists who have examined previously unstudied languages (including signed languages) and non-standard dialects of languages. Because such languages are unfamiliar and "strange" to those who do not know them, it is automatically assumed that they are inadequate and primitive. William Labov, an American linguist who has studied the language of Black Americans, has said that prejudice against certain nonstandard dialects is caused by "ignorance of basic facts about human language and the people who speak it." This is exactly the case with the visual/gestural communication system used by the deaf community. While so-called experts on deaf education or deaf welfare remain ignorant and uninformed about the nature and function of Sign Language, the prejudice against this language will continue. So long as the general public, the vast hearing world, remains ignorant and uninformed about Sign Language and manual communication, the prejudice against Sign Language and against deaf people themselves will continue. When we change people's attitudes toward the language of deaf people, we change people's attitude toward deaf people themselves: in acknowledging the rightful status of the communication of deaf people, we are achieving a recognition of the rights and dignity of the whole deaf community.

At long last the battle to counteract ignorance about Sign Language has begun. In Britain at the moment, we are seeing remarkable developments in the awareness and understanding of the structure and functioning of the Sign Language used by the deaf population. Of course, ignorance about British Sign Language (BSL) is part of a wider problem since signed languages, in general, have been largely ignored even by people directly concerned with the study of human languages. The first steps towards repairing this neglect were taken by one man in the 1950s, the man to whom this book is dedicated, William Stokoe. The debt owed to Stokoe by the users of American Sign Language (ASL), by the present generation of American deaf children, and by linguistic and psycholinguistic researchers into ASL is immense. However, we here in Britain owe a similar debt of gratitude to Bill Stokoe: the remarkable revolution in learning which he initiated in the USA in 1960 is now being repeated here in Britain. A glance through the articles written about British Sign Language over the last five years shows just how difficult our current research efforts would be without the influence of this one man.

Most of us involved in active research can recall, sometimes quite vividly, that first contact with Bill's work which opened up new areas of understanding. His approach forced us to pay attention to observations and intuitions which had somehow remained dormant. Even those of us who recognized that it was ludicrous to think of BSL in terms of English structure, often failed to see BSL on its own terms without the sometimes distorting influence of preconceptions based on spoken languages. Only recently have we begun to acknowledge that signed languages may have patterns of organization quite unlike those common in spoken languages. The visual/gestural medium appears to impose specific constraints on grammatical structure in signed languages, just as the oral/aural medium imposes constraints on spoken languages. However, these constraints should not be seen as limitations, but can be viewed positively as providing new types of patterning which would be quite inappropriate within a spoken language. Signed languages, far from being primitive and 'barbarous', are unique visible signs of the remarkable ingenuity of the human mind.

In the following pages we would like to indicate some of the new developments in research, education, social welfare and community awareness which can be directly related to changes in attitude towards BSL. We cannot possibly describe all the individuals who are promoting greater knowledge and understanding in this area, but we hope we can give some sense of what may be the renaissance of Sign Language in Britain. Recognizing the real worth of Sign Language is bringing about a *renewal* at various levels within and around the deaf community. We hope that this renewal will develop into a true linguistic and cultural renaissance which will benefit both deaf children and the deaf community as a whole. Bill Stokoe has had a dual role in this renewal: as an eminent pioneer in Sign Language research whose classic works provide a foundation for present developments, and as a friend actively encouraging research in a more personal way.

Current Programs

In 1977, the Northern Counties School for the Deaf at Newcastle-upon-Tyne and the British Deaf Association (BDA) arranged a Sign Language Seminar at the Newcastle School. This seminar was important in many ways. It clearly indicated that Sign Language usage was becoming the common concern of a variety of individuals and groups. Represented at the seminar were the British Deaf Association, the Royal National Institute for the Deaf, the Department of Education and Science, and the Department of Health and Social Security. Individuals included psychologists, linguists, teachers, and members of the deaf community. Visitors from abroad included Brita Bergman and Lars-Åke Wikström of the Swedish Sign Linguistics Group at Stockholm University, and Willard Madsen and William Stokoe of Gallaudet College. Contact with these well-known researchers in Sign Language helped all of us participants to realize that we had reached a turning point: we recognized that research into Sign Language was now both possible and essential. Several of the participants already had research plans, some of which they modified or amended in the light of advice from more experienced participants. Now, three and a half years later, we can report an upsurge of activity. In the research and development area, some of the most important activities are:

- *The Communication Skills Program*
  This is being conducted by the British Deaf Association and is supported by a grant from the Department of Health and Social Security.
- *Sign Language Learning and Use*
  A project established at the University of Bristol and directed by Dr. Jim Kyle; also supported by the Department of Health and Social Security.

- *The Edinburgh British Sign Language Research Project*
  Established at Moray House College of Education and funded by the
  Scottish Education Department; directed by Mary Brennan.
- *The Sign Linguistics Research Group*
  Set up at the University of Newcastle and supported by the Northern
  Counties School for the Deaf, the British Deaf Association and an
  anonymous benefactor; directed by Lionel Evans.

While there are other research projects that relate to deafness and
the deaf community, we will describe here only those which focus
directly on Sign Language studies.

The Communication Skills Program.

When the British Deaf Association was founded in 1890, one of its
primary aims was to encourage the use of manual communication,
including both fingerspelling and signing. During the last 90 years,
the BDA has, of course, had tremendous difficulty in convincing
policy-makers within education that Sign Language has an important
part to play in the lives and education of deaf people. The changes in
educational policy at the turn of the century meant that Sign Language was banished from the majority of the schools and treated as
an inferior and even invalid form of communication. Although the
BDA has spoken out strongly over the years to promote Sign Language, only in the last decade have we had the right "tools" to support this approach fully. As with many other historic developments, a
combination of the right information, the right people, the right circumstances, made this very special venture possible. The "tools"
from linguistics (Stokoe 1972, Brennan 1975) and psychology
(Montgomery 1976) and evidence on the standard of education under
the predominantly oral system (Conrad 1979) together provided the
British Deaf Association with a solid foundation for their ambitious
program. As Allan B. Hayhurst described in his report to the BDA
Delegates' Conference in 1978, their aims are to help in the following areas:

- Publicizing the value of signing to deaf people, to their teachers, and
  to people who are likely to meet the deaf in the course of their work,
  or in other ways
- Helping teachers to realize the use of signing in school and the value
  of it to their children in after-school life;
- Studying British signing, reporting on its structure; recording British
  signs in reference form—books, films, video;
- Arranging courses to help people to learn communication skills;

- Training people to teach signing;
- Preparing materials for teachers of signing;
- Training interpreters (and the promotion of training);
- Establishing a Registry of Interpreters, as has been done in the USA and the Scandinavian countries, in order to give professional status to interpreters and to protect deaf clients.

The BDA has undertaken an enormous task, but already the effects of the Communication Skills Program are being felt within the deaf community and within deaf education and welfare. Over the last ten years the BDA has pursued a policy of bringing the experts, and hence the information, to the people. Overseas visitors who have contributed to BDA Congresses and Conferences include Edward Merrill, McCay Vernon, David Denton, Willard Madsen and William Stokoe from the USA; Ruth Madebrink, Brita Bergman and Lars-Åke Wikström from Sweden; and Britta Hansen from Denmark. In 1976, the BDA began to publish special supplements to the *British Deaf News*. Many of these supplements have been concerned with current work on Sign Language, developments in other countries, and the practical implications of the philosophy of "Total Communication." In one important contribution in 1978, *Sign Language research: What it knows and whither it leads,* William Stokoe examined ways in which "Sign" could be given central importance in education of the deaf. One suggestion was that we should "foster true intellectual curiosity about it as a language." Part of the present upsurge of interest is due to such curiosity or fascination. Of course, fascination should lead not only to dry and abstract theorizing, but to practical developments in education and welfare. As Stokoe himself puts it, "Much of the justification for ways of applying Sign Language comes from the realm of theory." There is now more hope than at any point in the past that theory and practice can be truly integrated for the benefit of deaf people.

The Communication Skills Program aims to encourage people to develop sign communication skills and to enable teachers of Sign Language to be more adequately trained. However, training and competence are to some extent dependent upon the existing state of knowledge about the communication system itself. The BDA along with other groups (see below) is actively studying the nature and structure of British Sign Language. For several years now, a team under the leadership of Allan Hayhurst has been working on a dictionary of BSL signs. The book *Sign-It* will provide information on over 2,000 signs and will include photographs, art work, and written

descriptions. We do not suggest that this book will be a complete
listing of all the possible signs in BSL; such a list would be impossible to write for any living language, since all human languages have
within themselves the potential to create new lexical items as required. However, *Sign-It* will contain more information on the vocabulary of BSL than has ever been produced before. It will super-
sede previous works because it is based upon a comprehensive investigation of BSL and will reflect actual usage within the deaf
community, rather than the hearing person's view of appropriate
usage. Deaf people have been fully involved in the project; indeed,
it would have been quite impossible to produce a work of this type
without the close cooperation of deaf adults. While *Sign-It* is concerned with the vocabulary of BSL rather than the grammar, some
general information on the nature of Sign Language will be provided
to guide newcomers to signing.

Sign Language Learning and Use: The Bristol Project.

It is obvious that training interpreters, teachers, social workers,
and others to communicate efficiently in Sign Language requires
knowledge and understanding of the system being taught. It also
requires information about the specific kinds of processes required
for learning a visual/gestural linguistic system. We cannot simply
assume that these processes will be similar to those involved in
learning spoken languages. Members of the Bristol Project are examining groups of individuals with varying levels of skill in signing.
They are investigating the appropriate skills or aptitudes necessary
for working and communicating with deaf people as well as attempting to characterize the underlying processes of such communication.
This research is now well into its second year and the researchers
have completed much of their testing. There is little doubt that this
work will be of fundamental importance in providing adequate help
to parents, teachers and social workers who are keen to acquire Sign
Language skills.

The Edinburgh British Sign Language Research Project.

This project is concerned more directly with examining the linguistic structure of BSL. At such an early stage there is so much to be
discovered that it can be quite difficult to know where to begin. The
research team, consisting of Mary Brennan (Linguist), Martin Colville (Lecturer in Communication Skills), and Lilian Lawson, whose

involvement as a deaf Research Associate is essential to the project's success, decided to focus on one particular area of grammatical structure: the tense and aspect system of verbs. However, from the outset we recognized that to examine how these categories operate in BSL it would be necessary to work through layers of structure and indeed "cope with" some of the fundamental issues in Sign Language research.

Given that signed languages make considerable use of such features as simultaneity and spatiality, what criteria can one use to decide whether a given signed utterance is a "word" or "phrase" or "sentence" or "text"? Are these units relevant to signed languages? How can we record signed utterances without relying on the distortion of English glosses? What kinds of transcription are appropriate for different kinds of linguistic analysis? Again the research team can only hope, at this stage, to provide clues to likely answers to some of these questions. However, already there are clues. The filmed material on BSL provides a rich source of information on natural conversational BSL, and we hope that the next few years will see a steady stream of descriptive and theoretical accounts of the structure of BSL.

The Newcastle Sign Linguistics Research Group.

This group is concerned with examining the structure of BSL but with the aim of developing new and more appropriate ways of teaching Sign Language at all levels. The important involvement of deaf people is shown by the special contribution of Dorothy Miles, who is not only an accomplished sign poet, but an innovator in the field of Sign Language teaching. Lionel Evans, Headmaster of the Northern Counties School for the Deaf, has been particularly active in promoting research on Sign Language. The Sign Linguistics Group hopes to start a further investigation in the near future into the acquisition of BSL by a child of deaf parents. Many of us have long felt the need for studies of BSL acquisition, and we hope that this important study, proposed by Alison Menzies, will begin a new field of Sign Language research in Britain.

Cooperative Ventures

One of the most encouraging recent developments in Britain has been the willingness of all these groups and individuals to share their enthusiasm, their information and, of course, their problems. The BDA Communication Skills Program has close links with the Sign Linguistics Research Group at Newcastle. Both Dorothy Miles of the Newcastle Group and Martin Colville of the BSL Research Group have developed new approaches to teaching BSL which take into account the special properities of visual/gestural languages. Both Dorothy and Martin try to help the learner see the manual sign not in isolation, but within a communicative context. Within normal signed conversation, a sign may be modified in a variety of ways and for a variety of purposes. It may be placed in a particular position in space to indicate particular grammatical relationships (e.g. subject-object); the movement of the sign may be modified (e.g. to indicate continuity); or a sign may be produced with differing speed and intensity to express changes in degree (e.g. CLEVER versus VERY-CLEVER). The learner thus begins to realize that, as with any other language, knowledge of single signs is but one part of competence in the language. Several courses have now been provided using new techniques and materials. The results so far are most encouraging. All those involved recognize the need to employ deaf people as teachers in such courses and the need to ensure that the "natural resource" of competent signers within the deaf community is used in the best possible way.

In May 1979, the four research groups and other interested individuals came together at Newcastle for the first BSL Research Workshop. Individual researchers included Margaret Deuchar from Lancaster, whose work on varieties of BSL is already well-known; Liz Dawson and Rob Baker from Southampton University, who are interested in fingerspelling and subtitling, respectively; William Edmondson, who is examining communicative interaction in classrooms with deaf children; and Irene Smith, another deaf participant from Newcastle, who has done a considerable amount of work on the identification and description of BSL signs for *Sign-It*. The subject of this first workshop was the enormous problem of transcribing BSL. We realized that transcription is a problem faced by all researchers and that if our work is to be mutually intelligible we must establish a common notation system.

The workshop was keen to examine the feasibility of using the system originally devised by William Stokoe for the transcription of ASL. We modified the system and agreed to try it out in practice. We also examined the huge problem of transcribing features of discourse, and discussed several preliminary approaches to this task. The Bristol Sign Language Group compiled and produced an account of the suggested methods in a booklet called *Coding British Sign Language*. When Lionel Evans, on a recent visit to the USA, showed Bill Stokoe a copy of this account, Bill took the trouble to make detailed comments and suggestions; this is typical of Bill's personal encouragement of research. Although he had very little time, Bill provided a written report on his suggestions and this report was discussed in detail at the second meeting of the workshop in November 1979. Lilian Lawson of the Edinburgh Project reported on the problems with the amended system from her experience in transcribing citation forms of some 1,200 BSL signs. Further changes and modifications were then made, and the revised coding system will be presented in the new edition of *Coding British Sign Language*, which is being prepared by the Edinburgh Project Team.

Cooperation among researchers is continuing; this year (1980) there will be further workshop meetings as well as a conference involving workshop participants, organized by the Bristol Sign Language Group.

Practical Implications

As we suggested earlier, theory and practice must go hand in hand. Alongside the recent research of BSL, there has been a gradual change in attitudes within education. It would be false to suggest that Sign Language is now accepted within the British education system, but there have been important policy changes. In Scotland, over half the schools for deaf children, including the largest, have adopted a policy of "Total Communication," and are using some form of signing in the classroom. The Scottish Centre for the Education of the Deaf, which is the center for training teachers of the deaf (including overseas teachers), now includes Manual/Visual Communication as an essential part of the training course. The Centre has also been responsible, sometimes in conjunction with local authorities, for special in-service courses to teach manual communication skills to teachers and parents. The demand for such courses is considerable.

In England and Wales, while some individual schools have adopted a policy of "Total Communication," an oral-only policy still prevails. However, several of the schools using "Total Communication," including the Northern Counties School for the Deaf in Newcastle-upon-Tyne and Royal Schools in Manchester, are attracting considerable interest. Cetainly there is more open and positive discussion of this communication issue than there has been for years.

As is well-known in other countries, even where the decision to use "Total Communication" has been made, the problem of what kind of signed language to use remains. Many of the fears about using BSL in schools can be directly related to insufficient knowledge about the nature and function of BSL as the natural language of the deaf community. Many also claim, of course, that deaf children must at least develop English literacy skills, and therefore some kind of Signed English is essential. However, Stokoe (1978) has suggested that "the ability of such a system for helping a deaf child acquire English competence has yet to be shown." Stokoe added that he would expect to see three languages used in an ideal school for deaf children: BSL, English, and one of the natural or artificial pidgins (e.g. Sign English or the Paget-Gorman Sign System). In Britain, it is too early to say how many schools will adopt such an approach. It does seem certain that the right decision will not be made if teachers and parents are not given all the information available on both BSL and Signed English systems. More research is needed on the kinds of processing used by the deaf child in reading and writing, and we need to continue intensive investigation into the nature of all visual/gestural systems of communication.

There have also been developments in setting up a Registry of Interpreters. Because there are formal differences in organization between England and Wales on the one hand, and Scotland on the other, slightly different approaches have been taken by the groups concerned. However, the guiding principle is the same: interpreting is a highly professional and demanding skill and if deaf people are to be given the best possible service, then appropriate training and assessment procedures should be available to would-be interpreters. We have taken considerable steps towards establishing a framework for training and assessment.

One encouraging development over the last five years has been the increasing involvement of deaf individuals in research and discussion. All the activities mentioned in this paper have depended upon hearing and deaf people cooperating closely. Those deaf people involved are not merely token representatives but are essential workers in the field. Of course, the situation is not ideal. There are still very few deaf teachers, and those few have had to struggle through courses aimed at teaching hearing pupils before they can achieve their aim. Relatively few schools employ deaf classroom assistants, and it is still possible for children in some schools to remain quite unaware that deaf adults exist.

Again we are battling against ignorance, including the deaf child's ignorance of his or her own rightful heritage. In these few pages we have indicated how several groups in Britain are replacing ignorance with knowledge and understanding. We are encouraged that deaf people are becoming more and more aware of the real worth of the complex linguistic system which they manipulate with such ease. Richard Mulcaster said of the English-versus-Latin controversy in the sixteenth century:

> Is it not indeed a strange bondage to become servants of one language [Latin] for learning's sake . . . whereas *we may have the very same treasure in our language* . . . our own bearing the joyful title of liberty and freedom?

William Stokoe's work over the last three decades has helped open our eyes to the very real treasures within human Sign Languages and to the undoubted freedom they can provide to the deaf children of the world.

References

Brennan, M. Can Deaf Children Acquire Language? An Evaluation of Linguistic Principles in Deaf Education. *American Annals of the Deaf, 120*, 95–107, 1975.

Bristol Sign Language Research Group. *Coding British Sign Language.* Bristol University, July 1979.

Conrad, R. *The Deaf School Child.* London: Harper & Row, 1979.

Evans, L. Psycholinguistic Strategy for Deaf Children. British Deaf Association, Carlisle, February 1979.

Hayhurst, A. B. Communication Skills Programme. Report presented to the BDA Delegates' Conference. British Deaf Association, Carlisle, October 1978.

Labov, W. The Study of Nonstandard English. NCTE Publications, 1970.

Montgomery, G. Changing Attitudes to Communication. British Deaf Association, Carlisle, June 1976.

Stokoe, W. C. *Semiotics and Human Sign Languages.* The Hague: Mouton, 1972.

Stokoe, W. C. Sign Language Research: What it knows and whither it leads. British Deaf Association, Carlisle, August 1978.

Research on Danish Sign Language and Its Impact on the Deaf Community in Denmark

by Britta Hansen

Introduction

Denmark is a small country in Scandinavia with 5 million inhabitants. Approximately 4000 are deaf, and 2000 of these belong to the National Association of the Deaf. There are more than 60 clubs for the deaf spread throughout Denmark. Most deaf children attend segregated schools for deaf students, but some are mainstreamed into the normal school system, either in "center-schools" using "total communication," or individually integrated into schools with no manual communication at all. In Denmark approximately 5000 hearing people attend courses in manual communication every year. Of these, 1000 attend courses organized by the Center for Total Communication.

Britta Hansen is currently Director of the Center for Total Communication in Copenhagen. She graduated in 1969 from the School of Social Work in Copenhagen and then spent three years working with deaf people, first as a counselor and then as a psychiatric social worker. In 1972, Britta studied psychiatric social work with deaf people in the United States on a Fulbright Scholarship, and later made several visits to the U.S., Sweden, Israel, and England to learn more about Sign Language research and teaching. As Director of the Center in Copenhagen since 1973, she has been involved in establishing a program for teaching Danish Sign Language, for training interpreters, collecting and analyzing Danish signs for a dictionary, and conducting other related research.

Ten years ago Danish Sign Language was not considered a language, but a simplistic means of communication. It was thought to be a private system for deaf people communicating among themselves, either at home or with their peers. The deaf community itself felt that their Sign Language was inferior to the Danish language. Deaf people felt that using Danish language structure in their signing was more acceptable to both the deaf and hearing community.

During the past ten years there have been noticeable changes in attitudes towards Sign Language among some professionals who work with deaf people. These professionals questioned previous views of Sign Language and felt that it might instead be a dialect used by an oppressed minority group who had limited means of communication. Therefore these professionals, while recognizing the use of Sign Language, were still of the opinion that it was a limited means of expression and thus incapable of expressing what the hearing community feels are the more abstract kind of language.

In the early 1970s, the teaching of Sign Language was completely based on Danish. With two exceptions, the teachers were hearing, and even the two deaf teachers taught Sign Language in Danish word order. The result was that parents and teachers of the deaf who learned this way were unable to understand the Sign Language as used by the deaf community. The major consequence of this failure in communication was that hearing people believed that deaf people could not sign correctly. Deaf people accepted the hearing community's assessment of their language and also looked upon Sign Language as an inferior means of communication, just as they had for the previous one hundred years.

In order to learn about the attitudes toward Sign Language that existed in 1973 and to seek guidance on how the Center for Total Communication should develop, I traveled around Denmark to interview respected and influential deaf and hearing persons. The hearing people had a number of concerns:

- We cannot understand deaf children when they communicate with each other, and we wonder whether deaf children actually understand each other.
- We don't like to attend social evenings in the deaf clubs because we cannot understand the way deaf people are signing.
- It is impossible for us to learn to sign the way deaf people sign.
- Sign Language should be improved, so that it can be used for the teaching of Danish, and therefore allow deaf people greater access to abstract discussions.

Deaf people had different concerns:

- Communication with hearing people is boring and superfluous.
- Hearing people who sign always control the conversations, and in most cases they win any arguments.
- We don't really understand TV or the videoprograms produced for deaf people, even though they are produced with the simultaneous use of speech and signs.
- The majority of the teachers of deaf children cannot sign properly.

During this period I interviewed a deaf "activity" teacher who worked in one of the schools for deaf children. I will never forget his astonishment when I naively asked him if he understood what the children were signing to each other. He replied, "Of course, otherwise I couldn't teach or communicate with them properly." I then asked, "Why don't the teachers and parents understand them?" His answer was, "Because they are hearing and hearing people sign differently." We then had a discussion about teaching Sign Language and he informed me that he was teaching parents and teachers to sign in Danish word order. He taught this kind of Sign Language because his class requested it and because he felt that this was the most appropriate thing to teach. Was this because he believed that they would be unable to learn Sign Language, or because he believed that the Sign Language used by the children was inferior and signing in Danish word order was superior?

Studying the Sign Language of Deaf Children

We started two different projects: the first, to study spontaneous communication between deaf children; the second, to analyze the way deaf children communicated under controlled conditions. With the results from these two projects we hoped to help parents and teachers to develop their communication skills with the children.

Inevitably we had problems, and we had to overcome traditional attitudes to the children's communication system. No one had ever studied the deaf child's sign communication before. Although they were sometimes able to communicate in Signed Danish with adult deaf people, parents and teachers were unable to understand the children, so they naturally felt that the children's Sign Language was not a real language. Parents and teachers felt that the children's language had no recognizable structure and therefore led to misunderstanding among the children as well. While interest grew and discussions continued regarding which types of sign systems and

Sign Language should be emphasized when teaching the deaf child, still no one seemed to believe that the children themselves possessed a sufficiently structured and varied Sign Language which could be used for teaching and teacher/pupil communication. If we had recognized the size of the task we had undertaken, we may not have continued. We had no methods or tradition to use in our studies. Our expertise was in psychology and education, not in linguistics, and many people thought we were trying to achieve the impossible. Early in 1973 there was a conference in Israel where I met Bill Stokoe—he gave me the stimulus I needed to continue our preliminary work. Bill Stokoe listened to my problems, discussed them with me, supported and encouraged me, and invited me to the Linguistics Laboratory at Gallaudet College. His advice was "Just get started, work within the Deaf community, and face the problems as they arise." Over the next two years, I visited the Laboratory several times; the advice, support, and information I received from Bill Stokoe and his staff was invaluable. Just to realize that American linguists were studying Sign Language as a *language* in its own right was invaluable.

It was valuable for us to learn that some staff of Gallaudet recognized that the majority culture oppressed the deaf community, its language and its culture, and that this reflected the problems of other minority groups. This gave a perspective and direction to our work and the stimulus to try and combine our theoretical studies with practical work among deaf people in their own communities, and among hearing parents and professionals.

The support and encouragement we received enabled us to continue our analysis of deaf children's communication. The deaf activity teacher and I videotaped 5 children who were between 7–12 years of age. The focus of conversation was telling stories to each other, which at times lasted 10 minutes. When I began to try and understand the children's signing I was totally unaware that the stories contained humor and many subtle details. Not only was I unaware of these facts, but I also found that I was unable to understand the basic information being conveyed. This concerned and puzzled me because I had been using what I considered was Sign Language for 8 years.

With the help and support of the deaf teacher, who spent several hours every day for 3 months patiently translating the children's signing, we finally recognized that the children had actually mastered Sign Language to a degree that both of us felt was unattainable.

Here we were, without a transcription or notation system, without a linguistic background to help us make a linguistic analysis, but convinced that we had found something which was possible for hearing people to learn.

Another interesting fact was that by immersing myself in the children's signing, I found that after 3 months I was able to understand most of the children's signing in the playground, and for the first time could relax and fully participate in the deaf adults' conversation in the deaf club. This raised many questions about how I had been taught Sign Language over the past 8 years. I felt frustrated and cheated by the traditional teaching I had received from both deaf and hearing people. My perception of Sign Language had been shattered and my thoughts reverted to all the clients I had worked with as a social worker, and how I had struggled to understand them. I had thought all the time that they were signing incorrectly and that their Sign Language skills were inferior to my own.

The second project started in 1974 with a teacher of the deaf, Ruth Kjær Sørensen, as the principal researcher. We wanted to investigate how deaf children understood each other's Sign Language. Was the children's Sign Language the same or similar to deaf adults? How did they convey certain grammatical or semantic features, e.g. nominal phrases, cause-effect, and prepositions.

We analyzed the signing of 44 deaf children in pairs. We asked the children to describe a series of pictures to each other. Each picture in the series had the same content, but the position of articles in the pictures varied. Both children had the same series of pictures, but they were given in random order, making sure that the other child was unable to see the picture that was to be described.

The children chose the medium of communication; we videotaped them. We obtained 100 hours of videotapes, and we transcribed and analyzed them to search for grammatical structure. We found that:

1. The children understood each other's Sign Language; 70% of all the problems were solved correctly.

2. They generally used the same Sign Language—the same signs and grammatical rules—as deaf adults.

3. The younger children used more pantomime, probably because they had not yet acquired sufficient signs. Most children do not learn the Sign Language of the deaf until they start school.

4. Deaf children of deaf parents use Sign Language more fluently and confidently. They also occasionally use a slightly different structure, but they will adjust their signing to the person they are talking to if neces-

sary. This becomes obvious with sign order which deaf children of deaf parents use more extensively. Localization and spatialization are the most commonly used grammatical features for deaf children of hearing parents. Deaf children of deaf parents repeat their sentences using localization and spatialization as an extra safeguard when the other person has difficulty in understanding the message.

These two investigations have supported the growing realization that it is necessary to learn the Sign Language of the deaf to be able to understand the children's spontaneous Sign Language. The children possess a rich functioning language, through which they acquire necessary information, and this Sign Language could be used as a basis for learning Danish.

The results of our research made us consider how to start courses in Sign Language as it is used by deaf people. We invited parents and teachers to participate, but how were we going to teach them? We had the following problems:

- No deaf or hearing person was trained in Sign Language teaching;
- We had no teaching materials and no methods of teaching had been developed;
- Both deaf and hearing people were still unwilling to recognize Sign Language as a language in its own right.

In 1974 we presented on Danish TV our findings on deaf Sign Language expressions. A number of deaf people throughout Denmark made these kinds of complaints:

"This should not be shown in public, it isn't good language."

"We never use that kind of signing, it is only the low verbal deaf person who uses it."

"We don't want the stigma of Sign Language placed upon us."

However, we also received some positive reactions:

"This was the first time we actually understood what was said on TV."

"It was so good to be able to relax and enjoy Sign Language."

At this time, we found that deaf people voluntarily offered their time to participate in the work of the Center. Two profoundly deaf people were employed to develop materials and methods for the teaching of Sign Language. Groups were formed all over the country to collect, describe, and translate signs which had no equivalent in Danish, or were not known to hearing people. Close cooperation developed between us and the Sign Language Committee in the

National Association of the Deaf, and representatives were exchanged for all meetings and projects.

To develop our relationships throughout Denmark, the staff of the Center embarked upon a series of lectures to explain to the deaf community the function and work of the Center. This gave the deaf and hearing members of the staff the opportunity to explain fully the reasons for investigating Sign Language as an independent language and how deaf people themselves could become involved in the work of the Center. Through this contact we saw the development of an interest and pride within the deaf community: the recognition that the deaf themselves had a role to play in the teaching of Sign Language—and the inevitable period where some people claimed that only deaf people should be authorized as Sign Language teachers.

The first course organized by the Center was undertaken after six months of preparatory work. This was an intensive one-week course in the Sign Language of the deaf. There were 16 students, all of whom were experienced teachers of the deaf, and four staff members, two deaf and two hearing. Our basic teaching materials were videotapes of deaf children telling stories to each other and deaf adults using different varieties of Sign Language. By the use of pantomime, signs, and Sign Language structure, we trained the students to express themselves and also to read Sign Language in sentences and conversation.

During the first year we organized six courses for teachers and parents of deaf children and we were astonished by the results. We quickly recognized that people would be unable to learn Sign Language in such a short period, but the change of attitude in the students toward deafness and Sign Language was the most important consequence of the courses. The students became aware that here was something that was functioning as a real language and that they would benefit from learning it. During one of these courses, a teacher burst into tears. She had been watching a videotape of one of her former pupils, and had found that she was unable to understand him. Later she explained that she had always lived in the hope that her former pupils would continue developing their speech and lip-reading skills. The realization that they in fact became deaf adults who used Sign Language as their main means of communication was a tremendous shock to her.

This fundamental misunderstanding and the lack of knowledge in teachers of the deaf of what a deaf child grows up to be is one of the major problems in the education of the deaf. Research can help to inform teachers of the linguistic rules of Sign Language—the lexical, phonological, morphological, and syntactic rules—so that Sign Language can be recognized, used, and taught as a language to deaf children, parents, teachers, and other professionals. This can only lead to a greater awareness of the language and the active exchange of information between the schools and the deaf community.

Many of the observations we make during our research into Sign Language are immediately analyzed, discussed, and then used in courses run by the Center. This means that the courses organized by the Center, whether on the use of Sign Language, interpreting, or teaching Sign Language, are constantly changing. This depends on the type of information being shared, but it can and does result in the changing of teaching methods and materials.

I would now like to try to explain a few of our research findings and how they have been used to benefit both deaf people and students of Sign Language.

Visual "Intonation"

In 1979, we started a project to study the grammar of Sign Language as it is used by deaf adults who had deaf parents. There were many things we wished to discover, including what a sentence was in Sign Language, and how deaf people understand when a sentence is finished. There did not seem to be any formal or constant rules for constructing sentences.

While we were watching the tapes we suddenly started to notice that all our informants not only moved their hands, but their head, body, and eyes, as well. We then started to study these movements to see if they meant something and if they carried a linguistic message. After some time we were sure they did, because there was a pattern which was constant through all the discourse. Every time a deaf person started or finished a sentence, there was a shift in either body, head, or the direction of gaze, or all three at the same time. In some of the informants the shift was quite noticeable: for others it was a very discreet movement, but still there.

When we presented this information to the informants and the deaf members of our staff, they were incredulous. The idea that they were systematically moving their head, body, and eyes while they were signing seemed impossible to them. However, after showing them the tapes and discussing our findings with them, they agreed that these movements seemed to be part of their communication system. From these discussions, we found that although the deaf accepted and agreed that they were using these movements, they did not recognize what they were actually doing. This led us to question the use of Sign Language by hearing people: could this be one of the reasons why both deaf and hearing people have such great difficulty in understanding each other? Were these movements the markers of the language which allowed such fluent communication between deaf people, because they told them when one utterance was completed and another was starting? Might this be the reason why deaf people had such difficulty in following an interpreter: not because the interpreter had insufficient signing skills, but because he was unaware of the Sign Language markers which allowed deaf people to *comprehend* what was being conveyed?

At the same time, we studied simultaneous communication and found that intonation and rhythm in the spoken language were often ignored by the interpreter or the hearing signer when signing and speaking at the same time. Intonation and rhythm are important parts of a message in spoken language—so important that some linguists have said that about 30 percent of our understanding of speech is based upon this information. What was new for us was this "visual intonation" in Sign Language. This visual intonation was made in different ways, but had the same function: among other things, to separate utterances and to stress important messages and signs. To watch a person signing without this visual intonation must be like watching a kind of written language performed in the air without any periods, commas, dashes, or semicolons, and without any clues about what is important, because most of the signs are performed with the same intensity.

Now we have started to incorporate this knowledge in our training of interpreters and in the teaching of simultaneous communication. It is necessary that a deaf and hearing teacher cooperate very closely when doing this, because the deaf person does not know about intonation in the spoken language—and most hearing people cannot determine if visual intonation is correctly performed in Sign Language.

Signs With No Equivalent in Danish

As I mentioned previously, groups of deaf people throughout the country collected signs which seemed to have no direct equivalent in Danish words. At this time the deaf community looked upon these signs as "slang" signs because they were traditionally used only within the deaf community and were very rarely known to the wider hearing community. While we were collecting these signs, we soon realized that these signs were an important part of Sign Language and should be recognized and taught as part of the language, if hearing users wished to communicate fluently with deaf people.

To find an exact Danish translation for many of these signs was very difficult, but by incorporating the signs into different contexts and various teaching materials, we were able to help the participants in our courses to understand the root meaning of these signs. Many deaf people were hesitant to share these signs because they considered them to be either "bad" or "private" signs for use only within an exclusive deaf culture. Some deaf people actually felt that we were intruding into an area of their culture where we didn't belong. Hearing people also at this time were reluctant to learn these signs, because in their minds a sign that had no equivalent in Danish was nonlinguistic and therefore unimportant. In addition, these signs often required a facial expression or a mouth movement which prevented the use of a traditional lip pattern for the Danish word.

An example of this sign is shown in Figure 1: TO-GET-READY or TO-PREPARE-IN-GOOD-TIME. However, if this sign is performed while mouthing the Danish word for "white," it means WHITE (Figure 2). The mouth movement is the only distinct difference between these two signs, and it is therefore a necessary piece of linguistic information.

After this initial period of resistance, it now seems that both hearing and deaf people are beginning to accept the teaching of these signs as part of the Sign Language program. There has been a positive reaction among hearing teachers and parents, and we find them saying: now I understand more of what the children are signing and I find it easier to explain new Danish words to them, especially when I know they are already aware of the concept in Sign Language. An example of this was where a teacher had a problem in making the children understand the idea "let's pretend." She had used the signs PLAY and IF, but could not make the children understand the concept "pretend." She thought one of the reasons was that they had very concrete thinking. In one of our courses she was taught that there was a specific sign LET'S-PRETEND (Figure 3), but she didn't believe it. She went home and tried to use it. The children understood her immediately, although they laughed at her too, because she couldn't make the correct facial expression that must accompany the sign. She was an experienced signer, and had used simultaneous communication in the classroom for more than 20 years.

In our work with the description of these signs, we are still having a lot of problems. We do not have a notation system to record the exact facial expression or the movement of the hands. This means that we can only make teaching material on videotapes, which makes it very difficult for hearing people to have the opportunity to do homework and memorize the signs. This is one of the main problems

Figure 1. TO-GET
READY, TO-
PREPARE-IN-GOOD-
TIME

Figure 2. WHITE

Figure 3. LET'S-
PRETEND

in Sign Language teaching. We are still unable to produce written
teaching materials which are based upon Sign Language instead of
using Danish glosses (word-based translations), which often do not
cover the precise meaning of the signs, or instead of using pictures,
which do not give the exact information about the movements of the
signs.

Modifications or Inflections of Signs

Individual signs in Danish Sign Language often behave differently than words in Danish spoken language. They are modified
and inflected without the word endings that we know from Danish,
but with changes in the direction, location, speed, size, and handshape. We are just beginning to describe some of the rules and patterns in the grammatical changes of signs—but the awareness among
deaf people that there are rules and that they are important, has made
it possible to start teaching the inflections of signs to hearing people.
I would like to give an example of teaching materials on the sign
LOOK (Figure 4; Danish 'se'). This one-handed sign can be inflected
or modified with changes in direction, two hands (for two people),
speed, and facial expression.

Every time we think we have discovered a new grammatical rule
and discuss it with groups of deaf people, they say: "Of course, that is
what we always do—but we do not think it is of any importance, we
just do it." After a while watching and discussing each other's signing, we can usually start teaching the signs and include the grammat-

LOOK   LOOK UP   LOOK DOWN

LOOK TO THE RIGHT   LOOK TO THE   LOOK AROUND
                        LEFT

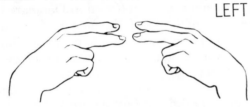

LOOK AT EACH OTHER

LOOK AT ME

SEE YOU LATER

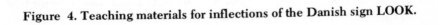

Figure 4. Teaching materials for inflections of the Danish sign LOOK.

ical features. To be a fluent user of a language does not automatically mean that one knows how the language is constructed and structured. It does not mean that one can talk about the language or teach it.

To know about the rules of Sign Language, one must study them, but first of all one must believe that there are some rules to study. Sign Language research in Denmark is still very young and we do not know enough to give full grammatical description of the language. That will hopefully be achieved within the next 20 years, with the close cooperation of researchers, deaf people, teachers of Sign Language, and teachers of deaf children. But we do not have to wait for perfect descriptions before we can exchange, discuss, and use the observations we have found along the road. Because the language is already there, it is functioning, and it has its experts, deaf signers themselves.

Dictionary of Signs

The first dictionary of Danish signs was published in Denmark in 1906 by the National Organization of the Deaf; the next in 1926; and the third in 1967. In 1967 the dictionary was meant to be a Scandinavian dictionary and therefore a Scandinavian committee had selected signs from the different Sign Languages of each country.

The dream was beautiful: to make a common Scandinavian Sign Language. But the deaf community did not buy the idea. They did not want to change their way of signing because of a dictionary. Dictionaries are usually not used by the people who know the language, but by people who want to learn it. What happened was that hearing people started to use the signs from the dictionary, and thought these were correct. Deaf people could not understand them, and a discussion grew in the deaf clubs of what was "new" and what was "old" Sign Language. Many deaf people wanted to learn the "new" signs, probably because they mistakenly believed that if hearing people used them, they must be the finest. But many deaf people also rejected the "new" signs, and wanted respect for their usual way of signing. The conclusion is that it is impossible for a dictionary alone to make people change a functioning, living language.

The next dictionary of signs was jointly published in 1979 by the Center for Total Communication, the Sign Language Committee, and the National Association of the Deaf. It contains signs for approximately 6000 Danish words and is called the *Danish-Sign Diction-*

ary. All the signs are commonly used in the deaf community; if several signs are used for the same Danish word, they are all included. The signs were selected by a group of four people: three deaf and one hearing. Following this section are two sample pages from the dictionary.

Some Practical Results

During the last couple of years we have seen an increasing interest in, and respect for, Sign Language at all levels of the hearing and the deaf communities. In the deaf community, the change of attitude towards Sign Language has had many effects. Deaf awareness is one of the most important ones. Deaf awareness includes a pride in Sign Language and a fight for the right to use and learn Sign Language from the very day deafness is diagnosed in a child. Also, in the teaching of Sign Language an important change has happened. Ten years ago we only had two deaf teachers of Sign Language, but today we have 24. They learn to teach Sign Language at courses arranged by the National Association of the Deaf and The Center for Total Communication. They themselves prefer to be trained without hearing participants at the courses, because they find that their methods, materials, and ways of presentation are different from those of people who can speak.

In the theatre for the deaf, "Deaf Film" videoprograms, and Danish TV programs for the deaf, a change has also been noticeable. Sign Language alone is now commonly used in the productions, instead of the simultaneous use of signs and speech.

In 1979, the Danish National Association of the Deaf passed a resolution on Sign Language that claimed the rights of deaf people to have their own language and that called for implementing bilingual education with Sign Language as the first language. This resolution was the first one in Denmark about Sign Language; it was later supported by the two parents organizations and the schools for the deaf.

The Center for Total Communication has grown through the years. We now have 16 employees and 40 people working on a free-lance basis. We set up approximately 40 courses in Sign Language, interpreting, and the teaching of Sign Language every year with about 1000 students. Schools for deaf children also arrange courses in total communication. About 5000 people attended courses in manual communication in 1979

902
god (godt)

GOOD

903
god (tid)
GOOD   (about time, to
have plenty of time)

904
godkende I
APPROVE I

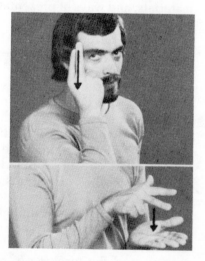

905
godkende II
APPROVE II

786
forvirring - forfjamsket,
kaos, krise, uro, virvar
CONFUSION (chaos,
crisis, unrest)

787
forældre

PARENTS

788
fotografi I

PHOTO I

789
fotografi II

PHOTO II

The deaf community has developed an interest and concern for deaf children because deaf people increasingly understand the importance of a Sign Language approach as early as possible. They are aware that deaf people, rather than hearing people should be models for the children. Deaf clubs have started children's clubs; they invite the parents to participate in the activities of the club. Deaf families have started to invite hearing parents with deaf children into their homes, in order to teach them Sign Language in the most effective way through conversation and mutual involvement.

Due to the politics of mainstreaming, more than 100 deaf children are placed in hearing schools with no exposure to Sign Language. Deaf people have strongly protested against this educational policy that enforces the isolation of these children. In order to set up alternatives, the Center for Total Communication has arranged courses in Sign Language with deaf adults for those individually "integrated" children. Parents have started to realize and accept that their children will grow up to be hearing-impaired, and will be a part of the deaf culture which uses Sign Language. The National Association of the Deaf has arranged summer courses for deaf and hearing families who have deaf children, where Sign Language is the main means of communication and the hearing parents learn about deaf culture and become involved in it.

Conclusion

A famous Dane, Hamlet, once asked, "To be or not to be? That is the question." I ask the question in my own way:

To be? a researcher into Sign Language. Or not to be? a researcher into Sign Language.

What are the choices implied by these questions? One is that you can involve yourself in Sign Language research by allowing yourself to be immersed in the language and the culture that uses the language. The other is that you can investigate a language without questioning how the language is used within the community.

The choice may seem obvious. It would seem impractical and unprofessional to investigate a language without recognizing how it is used and what your research may imply for the community that uses the language. Yet this is what often happens with Sign Language research. Researchers might study the language without prior knowledge of the language and without control groups to check that their findings and results are correct, and might ignore the damage that their results may do to the community that uses the language.

"From the little acorns big trees grow." Bill Stokoe planted the acorn when he said, "Be involved in the deaf culture," because from that seed we have grown, our tree has developed and we have fed and watered the roots, trunk, branches, and leaves. Far too often people forget to water part of the tree and it withers through lack of stimulation; the tree must be encouraged to take root again so that the trunk is reborn healthier and stronger.

If you wish to study Sign Language you cannot just tend the trunk, without looking after the roots, branches, and leaves, because over the past 100 years the roots of Sign Language have been systematically attacked and they have withered, but have never been completely destroyed. The branches and leaves in Denmark seem now to grow healthier and stronger, because we have tried to keep in mind Bill Stokoe's original message.

The roots are Sign Language.

The trunk is the deaf community.

The branches are the various organizations and institutions I have mentioned in this paper.

The leaves are the changes that happen in a living, growing culture.

We have tried to maintain a firm belief that to investigate a language, everything and everyone must be involved.

Afterword

by William C. Stokoe, Jr.

Despite the broad range of this book and the many pieces of the story that the authors have assembled, our story is incomplete without a short glimpse of what Bill Stokoe has written himself. The following brief description is an excerpt from a talk that he gave entitled "Language and the Deaf Experience." He made these remarks at the 30th Annual Georgetown University Roundtable, which was held in Washington, D.C. on March 22–24, 1979; the complete speech is published in the proceedings of that conference, edited by G. Alaitis and R. Tucker.

. . . With a dozen or more colleagues I joined the Gallaudet faculty in 1955 and began to learn how to produce signs, which were then presented to us as equivalents of specific English words. But I had recently enjoyed a sabbatical year, and it didn't look to me that simple. While trying to cope with various neglected problems in Old English, Middle English, and Middle Scots, I had been impressed with Robert Stockwell's treatment of the Old English vowel system. Through that I had come to study the 1951 Trager and Smith *Outline of English Structure* with more than usual care. Consequently, it occurred to me again and again, in our sign vocabulary drills in September 1955, that these signs with different meanings seemed to be alike in more ways than they differed.

When I told the Dean [George Detmold] that minimal-pair analysis seemed to work as well on signs as it had on words, he suggested seeking help here. The Georgetown University School of Language and Linguistics then was not here but on Massachusetts

Avenue, and it seemed to us the logical place to find a graduate student perhaps willing to study Sign Language as a linguist should.

The next events remind me of one of the early plays the Dean directed. The Director of the School, the late Leon Dostert, was unavailable the day I called. His second in command, Paul Garvin, was out of town; but I held my ground in front of the receptionist's desk and at last was sent to the office of the late Professor William Austin. He welcomed me, listened intently for awhile, but insisted I must be a scientist posing as an English professor, and became more and more excited as I tried to explain what Sign Language seemed to be. At the end he literally thrust me out of his office charged with orders, which for a mild mannered man he almost shouted: I was to go around the corner at once to Earl Brockman's office and say that I must have a summer grant-in-aid from the American Council of Learned Societies; next I was to phone Trager and Smith in Buffalo and arrange to join their summer institute a few months later in 1957.

Brockman, the ACLS, the summer institute, its teachers and participants, especially Trager, Birdwhistell, and Haxie Smith, were all as directly and immeasurably helpful as Bill Austin had been to a linguist in-spite-of-himself. I left Buffalo with a clear idea of what had to be done, but no clear idea of how to do it . . . Still, by the end of 1959 it had become apparent to me that sign morphemes, unlike spoken ones whose segmental components are arranged in time sequence, could be analyzed as if composed of *aspects* (the word has its most precise meaning) of the same unitary act, a sign. Smith was an ideal and enthusiastic mentor, for his theory of the morphophone held that segmental and suprasegmental morphemes too were simultaneous, not sequential, or trivial. Trager quite correctly observed that my initial study did not prove that American Sign Language was a language yet, but he thought the case well worth considering and published *Sign Language Structure* as Occasional Paper 8 in his *Studies in Linguistics* (Stokoe 1978 (1960)).

This, of course, was only the comedy's first act curtain. Publication in 1960 brought a curious local reaction. With the exception of Dean Detmold and one or two close colleagues, the entire Gallaudet College faculty rudely attacked me, linguistics, and the study of signing as a language. My function was to teach English they told me in a meeting to which I had been invited to talk about the occasional paper. If the reception of the first linguistic study of a Sign Language of the deaf community was chilly at home, it was cryogenic in a large part of special education—at that time a closed corporation as hostile to Sign Language as ignorant of linguistics. Even the general public joined in the outcry. One instance: When the National Science Foundation first granted support for research in Sign Language, two letters attacking the foundation, the grant, and the research purpose appeared in the *Washington Post*. Both letter writers, descendants of A. G. Bell, based their objections on the claim that grandfather had proved once for all that Sign Language is useless and pernicious in the education of the deaf . . .

What warmed me in all this cold was the intelligent, critical, challenging, interested, and continuing interaction provided by linguists at the Center for Applied Linguistics and at Georgetown University's School of Languages and Linguistics, especially in the informal arena provided by the Washington Linguistics Club . . . [Many there] provided the encouragement an idea needed to grow and spread.

In fact, now looking back, the growth and spread seems exponential. Literally hundreds of programs, schools, and classes for deaf children have changed in the last five or six years from narrowly conceived oral instruction to that mix called "total communication." And if this is not full recognition of natural Sign Language as part of bilingualism, it means at least that signs will be used in the presence of deaf pupils. Sign Language courses, still largely of the sign-for-word vocabulary kind, are being taught to parents, teachers, and others who may expect to interact with deaf persons.

With all this attention on their language, deaf people themselves have more visibility now, more public acceptance, more self awareness (as far as this can be seen by outsiders), more pride in Sign Language, and even more motivation to learn English as a second language. More and better positions are open to qualified deaf persons, and the opportunities for them to qualify in a great many more professions and vocations are opening up as well. Though deaf persons and their language and culture are still the object of study, the nature of the study and its emphasis and focus have radically changed. It is currently not a study of pathology or deficiency but a sympathetic study by linguists, sociolinguists, and anthroplogists of humanity complete and articulate. Best of all, deaf persons themselves are finding real acceptance as professionals in anthropology, its linguistic branches, and in many of the social and political decision-making positions formerly closed to them.